FARRAR
STRAUS
GIROUX

HOUSE of HAPPY ENDINGS

HOUSE of HAPPY ENDINGS

* * *

LESLIE GARIS

FARRAR, STRAUS AND GIROUX

NEW YORK

FARRAR, STRAUS AND GIROUX
19 Union Square West, New York 10003

Grateful acknowledgment is made for permission to reprint the following:
pp. 218–20, excerpts from "The Pasture" and "Take Something Like a Star"
from *The Poetry of Robert Frost*, edited by Edward Connery Lathem. Copyright © 1949, 1967, 1969 by Henry Holt and Company. Copyright © 1977 by
Lesley Frost Ballantine. Reprinted by permission of Henry Holt and Company, LLC; pp. 263–64, excerpt from "Portrait of a Lady" by T. S. Eliot, from
Collected Poems by T. S. Eliot, courtesy of Faber and Faber Ltd.

Library of Congress Cataloging-in-Publication Data
Garis, Leslie, [date]
House of happy endings / Leslie Garis. — 1st ed.
p.   cm.
ISBN-13: 978-0-374-29937-8 (hardcover : alk. paper)
ISBN-10: 0-374-29937-4 (hardcover : alk. paper)
1. Garis, Leslie, [date]   2. Journalists—United States—
Biography.   I. Title.

PN4874.G326A3 2007
973.9092—dc22
[B]

2006036321

Designed by Gretchen Achilles

www.fsgbooks.com

1   3   5   7   9   10   8   6   4   2

for ALEX, BEN, and KAT

Through lane it lay—through bramble—
Through clearing and through wood—
Banditti often passed us
Upon the lonely road.

The wolf came peering curious—
The owl looked puzzled down—
The serpent's satin figure
Glid stealthily along—

The tempests touched our garments—
The lightning's poinards gleamed—
Fierce from the Crag above us
The hungry Vulture screamed—

The satyr's fingers beckoned—
The valley murmured "Come"—
These were the mates—
This was the road
These children fluttered home.

c. 1858
no. 9 in *The Complete Poems of Emily Dickinson,*
edited by Thomas H. Johnson

HOUSE of HAPPY ENDINGS

November 1962

That night I fell into a sound sleep almost as soon as I pulled the covers around me. But I awoke at dawn with words, sentences, half-effaced thoughts insisting on being heard. "Maybe he'll be okay now" was tumbling around in my mind like a mantra. Maybe he'll be okay now—now that his father is dead. Maybe that's what he needed . . . And what was that thought about J. D. Salinger? Salinger, Salinger— "Uncle Wiggily in Connecticut." I'd read the story a few years ago. What was it I was just thinking about . . . just before I woke up? I sat up straight in bed. I tried to remember the story.

Two women, one married, meet in the married woman's suburban house on a winter afternoon. They were friends in college. The unmarried one thinks the married one is lucky to be prosperously set up, but we see that the married one is drinking too much and is fiercely unhappy. There's a little girl named Ramona who has an imaginary friend. The drunken mother doesn't seem to like her daughter very much and has absolutely no sympathy for a girl who is such a loser that she has an imaginary friend. That much I remembered. Where did Uncle Wiggily come in? I lay back on the pillow and looked at the ceiling. There were no sounds in the house, which was a relief.

The married woman tells her friend that she had been in love with a man who was killed in the war. She says he made her laugh. She remembers that while she was running for a bus, she twisted her ankle and the young man said, "Poor Uncle Wiggily." As she recounts the story, you can tell she thinks that was the sweetest, wittiest, and most original *thing anyone ever said to her. She repeats the words, only I think this time she says, "Poor old Uncle Wiggily."*

The story ends with the mother asking her friend plaintively, "I was a nice girl, wasn't I?"

What did it all mean?

The man who talked to her of Uncle Wiggily is dead. All that innocence is gone, and with it any tolerance for whimsy she may once have possessed. Yet her memory of a kinder past is more real than the alcohol-blurred present in which she's living.

The man who created Uncle Wiggily and embodied innocence in our lives was gone, too, along with his last despairing years as he watched his son disintegrate. By some alchemy of thought, those events were falling away in my mind and an innocent past was coming into focus. I fastened on the idea that all the horror would disappear now and my father would emerge as a healed and happy man.

We were a nice family once, weren't we?

PART
ONE

* * *

CHAPTER ONE

1953: Amherst, Massachusetts

In those years I spent a lot of time in the dumbwaiter, moving up and down behind the walls, listening to voices. I sat with my knees up: sometimes I clasped my arms around my legs, sometimes I kept my hands on the rope that extended in a loop from the top of the house to the bottom. Two lengths, thick and prickly, were suspended side by side. One for up, one for down. It was dark inside the box, but never entirely black. Faint light seeped in from the square doors that opened on each floor.

No one knew I was there. I was invisible. I could eavesdrop to my heart's content. I was like blood flowing through a vein, silent and purposeful. There were certain confusing incidents I was trying to interpret, and I hoped I was on the trail of truth. The problem was, I had too much information.

A good person is happy; a happy person is good. I knew this without a doubt because we were wrapped in a dream of perfection, a dream created and refined in vivid detail by the collective imagination of my family.

How warm and cozy it was in Snow Lodge! How bright were the lights, and how the big fire blazed and crackled and roared up the chimney! And what a delightful smell came from the kitchen!

I could jump right into that world. *The Bobbsey Twins at Snow Lodge.* Granny or Grampy—I wasn't sure which—wrote it. I was inside the boundless optimism and could hardly wait for time to unfold its treasures. The fact was that when I looked around my own life, I saw something so similar in its physical outlines to that mythic ideal that fictional boundaries tended to fade in my unformed, overactive mind.

Our family was suffused with stories. Dad's often-told tales of traveling through the desert with an Egyptian prince, Mom's romantic memory of falling in love with the most debonair, handsome, sophisticated man she had ever met: my father. The stirring story of my grandmother's life: suffragette, pioneer newspaper woman, author of books . . . But the stories that held us most in thrall were fashioned by my grandfather, and their most distilled form was also the most improbable. After writing hundreds of books in numerous popular children's series, he became rich and famous by creating a rabbit who wore a top hat and tails and lived in the most idyllic small town America ever produced. His name was Uncle Wiggily, and he inhabited Woodland with Nurse Jane Fuzzy Wuzzy and their animal friends. A rabbit! Yes. *The Uncle Wiggily Stories* were the bestselling children's books in America for decades before I was born and my grandfather was still a celebrity on their account. I was known at school as the granddaughter of Uncle Wiggily.

My mother expected my brothers and me to be as kind and well-mannered as Uncle Wiggily, and also as energetic, successful, and well-groomed. I was being brought up on the morality of a make-believe rabbit.

Was she right? Perhaps Woodland was the best place to look for an ethical model. But if that were so, where would I find reality? If, as I was beginning to believe, life wasn't like my grandparents' books, was happiness merely a fantasy? I didn't accept that, but my self-appointed mission was to discover the unvarnished truth. My survival, I sensed, depended on it. I was sure the answers were here in this house, this enormous, magical house—the first great love of my life.

IN 1948 Dad left his job at *The New York Times Magazine* to be a full-time writer, and in celebration of his release from formal employment he bought a "nicer" house in a sleepy New England college town: Amherst, Massachusetts. The house had its own name. It was called The Dell.

That was all I knew—except that I gathered my mother was unsure The Dell was right for us. At age five, I had no idea why. When we drove into Amherst, I was spellbound by the town's aura of settled calm. Its generous village green was bordered on one side by the princely buildings of Amherst College and on the other by a craggy town hall, a brooding, ivy-covered church, and a group of small stores. The leaves of the old maples on the Common were beginning to turn gold.

At the bottom of the Common, where the white brick Lord Jeffery Inn sprawled in calm splendor, we turned down a narrow road called Spring Street. My three-year-old brother Brooks and I were looking out of the car with the windows cranked down. We came to a shaded crossroads, the air moist and fragrant. Down on the right was a long building with a white porch, which formed a T with the end of the street. It defined the view like a stage set, its windows sparkling in the afternoon sun. Dad said it was called Valentine Hall—such a romantic name!—and it was where the Amherst College students took their meals. Looking to the left from the crossroads, we could see a large stone church with a hefty spire. I can't recall any people at all on the sidewalks that afternoon; in fact there was an eerie sense of isolation from the real world, almost of a lost village under an enchantment.

Mom held five-month-old Buddy in her arms. Was she apprehensive? I cannot recall. As we entered the driveway of 97 Spring Street, our car tires crunching on gravel, I found myself repeating silently, "The Dell, The Dell," as if the name could explain the kingdom that opened before us. Dad stepped out of our Packard and looked at a house wrapped in shingles, its rooflines and corners as softly contoured as the land. He smiled like a man who has taken possession of his magic castle, within which his life will be blessed.

It looked to me like a giant playhouse. I couldn't see the whole shape of the place at first. The sheer size of it prevented me from taking it all in from my low perspective.

Knowing my father's innate modesty, his shy, deferential, soft-spoken manner, I was surprised that he had bought this imposing place. It's true that in private he was unusually elegant. He carried a vermeil-engraved cigarette case and kept his many pairs of gold cuff links in a silver box that said ASPREY on it. He wore silk bathrobes (from Sulka, I would later learn), ascots in cool weather, and finely cut clothes even for gardening. Now his public image would match his private preferences.

I ran around the side to a wide terrace of rose-colored stone overhung by a white arbor encircled by thick arms of wisteria.

Tall doors, their leaded glass panes divided into beautifully balanced curves and angles, completely shaded from the bright afternoon light, looked black under the arbor. I peered through them at a diorama of dark wood.

I ran around another corner of the house past a giant beech tree. The terrace opened up to an even larger expanse bordered by a low stone wall. Looming at one end, and looking alive with power, was a massive stone table in the shape of a mill wheel set on a pedestal. Dotted along the lawns, with tranquil distances between them, were many kinds of trees, one laden with apples. I was tempted to run down there and pick one, but I could hear my mother calling me.

She and my father simultaneously came out of the house from two different doors that opened onto the terrace. They were laughing. Brooks stepped carefully, his blue eyes wide with discovery. My father lifted me up into his arms.

"What do you think of your new house, Les?" he asked.

"I love it, I love it, I love it . . ."

"We're going to be happy here," he said.

"Oh, yes!" I answered, hugging him hard, my arms entwined around his neck.

Inside, standing in the hall, I felt dwarfed by the scale of the rooms. The house was designed so that windows were always in view. No matter where you were, light shone in—prismatic and softened by the extraordinary windowpanes. The outdoors was so present that even though the walls were dark, I had the impression that the slightest change of sky, like a cloud passing by, would be reflected inside.

I could see that Dad was in another world. It seemed, even to my five-year-old eyes, that there was something about the feeling he had inside the house—perhaps the dimensions of the rooms, or something as simple as the color of the woodwork, or a particular smell, or maybe a sliver of light on a floorboard—something that made his heart beat faster, a flutter of joy that invaded his chest, a sudden tearing of his eyes. My mother watched him with love.

Everything about The Dell amazed me. The carved crystal doorknobs felt smooth and sharp in my hand, on the walls were lights that looked like old-fashioned oil lamps, doors slipped into wall pockets, and the walls were as thick as my forearms were long. Each door had a large brass plate with a medieval-sized keyhole.

A peach marble fireplace adorned the dining room, and I recognized the Dutch door from which my mother had emerged when I was standing on the terrace. To the left of the fireplace was a swinging door that led to the butler's pantry and a peculiar kitchen. Stretching along one whole wall, beneath mullioned windows, were a black sink and counter. I'd never seen a black sink before. Red birds congregated in the arborvitae hedge that walled one side of the back driveway.

I ran from the kitchen into a narrow corridor from which you could walk up a back stairway or down gray steps into the cellar. Several feet up from the floor, at the level of my shoulders, was a small, square door with a round brass pull. Why would a door be up there? I called Mom: "What's this?"

"Look and see," she said, opening the door and lifting me up. "It's a dumbwaiter, and it goes all the way up to the top of the house and all the way down to the cellar."

A dumbwaiter! Plans began forming. Ahhhhh . . . What possibilities.

"Here's something else, Les. Wait till you see this!" Mom opened the door at the end of the corridor. It led to the front hallway, past paneled woodwork under the main staircase. It was made of what Mom called buttonwood—a buttery light brown. Her fingers searched and found a tiny wooden knob. The panel came away to reveal a dark space with a long coiled hose.

"Mrs. Churchill, who built this house, was afraid of fires. That's why the walls are so thick, and that's why this hose is here. It reaches to every single corner of the house. Isn't it wonderful?"

It surely was. A dumbwaiter, a secret panel . . . I was awestruck.

Back in the hall and through another door, I found the best room of all—a big library with yet another marble fireplace, bowed windows, a very large desk, and floor-to-ceiling bookshelves. Boxes of books were strewn on the floor. I figured we could put them all away and still have space for more. We would fill up the whole room with books. What bounty.

Later, in a state of restless ecstasy, I was taking a bath in a tub that was so long, my mother had to hold me so I didn't slip under the warm, soapy water. When she helped me out over the side and wrapped me in a towel, our voices echoed. The floor was covered with thousands of tiny diamond-shaped white tiles in gray grouting. I couldn't get over all those minuscule tiles; there was something so precise and exorbitant about them. They gave me a strange joy.

A white radiator sat fat and placid under a big window through which the day moved into its last pale moments. The porcelain sink was almost above my head. But that was because I was so small. I stood on a chair and looked into an old, dark-streaked mirror. My eyes looked back at me. Behind me was my strikingly vivid mother, darkly beautiful. She leaned down to pick up Brooks and was gone from the mirror. I studied my face for signs of something. I appeared more knowing than I had yesterday in our utterly familiar Rye home. Today was the beginning of the adventure that would be my life.

Filled with the manic energy of a freshly scrubbed child, I ran downstairs to find my father, who, I believed, was the one person in the world who truly understood my feelings. He stood in the kitchen, playing with an odd-looking contraption attached to the wall.

"Look at this, Les!" He was excited. "This microphone connects to tubes in the walls that go to all the rooms. We can call
someone upstairs from here."

Indeed, a small metal megaphone protruded from the wall.
Next to it hung a black disk with tiny holes in it. My father put it
to his ear.

"Let's call Mom and Brooks!" I said.

"Mabs! Mabs!" he yelled into the opening. Everyone called my
mother Mabs. Her name was Mabel. "Mabs!"

After waiting some minutes and yelling some more, his face lit
up.

"She's there, Les! Listen."

I put the receiver to my ear and heard a muffled noise. It was
my mother's voice sounding as far away as a star. I yelled hello to
her.

"I think mice have gotten in there," my father said, not at all
concerned. "Anyway, isn't it marvelous?"

Oh, it was marvelous. Everything was marvelous.

My mother showed me the bedroom she had chosen for me off
a spacious rectangular hallway. I loved its central position, so close
to the grand staircase and not far from another set of wide stairs
that climbed to the third floor. I had my own fireplace, with a deep
mantel, and cabinets behind the woodwork, which I imagined I
would fill with secret papers.

The walls were a muddy color, which didn't bother me in these
heady circumstances, but Mom promised that soon I could pick
out my own wallpaper. There was a door between my room and
Brooks's, which I intended to lock.

My father sat with me, as he often did while I said my prayers.
I got on my knees next to the bed and prayed fervently for bless-
ings on everyone in my family. Then I said the Lord's Prayer,
knowing, with absolute certainty, that God was listening to me—

even in this strange, new room. For my father's benefit, I recited slowly, drawing out my moment of stardom in the universe, breathing into the syllables, making words like "art" and "hallow-ed" sound as round and resonant as possible.

Then my father tucked the sheets up under my chin. His face registered the radiant contentment of a man who has just stepped into his chosen role in life. He was lord of a castle, with a sweet princess for a daughter, and I fell under the spell of his design as deeply as Sleeping Beauty.

As he stroked my hair, he read to me from Stevenson's *A Child's Garden of Verses*:

> *"I shut my eyes and sail away*
> *And see and hear no more."*

FIVE MONTHS LATER, the shades were down and the drapes drawn in my mother's room, but on this bright winter day, the light soaked through anyway.

Laughter hurt her, she told us, even if it came from downstairs and was barely perceptible in her room. So we kept ourselves quiet.

I saw her rise halfway up from the bed and face the wall behind her. She raked it with her fingers, as if the wall were between her and the absence of pain. Tears soaked her cheeks. Then she vomited.

My mother's migraines were scary. She was so small—barely five feet, and one hundred pounds—and the headaches were so powerful that I was afraid they would break her entirely. Sitting by her side, trying not to make any sound, changing the washcloth every half hour to keep it cool, I liked feeling the curve of her brow, her bone structure so delicate and vulnerable under my hand. She needed me, and I could help. It was a simple exchange. Satisfying, in the way caregivers understand that on a basic level they can meet life's demands.

Recently, though I was barely six, I'd begun to have the uneasy sense that my mother was feeling inadequate to the demands of her own life. She had contributed a backbreaking amount of physical labor bringing the house up to her standards—which meant abolishing the pervasive darkness of the original walls. She tore down the brown flowered wallpaper and put up white fabric on the walls in the hall and living room. She'd also made sweeping living-room curtains on her big sewing machine.

Every Saturday she assigned me a cleaning task, usually emptying the baskets and dusting, while she vacuumed. We had a cleaning woman who came for only a few hours once a week, not enough for a house that size. As a helper, I alternated between being fiercely efficient and subversively dreamy, so I was either, in her words, "perfect" or "impossible." There was little in between.

One Saturday morning soon after her migraine, I was humming and finishing up dusting the upstairs, in my perfect mode. Buddy was asleep in his playpen, and Brooks was in his room building a toy log cabin. Even as young as that, I was subject to wild mood swings. But that day—perhaps because of my mother's recovery from her migraine, which always seemed like a miracle after the maelstrom—I felt steady and limitlessly capable. When my chores were done, I decided to ask Mom if there was anything more I could do.

I found her sitting on the floor of the hall, a dust rag in her hand, crying. Aside from the headaches, which happened about once a month and lasted two days, my mother was resolutely cheerful. She was a person who believed in the power of smiling and singing, who spoke of birds as if they were her friends—*Oh look! A yellow warbler is visiting our tree. Isn't it lovely!* Her greatest insults were to call a person "unattractive" or a situation "unpleasant"; to her mind it was everyone's duty to make the world a happier place. I was shocked to see her in tears.

"We should nevei have bought this house . . . I told your father . . . With you children . . . all I have to do . . ." She put her head in her hands and wept. "It's too much . . . I can't cope." Her shoulders shuddered with her sobs.

Instant alarm. Headaches were one thing. They were caused by something physical, I thought, and as such weren't threatening, because they passed away like mumps and flu. But her words undermined my fierce belief that this house and our lives were virtually perfect.

"I can help you," I said, hoping to sound convincing. "We can do it together, you'll see."

She looked up at me, startled. She hadn't meant to speak. Her round brown eyes looked like dark stones at the bottom of a stream.

"Would you get me a Kleenex, dear?"

I ran to the bathroom and brought back toilet paper.

After she blew her nose and wiped her eyes, she patted my back. I would have preferred a slow rub or a still hand on my shoulder, but her way was to pat quickly, as if she were sending a friendly telegraph.

"I didn't mean anything, Les. Forget what I said. I was just in a state, just a little tired."

"Don't you like our house?"

"Of course I do. I was just feeling a little low. It's nothing."

She got to her feet, squared her shoulders, and lifted her head so her lovely neck lengthened. She wore her cleaning clothes: gray trousers, a white blouse, and sneakers on her size-three feet. She ordered her shoes from the catalog of Cinderella, which stocked tiny shoes for grown-up women. She had tied a red scarf around her head to protect her hair from the dust. The whole affect was acutely feminine and pretty.

"I would never want you to think that I didn't agree with your father on something as important as our home. We're very happy we moved here. Your father and I are in complete agreement."

It was like an icy breath from the universe when she talked that way. It was confusing when she said things like "your father and I are in complete agreement," because it was hard to find the truth in formal pronouncements.

"Okay, Mom."

"Did you finish upstairs?"

"All finished."

There was a silence then, the two of us breathing quickly, stifling the unspoken.

"Would you like to make a snowman on the terrace with Brooks?" she asked, her voice achingly hopeful.

"Sure." I didn't want to. Brooks was too young for me to play with. He was so sweet and vulnerable that I felt alternately protective and resentful.

"Let's call him and get on your snowsuits."

Instead of the snowman, we made angels. Brooks's enormous blue eyes fixed gravely on the gathering clouds. His breath made mist in the frozen air, creating droplets of ice that fell back onto the perfect features of his handsomely formed face, which was pink from the cold. His arms and legs moved to form the wings and skirt of the angel in the fluffy snow.

I peeked into the library windows and saw my father standing at his desk. I knocked, and he turned around and waved back.

When we came inside, Mom made us cocoa, then took Brooks upstairs for his nap. I wandered into the library.

My father was sitting on the couch, reading typed pages from a loose pile of papers beside him. A fire popped behind the black mesh screen. I loved fires. I picked up a poker, moved the screen aside, and pushed the logs around, rearranging them on the andirons so that air could move through.

"Thanks, Les," he said affectionately.

As so often, he had a distracted, distant air that night, which I took as a challenge to draw him into our world. His thank-you told me I had succeeded, though I had noticed lately that there was also an uncertainty in his manner that I couldn't breach. I sensed it as the merest wisp of a chill that the fire did not touch.

CHAPTER TWO

As you perhaps know, some authors are so modest that they hide their real identity under pen names, and this is a case where we are sorry to state that we can give you no information concerning this author further than to say that he is a live, wide-awake American who is well known not only in the book field but also in other lines of literary endeavor.

—Edward Stratemeyer to an inquisitive Tom Swift fan,
March 19, 1930

To the right of the fireplace was a wall of books in faded, once-bright colors with spirited titles: *Tom Swift and His Airship, The Bobbsey Twins at Meadow Brook, Baseball Joe in the Big League, Dave Fearless Wrecked Among Savages, Through Space to Mars, The Motor Boys Over the Rockies, Six Little Bunkers at Uncle Fred's, The Curlytops at Sunset Beach, The Moving Picture Girls Snowbound, Dorothy Dale's Camping Days, The Racer Boys to the Rescue, Bunny Brown and His Sister Sue and Their Shetland Pony, The Outdoor Girls at Rainbow Lake* . . . There were hundreds of volumes here grouped together, all with similar bindings and titles. The authors were Victor Appleton, Laura Lee Hope, Frank V. Webster, Clarence Young, Roy Rockwood, Roy Eliot Stokes, Lester Chadwick, and others with equally stalwart names.

I started having a near-hallucinatory reaction to these books— almost as if I heard voices behind them—when my parents told me the most incredible thing: my grandfather wrote them all, except for around forty written by my grandmother, and half a dozen written by my father when he was in his twenties. How could that be? Why all these other names? The concept of pseudonyms was explained to me, but the problem was that the names had strong identities and shimmered with specific associations. Richard Barnum, Alice Dale Hardy, Margaret Penrose . . . I simply couldn't accept their unreality. Didn't Elmer Dawson and Nat Ridley live somewhere in houses with staircases and kitchens and families?

My grandfather was known to me as the author of *Uncle Wiggily*, but if, as Victor Appleton, he also wrote *Tom Swift*, it meant that he had another identity—in fact many identities, like a master spy. And what about Granny—Lilian Garis—or was she Laura Lee Hope? Family lore had it that besides her Judy Jordan, Nancy Brandon, Connie Loring, Barbara Hale, Joan, Gloria, and Cleo books (under her own name), she had written all the early volumes of *The Bobbsey Twins*, but I later discovered that only the first two were hers. Grampy actually wrote the next twenty-five, but he allowed her to take credit for them among family and friends. Why would she want credit for those books when she'd written so many of her own? Why would Grampy allow it? Why didn't the world know what they actually did write? Was it a secret? I wanted to understand, but every time I got an answer, another question presented itself.

My parents often mentioned the name Edward Stratemeyer. They said Granny and Grampy signed fake names because Edward

Stratemeyer asked them to. Dad, who also briefly worked for Stratemeyer, had explained it to me several times. Stratemeyer hired writers to write books for his "syndicate." He owned the copyrights and paid his writers flat fees, usually seventy-five dollars. The writers signed contracts giving away their royalties and promising never to reveal their identities. That way Stratemeyer could hire other writers if the first ones died or didn't please him, and the phantom authors could go on and on earning him profits.

No one wrote as many books (more than three hundred) for the syndicate as Howard Garis, who was good friends with Stratemeyer. Well, if they were such good friends, how come Stratemeyer didn't give Grampy more money when *The Bobbsey Twins* and *Tom Swift* took off? Dad shrugged. "That was the deal, and your grandfather never asked for more. He's a very gentle man."

A very gentle man. Not a satisfying answer.

"Dad never bothered much about money," my father said. "Anyway, he made so much on *Uncle Wiggily*, which, of course, had nothing to do with Stratemeyer, that he put all that work-for-hire business behind him."

What about other Stratemeyer writers? My father explained that *Nancy Drew* and *The Hardy Boys* were also ghostwritten.

"So Carolyn Keene and Franklin W. Dixon aren't real either?"

"No." Dad shook his head. "Those writers are actually Mildred Benson and Leslie McFarlane."

"And they didn't get paid more when the books sold so well?"

"No indeed."

"Did they mind?"

He didn't know. A somber, veiled smile played on his face whenever we talked about Edward Stratemeyer. My impression was that Dad admired Stratemeyer for his enterprise in getting rich but hated him for taking advantage of our family. Another uncomfortable subject for Dad was that Grampy seemed to be an endless source of creativity. The stories just flowed out of him. I sensed there was something potentially crushing in such an avalanche of words.

Dad had had his successes, but he'd never been able to match his father's. How could he ever measure his power as a writer against the mythic influence of the wonder boy Tom Swift and the model of American domesticity embodied in the Bobbsey Twins?

Those series books, published during the first great surge of mass marketing in the United States, were devoured by generations of children who absorbed the enthusiasm, propriety, confidence, and general can-do flavor of these stories. The children grew up with these fictional models embedded in memory. It was a picture of the American dream that was measured against the realities the children encountered, and the influence of these books was incalculable. Even today, in the twenty-first century, families still name twins after Freddie and Flossie or Nan and Burt—the two sets of Bobbsey Twins. Stephen Wozniak, cofounder of Apple Computers and the man credited with starting the PC revolution, says his inspiration was Tom Swift. "He's always been a hero to me."

What is it like for a son to be born into the family who created all that? As an emerging person, he had a lot of fictional heroes to live up to, and as a writer, he had a preposterously enormous output to compete with. Mom had told me how proud Dad was when he got a ten-story contract with *Liberty* magazine in the late 1930s. I also knew, but couldn't begin to comprehend, that when Dad was offered the contract, Granny told him he was in over his head. He'd shown her! Every one of his stories was featured on the cover. But why would she say that to him? Did she think he had no talent? Or that he was lazy? Or did she suspect some hidden flaw that would doom him to failure? She apparently tried to stop him from covering a state corruption trial for the *Waterbury Republican*, insisting that he turn down the job because it would be too difficult for him. Granny was ignored, Dad took the assignment, and the paper won a Pulitzer for his articles. Why she underestimated him was a mystery to me, but I was proud of him for standing up to her.

As soon as *Uncle Wiggily* became a bestseller, Howard Garis was followed around by groups of adoring children wanting him to tell a story. I tried to imagine how Dad must have felt, perhaps walking home from school, seeing all those children clustered around his father on the sidewalk. I should think it would have made him feel left out.

Here he was now, though, encircled by his own family, sitting in his own library, with only one wall of books to remind him of his heritage. The rest of the room contained his collection of European and American literature, in stark contrast to the children's fare produced by his parents.

"Les," Dad said to me from the couch as I warmed myself by the fire. "I have something to tell you. Something exciting."

His voice was strong with certainty.

"Look, it's snowing again," he said. I sat beside him on the couch. We watched wet white flakes float outside the window against the gray sky.

"What's the exciting thing?"

"I know why I bought this house."

This was a startling piece of news on many levels.

"I bought it so I could start a magazine."

A magazine! Did he always think The Dell was for a magazine, or did he just figure it out? I thought he bought the house for us.

"I'm calling it *The Pioneer*. A lot of people will be coming and going. It will get pretty interesting around here. Your mother will have her hands full, so I want you to be a big help to her."

"Does she know about the magazine?"

He laughed. "Of course!"

"Is she excited?"

"Sure, she's—well, it may take her a little time, but . . . no question she's excited."

But just because he said it that way, there was a question. She was already so busy! As if reading my mind, he added, "She may be a little nervous now—naturally—it's a big step. But believe me, she's going to love it." He explained that the library would be the main office, but that people might be off in other rooms, too, working on "copy." And, of course, they'd be using the third floor, that huge space with my favorite windows under the eaves.

Dad reminded me that he and Mom had met when he worked for the *Waterbury Republican* and she was writing drama reviews. A generation earlier, he said, in 1896, his own parents had met in the city room of the *Newark Evening News*. So publishing a magazine was the most natural thing in the world for him. It was in his blood.

"Your mother will be writing for the magazine," he said solemnly, by which I was to understand that he was bringing her into a noble cause. It occurred to me that Mom might get more headaches, but then again maybe not, because she might prefer working on the magazine to caring for us. I had a fleeting moment of panic imagining that responsibility for the house would fall on me.

"I'm counting on you, Les, to be a big girl." Dad put his arms around me.

I snuggled up against his tweed jacket. "I'll help a lot, you'll see."

TWO MONTHS AFTER DAD'S ANNOUNCEMENT, I lay on my bed with my hands behind my head. The cold New England sun imbued the surfaces in my room with a flat vitality. I stared at the wallpaper. "Are you *sure?* Really sure you want that one?" my mother had asked me when I chose this paper at the North Adams outlet. So sure, so absolutely sure I was, and I was right.

She couldn't understand why I was drawn to something that was not only without color, but looked unfinished—simply line drawings of figures on a white background. A woman on a swing, a man nearby, a tree, a split-rail fence, a bush, and flowers. That was all. The woman is smiling, her whole body animated as she kicks her legs in the air to propel her higher. The man is seen from the back; his arm reaches out to gesture to the woman. The woman is looking in his direction, possibly staring past him, possibly connecting with his eyes. What makes this picture unusual is that the lines never meet each other; they taper out into space or drift from one figure to another, casually supplying the shape of a face and the beginning of a leaf with one stroke, then drifting away before completing fully any form. The woman's body never quite reaches the swing; the man's foot doesn't touch the ground, as if the drawing were still in the process of being completed.

I never tired of studying it, dreaming into it, analyzing it, filling in histories, and finishing lines. Some days I thought the man loved the woman, but the woman was more interested in her solitary swinging than she was in him. In another mood, it seemed to me the woman was only killing time on the swing, hoping, praying, that the man would come, and now there he was, and her happiness was complete. When I didn't make up stories, I studied the lines—how one fed into the next and the next, flowing into the repeat, where it all started again. I looked for someplace on my wall where the lines were different, trying to memorize their exact placement so I'd be able to recognize any deviance.

I never found the slightest change in the drawing, but, in the same way I searched for a four-leaf clover (which I had also never found), I kept on the hunt. The man and woman were completely real to me. What's more, they knew by now that I was watching them, but they didn't care.

I was watching everything, and there was much to see. Somewhere in this house was John Hackett, the man my father had hired from *Look* magazine to help edit *The Pioneer*. I thought he was in love with my mother, the way he stared at her, and he always seemed to have a glass of whiskey in his hand. He had the whiff of a big city about him, not only because of his rumpled dark clothes and boozy voice; there was something sophisticated and rough about his wide-gaited walk, something tough and attractive about his knowing face. But I was sure my mother only loved my father—except possibly for Pancho Gonzales, whom she had never met but whose tennis career she followed and talked about as if he were a god.

John Hackett had left New York and was living with us. He stayed in the guest room at my parents' end of the upstairs. The room had a balcony, lucky him.

There was another man named Robert, who peeled out of the driveway in a secondhand car my parents bought for him to sell advertising in the area. He was handsome but very short.

True to Dad's prediction, people were coming and going like crazy, and my mother was on the verge of hysteria, except during the cocktail hour, which calmed her down. My father was very much in charge. I heard him say to Mom, "I want lunch for seven," and she spat something back at him. But she made the lunch, and the voices in the dining room were loud, including hers. One night, when Mom and Dad were slowly climbing the stairs together after a long day, she said, "Roger, I'm so stretched."

I wasn't called upon to clean more than usual. I think Mom resigned herself to the constant messiness of papers and coffee cups. To take up the babysitting slack, Mom gave a young couple the upstairs apartment on the other side of the landing (separated from my room by a linen closet) in exchange for working on the grounds and watching after the three of us. Their advent provided me with two more avenues for spying. The dumbwaiter stopped behind their apartment, and I would wait in there, yearning to be part of their love for each other and listening for signs of the intimate things grown-up couples did. I never heard anything conclusive, just provocative murmurs and laughs. At night, after I turned out my light, I would creep into the linen closet and sit against the door that led into their space—a door I was forbidden to open. I was interested in the true life of a family that didn't make up stories for a living. But at night they listened to music, which lulled me into grogginess so that I hardly remembered making my way back into bed.

During those hectic days, I was in a state of constant excitement, not knowing whom I'd meet around the house, coming away from every encounter with the certainty that life was high adventure.

The Pioneer, A Magazine for New England, practically made me swoon with pride. The painting on the cover of the first issue was of the Old Grist Mill in South Amherst on a snowy day, seen behind the simple bridge that crossed a narrow stretch of river at that spot. I thought it the most romantic picture I'd ever seen.

Each issue started with the statement,

If you work in a town, work for it. If you live in a town, live for it. Help advance your neighborhood. Speak well of it. Stand for its civic and commercial supremacy. As long as you are part of a locality, do not belittle it. If you do, when the first high wind comes along you will be uprooted and blown away and, probably, you will never know why.

—*Charles G. Dawes*

Of course at the time I couldn't judge the content of *The Pioneer*. Looking at it decades later, I see that in fact it was a pleasant, atmospheric combination of articles on local issues; poems about New England; book, music, movie, and theater reviews (my mother wrote about books under the name Eleanor King); romantic short stories with names like "Escape in Egypt" (most by my father, some under his name, some signed with obvious pseudonyms like Roger Clark); drawings by the *New Yorker* cartoonist Lombard Jones; quirky columns like one about maple sugar houses; a sports column about area events; and cheerful ads by local merchants for fishing gear or fresh meat or new cars. There was also a column called "Household Hints," by Elizabeth Robinson Brooks—who was my mother using a combination of her family names:

If you are running a house you must realize you are performing the most important job in the world—creating the background of America. Prepare, then, for this job as you would for any other; see to it that you are well-dressed for your work in fresh, tubbable cottons or other suitable attire, that your hair is brushed and don't forget the lipstick!

The second most important item is Organization. Spare your nerves and those of the rest of the family by having a system in your home—it is the greatest single attribute of any homemaker . . .

. . . Monday, washing; Tuesday, ironing; Wednesday, mending and checking over clothes; Thursday, upstairs (or bedrooms and bathrooms if your rooms are on one floor); Friday, downstairs; Saturday, kitchen . . .

A daily schedule should start with the dusting and tidying of your living room first so that it is presentable if anyone calls. This can, in most cases, be accomplished while waiting for the morning coffee to perc or the cereal to cook; when you have done

*the breakfast dishes and the kitchen is straightened, finish the
downstairs, then the bedrooms and a quick rub around the bathrooms and you are ready for your Job of the Day on your weekly
schedule.*

She ends with a recipe for meat pie.

How 1949! And yet she was writing fantasy. My mother was
neither calm nor organized, but she was indeed dedicated to being
a homemaker, while not being unaware of how pretty she was or
how talented (she was an amateur opera singer), and dreaming of
maybe one day meeting Pancho Gonzales. She was an eager, tiny,
dark beauty, with three children and an impractical husband who
fancied himself a magazine publisher.

During that time he sat at his desk in the library greeting a
stream of people who hoped to be published. A handsome, dark-
haired poet named Doris Abramson emerged from the house one
day when I was sitting on the front steps. With the ceremonial re-
straint that would always characterize her movements, she slowly
lowered herself down next to me. It was the beginning of a friendship that would continue all the years I lived in Amherst. In her
low voice, she said conspiratorially, as if we were peers, "You know,
I was frightened to approach the man in the big house who had his
own magazine. But when I saw his eyes, I knew I had nothing to
fear. He is one of the gentlest men I have ever met."

Here was his first message to his readers:

*Writing the first editorial in a new magazine is a difficult task.
It has seemed to me (thus eschewing the editorial plural immediately) that an editorial policy is best achieved by saying what
you think at the time you think it. People have made fools of
themselves by carrying around opinions long after they have
worn themselves out, like mongrel shadows.*

There are lots of things I could speak of, that I could wrap with words which would echo as meaninglessly as a political harangue. But that would be useless, because I would not have an honest faith in those things; I would be writing what looked and sounded good but was not good. There is little sincerity in the editorials appearing in the large newspapers and magazines. Those editorials are fashioned as carefully and designedly as a bullet. They are the product not of one mind, but often of several. Their object is to stun the reader into remarking "Well, by golly, that is so, isn't it!"

Such fancy journalism is hard to achieve, and is highly paid for. Perhaps this whole piece is actually dictated by jealousy. But I honestly believe that I am not smart enough to know all the things an editorial writer is supposed to know. I shall not, therefore, be an editorial writer, at least for some time. I shall devote this page to letters from readers, and let them form the editorial policy of this magazine. I may, sometimes, get mad enough to fight back, just as anyone would, but for the most part each letter which appears on this page is going to be an editorial . . . So . . . I'm going to sit back and listen.

—R.G.

It seems to me, reading this as an adult, that Dad's statement is a curious amalgam of misplaced diffidence (after all, it was his magazine), hidden resentment, and just plain fear. Or it could have been simply a testament to his modest nature.

IN THE EARLY SUMMER of 1949 the magazine had published five issues and my father was working on the sixth. The house was upset.

Activity in The Dell had begun to shrink. People came less and less about the magazine, and my parents had an argument about John Hackett.

I heard Dad say, "He comes in here, and first he wants to take over the magazine, and now he wants to take over my wife!"

"Don't be silly, Roger! It's nothing of the sort!"

"He's a drunk!"

"He has a problem, that's true," Mom admitted.

"It's getting worse."

This was at night, and I was sitting on the landing in my seersucker pajamas listening to the goings-on downstairs. I wanted to keep on top of the forces that were threatening our family peace. If I knew the worst, maybe I could affect the outcome.

Recently my grandfather, a stocky man with bright white hair and kind eyes, had come on a sort of state visit. I always enjoyed seeing him. He and Granny lived in a rambling white house with large mullioned windows in East Orange, New Jersey, on a street called Evergreen Place. The few times I had visited, I felt embraced by the warmth of their deeply colored Persian carpets and the generosity implied by a box of chocolates with more choices than I'd ever seen. And I was charmed by the eccentricity of the sink Granny had installed in the music room so that her doctor, who examined her there on his house calls, could wash his hands without having to use the "lavatory." My favorite object, though, was a small steam engine Grampy had in his basement, which he kept polished bright silver. Granny was always afraid he would burn himself using it, but he would take us downstairs anyway to demonstrate the steam.

He was still writing six Uncle Wiggily stories a week for newspaper syndication, and he had a radio show, which we often listened to, gathered around our big Philco. His program was introduced by Brahms's Lullaby; then Howard Garis came on, saying that even if things got scary for a moment in the story he was about to read, everything would come out all right in the end.

On this cool April day when he visited us in Amherst, he

looked uncharacteristically grim. He and my parents entered the library and closed the door. "I just can't carry . . ." I heard Grampy's
booming voice, which he quickly lowered. When they emerged, my
mother was red-eyed; my father and grandfather both looked angry. Without staying for dinner, Grampy left for the three-hour
drive to New Jersey.

"If only we had more time," my mother murmured quietly to
my father when we came inside after watching Grampy's car pull
away from our door.

Soon John Hackett went back to New York. After he left,
Mom said, "Oh, Roger, wasn't it funny when John said Greenfield
was so small they pull the sidewalks in at night?" She always
reached for something cheerful when the mood turned bleak. Dad
laughed lightly and put his arm around her shoulders.

A man named Ralph Copelstone Williams, an artist who lived
in Amherst on Lincoln Avenue and who had done covers for my
father, presented himself, fedora in hand, to bid goodbye. "It's been
an uncommon pleasure," he said in courtly tones. He shook hands
with my parents and made his exit.

My mother, seeing me standing to the side, put her arm around
my shoulders, guided me out to the terrace, and sang,

> "'A,' you're adorable,
> 'B,' you're so beautiful,
> 'C,' you're a cutie full of charms.
> 'D,' you're a darling and . . ."

Dad was back in the library with the door closed.
I knew the magazine was over.

CHAPTER THREE

The year that followed the demise of my father's magazine was peaceful in our household. Dad seemed to take it in stride, continuing his routine of writing every day, but he was perhaps more subdued and tentative than before. I gathered he was sending stories to magazines and ideas to Hollywood. I had no idea whether he was selling anything, but he was amiable, and I continued to prefer his company to anyone else's in my life.

Always close, we had a new, unspoken alliance ever since my school debacle.

I had been attending the public Amity Street School, across from the town library. I was constantly in trouble in class for talking out of turn and generally disrupting the peace. A few months into the school year, Miss Bussell, who was the principal and also my first-grade teacher, called in my parents. Later Mom sternly told me that Miss Bussell had said, "I can take care of thirty-six children or Leslie, but I can't take care of thirty-six children *and* Leslie." Apparently, my parents pleaded with her to let me stay in that school, proposing that I be put back to kindergarten, since I was a year young for the grade anyway. According to my mother, the voice of power answered, "No. She'd be bored, which might make her an even worse problem. And she has so much promise."

The upshot was that my parents were going to have to find another school for me. Miss Bussell suggested a private school in Northampton, Smith College Day School. It had small classes and teachers' aides—a more suitable situation for such a restless, unruly child.

"Expelled from public school in first grade," Dad said mildly, with a mischievous smile. "I think that's a family first."

My mother was too insecure to brush aside this official disapproval. For the first time, I realized that she wanted me to please authority, and since I couldn't do it, I began to distance myself from her. Dad, however, seemed more than satisfied with me. It was as if we had a secret: the powers that be might turn away from us, but we knew we were all right. Being excluded from Miss Bussell's class wounded and shocked me, but my father's attitude soothed my bruised pride. I was more than ever devoted to him.

As far as I knew, no one else had a father anything like him. Everything about him was impeccable: his clothes, his manners, his lean physical form, his way of entering a room. He seemed the least demanding of men, but he made you hope you weren't letting down some inexpressible standard.

At five feet eleven, he was tall for those days, almost a foot taller than my mother—and fifteen years older. He had sandy hair and cornflower blue eyes that were so deep set they seemed to be flickering at the back of a cave. His nose was prominent, his chin scaled like an Englishman's. He looked remarkably like Leslie Howard.

He didn't own a pair of blue jeans and never wore T-shirts or turtlenecks, although he had a number of flannel shirts. He often wore a "sports" jacket, linen in the summer, heavy tweed in the winter. He never came to the dinner table without a tie. His shoes were wingtipped, his socks soft ribbed cotton or wool, and he wore an onyx ring in a gold setting. He carried off this style with a worn, distracted ease. His clothes seemed to have originated with his manhood, and because they were so well made, they rarely had to be replaced.

From my hiding place inside the dumbwaiter, I spied on everyone. The dumbwaiter was parallel to the laundry chute that deposited clothes next to the washing machine in the basement. The clothes made a whooshing sound as they fell past me into the cavernous stone room. My space was nothing like the chute. Mine was a palace compared to that.

Down there I could hear my mother singing as she did the laundry. She was studying with Madame someone or other. She had a true, expressive voice, touchingly light and pure. I would listen to her sing mystifying foreign words and feel energized. It had nothing to do with me, but it was so alive.

The main floor was more problematical from the point of view of detective work. Because the dumbwaiter was in the corridor between the kitchen and the front hall, voices were farther away unless someone happened to be walking from one place to the other. Still, I would sit in there feeling my heart, hearing my breath, waiting for something to happen. I'd hear the back kitchen door slam and Brooks calling to me or to my mother. I always thought his voice sounded too defenseless, too eager. It scared me because whatever it was he expected from the world, I couldn't help him. Even at that age I knew I was unbreachably different from many people around me, which made me feel somehow hard. I was beginning to realize that my temperament separated me from my mother. She and Brooks were very alike in their air of hopefulness. I couldn't tell yet about Buddy, since he was still a toddler. He was adorable, like a walking doll, and I loved him in an uncomplicated way, even though I hated dolls. Coiled inside my wooden box, hid-

den in the frame of the house, I felt myself separate, contented to
be a kind of outlaw. How innocent they all sounded.

IN 1951 Dad had an exciting idea. Television was just entering its
so-called golden age. Shows like *Lux Video Theatre* and *Kraft Television Theatre* were beginning to broadcast live drama, and soon
Omnibus, *Matinee Theater*, and *Playhouse 90* would join them. Dad
thought he'd be good at this new form. Household voices took an
upward turn. There was a perceptible rise in energy.

By winter of that year, he had accomplished his goal. "Flame
Out," an hour drama about a test pilot, was broadcast on *Lux Video
Theatre*. My parents had recently bought a black-and-white Zenith
with a twenty-four-inch screen, which we watched in great excite-
ment on Dad's night. I thought it was the best show I'd ever seen.
In truth, I preferred *The Lone Ranger*, but even though most of
Dad's play went over my head, I could tell it had excellent sus-
pense. And it made him happy.

So now he was a television writer. He talked about more tele-
plays to come. Mom was clearly in a buoyant mood. Boxes from
Cinderella shoe store arrived—always a good sign—and she sang
all the time, whatever she was doing.

One sunny spring morning I heard Dad screaming—or rather
yelping—outside the back kitchen door, "Yikes! Yikes!" I ran
through the kitchen onto the porch, by the bell my mother clanged
in the late afternoons when it was time to come home for dinner.
We could hear it all over the neighborhood. The porch stood high
over the back gravel turnaround from which a path led through
trees onto an open lawn. Apparently my father had decided to collect and burn brush. He'd dragged it to the gravel surface, doused it
with gasoline, and set it on fire. In his dreamy way he had somehow envisioned setting a fire around him—like a Wagnerian hero

in a ring of flames—and watching it consume the brush from the best seat in the house, the exact center. It had slipped his mind that such a satisfying conflagration might have dire consequences for his legs. He was jumping up and down in the middle, pulling his knees up high, and yet—here was the lovely part for the children— he was laughing at his utter folly. I knew there was something terribly wrong with a grown man setting himself on fire by mistake. How could he not anticipate the outcome? At seven years old, I would have known better. Why didn't he?

Around that time my parents were having many intense conversations that ceased the moment I approached. More than once, as I drew near them in the midst of this serial dialogue, it was obvious they were upset, especially my father. After a few weeks I figured out that they were talking about Dad's parents. But that was all I could glean.

Eventually they gave me a prepared explanation. As usual with my mother, there was a long preamble. Granny and Grampy were getting old now, and Granny was not well. You know, Granny has been ailing for many years . . .

Dad sat with his legs crossed, trying to look impassive. What I couldn't have known then was that Dad's parents had been giving him money every month, and that this present conversation had more than a little to do with Dad's inability to make enough to support our living in The Dell and his parents' decision to consolidate their own expenses.

"Granny doesn't want to go into a nursing home. And they can't handle that big Victorian house anymore. They'd actually like us all to go to New Jersey and move in with them . . ."

"But—," I began, panic rising.

"No, no. We're not going to move away. How would you like it if Granny and Grampy came to live with us?"

I thought it would be fantastic. I had already begun to keep a diary, writing in it every day without fail, and I was beginning to imagine one day becoming a writer in my spare time between acting in plays and movies, since I would also be a famous actress. Although my grandfather was familiar and cozy, my grandmother was an aloof figure of mystery and fascination. I'd never made much headway with her when we went down for visits; she seemed entirely uninterested in my small person. However, if I had her under my roof! What conversations we could have. And Grampy I adored. Possibly because he loved children, or maybe because he just loved to have children love him. Having him to ourselves! He could come to my school and tell Uncle Wiggily stories, and he'd take walks with us, and . . .

"When are they coming?" I asked. "I can't wait."

CHAPTER FOUR

One warm, heavy afternoon in the fall of 1951, a long, swank black car crunched into our drive.

"They're here!"

Brooks and I clambered down the stairs.

We all gathered on the front porch. My father stepped forward with great dignity and helped his mother out of the car.

"Hello, Mother."

"Hello, Roger."

He kissed her on the cheek, which she distantly acknowledged.

"Hello, son!" boomed his father, shaking hands, then brushing past him on his way to the front door. "Hello, children!"

A uniformed man carried suitcases into the hall. I was dazzled by the stately car and driver. Dazzled by the evidence of my grandparents' stature. Dazzled by my own reflected glory with such personages in my family. Life was about to become even sweeter. Grampy would tell us delightful stories with soothing endings, and he would infuse our days with his infectious, boisterous energy. I would burrow into the soul of my grandmother and discover the secret of having the ambition to write so many books and the courage to be the only woman working on a newspaper in the dark days of another century. Beyond that, I hoped also that I would discover in them the personalities of their pen names. This would all take time and sly attention to detail. Howard and Lilian were heroes. And here they were, about to be part of us. I could see a glorious future, in which happiness would be so taken for granted that my mind would be free to range over limitless possibilities for perfect fulfillment. I was eight. Lilian was seventy-nine. Howard was seventy-seven. I was eager to establish deep contact with them as soon as possible. Who knew how long they would live?

In the hall, Lilian let out a beset sigh. On this humid day she was wearing thick dark stockings and black leather lace-up heels of a stylishly narrow cut. She was tall and slightly plump. Her dress was black, with tricky open-and-closed pleating and a belt with a tortoiseshell buckle. At her neck she wore an ivory-and-silver brooch. Her long gray hair was gathered in a loose bun. Set on her small nose was a pair of wire glasses, which gave her sensitive, imperious expression an added element of studiousness.

"Of all outrageous things," she declared, "our driver wouldn't take the Merritt Parkway. He insisted we were a commercial vehicle because he was being paid. So he took an endless truck route. That's why we're so late! Have you ever heard of anything so ridiculous? I told him he was wrong, but he wouldn't listen to me."

The driver, looking abashed, began to carry in the luggage.

"*That's* what happened!" my mother said. "We were worried about you. We expected you two hours ago."

"And we would have been here then, if our driver—"

"Now, Lily," Grampy said, which immediately silenced her.

My mother, her tiny feet in sandals, her small waist exaggerated by a wide belt and full skirt, her dark hair brushed back dashingly, doled out directions.

To the driver: "Would you be so kind as to carry the bags to the upstairs hall?"

To Brooks and me: "Pipe down. There will be plenty of time to visit with your grandparents. I'm sure they're tired from their journey."

To Dad: "Roger, would you help me get your parents settled into their rooms?"

To Grampy: "Would you like a cup of tea or a cocktail?"

To Granny: "Are you very tired? Would you like to lie down before dinner?"

Howard—sturdy, broad-shouldered, shorter than his wife, and wearing a wide-lapel white linen suit with a bright tie of red design—boomed his voice into the close afternoon air.

"Mabs, you're a sight for sore eyes! Don't fuss, now, we're fine. The drive wasn't bad at all. Nice countryside you've got here. Lily, don't bother with that case; give it to me. I'll bring it upstairs for you. Mabs, I might just take you up on that cocktail. A sherry would be fine. What time's dinner?"

Buddy, barely three, tottered about at the edge of the group, while six-year-old Brooks shyly reached up for his grandfather's hand, which Howard took as naturally as a man buttons his jacket in a breeze.

My father, taller than both his parents, taller than everyone in the hall that afternoon, stood in the midst of the commotion and looked overtaken. He appeared in the grip of another reality. I had the impression that something was crowding into his mind, and for a moment I was afraid for him.

"Mother, let me help you," he said gently, taking Lilian's arm. "Mabs has done a wonderful job preparing your rooms."

They proceeded to the stairs and up. I cut in front of them and ran ahead.

"You'll love the curtains!" I said excitedly. "And wait till you see the wallpaper!"

Mom was behind us with Grampy, who was still holding Brooks's hand. The adults chatted about the weather. Brooks, wrapped in shyness, was quiet.

At the door to her new room, my grandmother stopped and silently took in her surroundings. She removed and put back one of her fine hairpins. Dad went on with his father and Brooks to the next room. Mom and I waited expectantly for Granny's reaction.

"I'm afraid this is entirely too bright," she said at last. "Since I'm to live here, I need a more calming atmosphere. I'm surprised you didn't know that, Mabel. I'll need darker drapes. I have to rest most of the time, you know."

My mother went white. "I thought this would please you. The curtains were very special. I made them myself. I think the room is lovely. So cheerful. I thought you'd want it cheerful."

I felt stricken.

"It's just not suitable for living in, Mabel. It might do for a guest room. You've made it very pretty—although I've never been partial to pastels. But I'm going to be in here most of the time, and you know my eyes are very sensitive to light. Are velvet drapes available? I'll make some arrangements tomorrow. It will all have to be changed."

"I think it looks like a picture in a magazine," I said protectively. How could Granny say these things? My mother had spent more than a month working on the rooms—this large bedroom/sitting room for Granny, a smaller bedroom for Grampy, and a long connecting bathroom. There were two entrances into the suite from the hall—the far one into a short corridor that led to Grampy's room, and the doorway in which we now stood, which opened directly into Granny's quarters. It had been my mother's summer project, mixing the wallpaper glue in a wide bucket, slathering it on the paper draped over an ironing board, and then fixing it on the wall with a wide, hard-bristled, long-handled brush. She made the curtains on her black sewing machine, which folded down into its own wooden table and had a foot pedal of filigreed iron.

Granny didn't bother to answer me. Instead she said, "I'm tired now. I need to rest my eyes. I'm going to lie down for a while." She stretched out on the bed after taking off her shoes.

Mom covered her with a light blanket. "Would you like a cup of tea?"

"A glass of cool water would be fine."

"I'll bring it right up. Come, Leslie, let's let Granny rest."

My grandfather came into the room. "Isn't this great, Lily? Haven't they done a bang-up job?"

"I'm resting now, Howard."

Mom caught Dad's eye. He started to go in, but she motioned him to stay out. I put my arm around her waist. I had a fearful intimation that these last moments were going to result in a migraine headache in a few days. I hadn't yet made a conscious connection between emotional stress and her terrifying headaches, but I had an intuition about them that wasn't quite a formed thought. How could Granny not consider my mother's feelings? It was so aberrational that I wondered for a fleeting second if it had, indeed, happened. What did it mean? Maybe it was one of her fictional personalities speaking, not her true self. Or maybe her characters *were* her true self. Did that happen with writers? I'd been told that Granny's favorite books were her mysteries, and they had frightening people in them. Unlike sweet Mrs. Bobbsey.

"Don't mind Lily," Grampy said to us when he saw that she was already on the bed with her eyes closed, although he sounded as if he minded quite a lot that she had immediately retired. He didn't even know about the terrible things she had just said to my mother. "How about that sherry, Mabs?"

"I won't be down for dinner, Howard."

"All right, Lily."

"I'll take it on a tray."

"All right."

"You know what I like."

"I'll take care of it, Lily."

"Are you going down?"

"For a little while. I'll come back and sit with you before dinner."

"Good. Close the door, please."

Later that night I opened *The Ghost of Melody Lane*, one of the books I had moved, a few days earlier, from our library to the bookcase at the head of my bed. The aqua spine had an imprint of an ink-black hand above the name LILIAN GARIS. Although I was younger than her adolescent audience, I was primed to come under her spell. I read,

The night was now dark and dreary, as fall nights are apt to be, and the massive trees with heavy shrubbery seemed to weave sinister figures into the very darkness.

Not far from me at this very moment, the woman who had written those words was lying in her bed. This, too, was a dark fall night, and outside her window were massive trees, just like the ones in her story. I had never thought their shadows were scary. Did she know something about life that I should learn? I was angry at her on behalf of my mother, but maybe I should reconsider. I went down the hall to the bathroom and heard raised voices in my parents' room.

THE NEXT MORNING the sound of typing was already coming from behind the library door by 8:30. It had to be Grampy, since I knew

Dad was still asleep. I thought it was incredible that he hadn't even had time to unpack and he was already at work.

I'd been told many times that his imagination was like an open faucet, a steady stream of ideas. I could hear slow tapping alternating with fusillades. When I came back to listen an hour later, it sounded just the same. Around noon he emerged, looking refreshed and happy.

"What did you write, Grampy?"

"Three stories, Les."

"Uncle Wiggily?"

"Yessiree."

"Three in one *day*?"

"Goodness me, I've been doing that for over forty years," he answered, beaming.

"But you just got here!"

He laughed. "Deadlines don't stop for a little thing like a move. And I like to keep ahead."

So Uncle Wiggily had had three new adventures. Maybe he'd gone over to Jackie and Peetie Bow Wow's house and found them scowling because they had new sleds and there was no snow. So Uncle Wiggily took wheels from their baby-dog carriages, attached them to the sleds, and off they went! And then . . . All this and more in one morning. I looked behind him through the library door. I could see the desk sitting inexpressively in front of the angled windows. But just moments earlier, all those characters were alive there, as if called up by sorcery.

"Do you like the room?"

"It's a beautiful room, a beautiful room."

"Would you like to go for a walk with me?"

"Maybe later, Les. I'd better go check on Lily, see if she needs anything."

He padded across the hall—although he was neatly dressed, he was wearing slippers—and made his way upstairs, holding the banister as he went. His forearms were as muscular as a laborer's.

Mom didn't get a migraine, but Dad stayed in bed later than usual. He came downstairs a little before noon and looked mutely toward his father's typing sounds behind the closed door, then disappeared into the kitchen to fix his breakfast of soft-boiled eggs, a piece of toast, and canned apricots in syrup. He'd suffered all his life from ulcers, and with his restricted diet he ate exactly the same breakfast every day.

Over the next weeks, my mother worked on changing Granny's room. Granny wore a succession of intricately tailored dresses and propped herself up against her bed pillows, cooling herself with one of her decorated accordion fans and directing the proceedings. Although my mother was obviously distressed, she was a good sport about it. When I asked her why she didn't seem angry, she said, "It comes from having British parents. Chin up, chest out, carry on."

Granny ordered dark drapes, changed the bedding from pale blue to claret, and hung icons of the Virgin Mary. I was mesmerized by the Virgin's maternal expression, which gazed down with distant benevolence from the small wooden pictures framed in burnished gold. A musty smell with a faint overlay of rose perfume began to permeate the air. The room was transfigured from a pleasant domain of uncomplicated sunniness into a sanctum of unfathomable mystery.

During these alterations I hung around, trying to engage Granny in conversation. She still had not come down for dinner, which disappointed, baffled, and intrigued me. What a rich private life she must have, I thought, being content to be by herself so much.

On top of her bureau were objects of intense fascination: a silver jewelry box, crystal perfume bottles, and a syringe on a gilded tray. Did she give herself shots? Mom told me she had diabetes.

I was eating an apple in her room under the guise of helping Mom, and when I got to the core, Granny asked me to hand it to her. She took three seeds and pressed each one to my forehead. They were sticky and stayed on my skin. "Close your eyes," she told me, "and make three wishes, one for each seed. Make sure you know which wish goes with which seed. The one that stays on your forehead longest is the one that will come true."

I don't remember what I wished for, but I remember believing that everything she told me was unimpeachable.

In the afternoons she listened to radio soap operas. "I just want to see how they work out this plot," she would say defensively. Sometimes I sat on the floor at the foot of her bed, where she couldn't see me, and listened, too. From my spot I had a view of the dark recesses of her fireplace, a tall wing chair by one bright window, and another shadowy window, outside of which were great evergreens dividing up the light. Of the radio shows, I especially liked *This Is Nora Blake*, and *Just Plain Bill*, but my favorite was *Backstage Wife*:

> *Now we present, once again,* Backstage Wife, *the story of Mary Noble, a little Iowa girl who married one of America's most handsome actors, Larry Noble, matinee idol of a million other women . . .*

Mary Noble had to fend off the women who tried to take her gorgeous Broadway star from her. Will she keep her man away from the scheming vixens? I felt for her. Will she lose Larry? No, he'll stay true if Mary can hold those women back! He loves his wife. As I listened to these juicy stories, thinking that Broadway was the epitome of glamour, deciding I would never be a backstage wife, I imagined my illustrious destiny, although I wasn't sure what it was. I hoped that the old woman on the bed above me might show me the way. Even so, I felt it was safest just now to remain curled up on the floor, hidden from view. She was tricky and would need much study.

Meanwhile, downstairs in the library, Mom and Grampy worked on the painstaking task of unpacking the boxes of books that had been sent ahead from New Jersey.

The most impressive was a nineteenth-century edition of the complete works of Dickens. These were oversize dark brown leather, and took up several shelves. They were Howard's most prized possession.

He had also brought the complete works of James Fenimore Cooper and H. Rider Haggard, two authors he'd been reading all his life. Cooper's Leatherstocking Tales took place in upstate New York, where Howard had spent his childhood, so they reminded him of his youth. But the first book he ever checked out of a library was Haggard's *Allan Quartermain*, a sequel to the famous *King Solomon's Mines*. Howard had been a Haggard devotee ever since. Fierce African warriors, lost civilizations, wildly romantic love, mythic physical beauty, jungle darkness; this was Haggard's world, now brought into our midst. What should I read first? My mother said they were too old for me and not appropriate, but Dad told me in private that in a few years I should start with Haggard's *She*. It was about the power of women, he said with a wry smile.

One day I was hovering in the upstairs hall, eavesdropping outside Granny's room. My mother was in there. I could sense the tension between the two women, which was thrilling in a creepy sort of way. Lilian was conveying some complaint to Mom, but I couldn't tell what it was. If I listened closely, I thought I might discover a reason for Granny's abiding crankiness. Suddenly her voice rose in anger, shrill with vitriol.

"But the Stratemeyers! Look how much *they* made!"

So she hates the people who hired them to write the books! I hadn't suspected that. Maybe Stratemeyer was the cause of my grandmother's pain; she was certainly angry about the money.

"Oh, but Lily, you've done *so* well!" my mother said.

I knew Mom's reassurance was futile. I already sensed that nothing would change Lilian's mind when it was set about something. I retreated to my own room, feeling sorry for my well-intentioned mother. Sitting on my bed, I stored the conversation away in my mind, to be reexamined when I had more information.

Later that day, Granny wandered into my parents' room. They had twin beds, and my mother had recently put a luxuriously soft blue blanket on hers.

"Mabel, what are you doing with that blanket?" Lilian scolded. "That is not for you! I brought that up here for Roger! That is for Roger!"

"Oh, Lilian." Mom sighed wearily. "I thought it was for both of us."

"No, Mabel. That's for Roger. I don't want him catching a chill."

Mom yanked the blanket off her bed with an eloquent show of exasperation and put it on Dad's. "There!" she said angrily.

Although Lilian didn't eat dinner with us, she often ventured downstairs around five o'clock to check on the food preparation. We had a cook who came in from four to eight, a soft-spoken round woman named Jean Bosworth. With seven of her own, she was used to children, and she treated us with tranquil indulgence, ignoring our pestering, moving us away from the sink, allowing us to lick the cake batter spoon, occasionally shooing us from the room so she could concentrate. Granny would wander into the kitchen and look around with grave intensity, like a bird scanning for sustenance or danger. And then, invariably, she would give directives to Jean: "Don't put too much salt in the potatoes" or "My son can't eat anything tough, you know. He has a delicate digestive

system. Make sure you cook it until it's tender." Or, "Is that rhu-
barb pie you're making? You'll need to put a lot of sugar in it for Mr.
Garis senior. He doesn't like anything sour." Her tone was chasten-
ing, and Jean's dignified "Yes, Mrs. Garis" made me ashamed.

After setting things straight, Lilian would mount the stairs to
her chamber, change into a Japanese dressing gown, reassume her
recumbent position on top of her bedspread, and close her eyes, an
expression of querulous suffering etched on her intelligent face. If
anyone came into her room, she would say, "I'm not taking a nap.
I'm only resting my eyes."

Down by our brook, through a parting of bushes only visible
close up, was a towering oak tree with a violent history embedded
in its trunk. At one time its massive trunk must have been struck
by lightning, and the landowners filled the burned-out hole with
gray stone. Bark had grown around the edges of the wound, forming a wavy frame, like the door to a house of wood spirits. From
high up, a long branch curved down and outward, with a dip in it
near the ground that made a perfect seat. I spent many aimless afternoons swinging on that branch. Since the arrival of my grandparents, I would sit there trying to figure out the lay of the land.
Was I imagining a change in my father? I thought perhaps it had
to do with giving up the library for his father, although when he
first made the move, he seemed happy to be leaving the house for
an office. Jones Library had given him a good room, part of a section they reserved for writers and academics. The room was free of
charge, and something of an honor. He told us he had at last found
the perfect working situation.

Yet now, when he came down in the morning and saw the library door closed, he looked mournful.

And even though he seemed to enjoy being with his father, he
deferred to him to a surprising degree. For the first time, I was seeing him as an unarmored son rather than my knightly father.

Why did Grampy sit at the foot of the dinner table opposite Mom? Why didn't Dad still sit there? Now he sat to Mom's left, and Grampy dominated the conversation. I would look across the table to my father and catch his eye, and he'd give me a private smile while Howard told a story. They were great stories, but I missed my father's quiet humor, which needed more silence to land.

Lilian's presence was another muddle. I couldn't decipher the look in my father's eyes that first afternoon when she arrived. It was as if there was something between them that threatened him in some way. I dismissed that thought as soon as I had it. It was too far-fetched—probably just another one of my overly dramatic notions.

However, there was one situation that troubled me deeply. Lilian came out of her room while Brooks was going to sleep. She stood by his bed, looked down at him, and said, "You must never disturb your father when he's resting. He's ill. He's very ill and needs quiet."

Her words terrified Brooks. He ran to Mom, crying, *Dad is sick? Dad is sick? What's the matter with him?*

I came into the tail end of that drama. I was across the hall in my bedroom when Mom, her voice quavering, stood just inside Lilian's door and said, "Don't you ever tell the children their father is sick! He's *not* sick! I will not have you telling them such a thing! Do you understand? You are never, ever to say that again!" I didn't hear Granny's reply.

What did the old woman mean?

Certainly he was not like other fathers. He wasn't physically active, he didn't have a regular job, he slept late, he didn't take his sons on outdoor trips. But he was available for deep discussions, he loved to laugh, he tucked me in every night even as I was growing older. He seemed perfect.

From my perch in the tree, I looked up into the mass of leaves turning gold. I could barely see the sky through the roof of dense color. I liked that. I felt entirely hidden. I thought about Amherst's great woman poet and wondered if proximity conferred any special meaning that might apply to my small self. Perhaps it was myth, but I'd been told that Emily Dickinson used to walk across the fields from her house to this tree and sit on this very branch, just as I was doing now. It would have been an easy five-minute walk for her, unless she stopped to daydream along the way; surely poets did a great deal of that. I learned about her in first grade when my mother told me she had gone to the Amherst school I'd been asked to leave. It was one more reason why being expelled had hurt. But Emily Dickinson had also briefly gone to our church, and we were members in good standing, so I still had two connections: the church and our oak tree. I was intrigued by the idea that she had lowered baskets of cookies by rope from her window to children below. Whenever I walked by her house, I stared at the upstairs windows, trying to picture the basket from the point of view of children standing in that very spot a hundred years ago, imagining a white napkin fluttering in the breeze. Intuitively I understood how a person's entire world could exist in one house. At that charged moment in my life it felt as if all I needed to learn about the universe was contained in my own home.

THAT FALL, when the heat wave broke, we had a tremendous thunderstorm, one of those New England events where the sky turns darkly livid and the air comes to life.

"Roger! Come outside!" Grampy called. "We'll watch the storm!"

Dad's father loved thunder and lightning. When Dad was a boy and the weather was calm, his father used to take him to a local amusement park that had a thunder machine. Whenever a storm blew up during Dad's childhood, it was a ritual to go outside with his father to see the sky change, watch the cataclysm until they got soaked, and come inside. But I knew nothing about that, and I was surprised when the two men stood on the terrace looking up at the sky while everyone else was running for cover. There was something thrilling about Grampy's childish excitement.

When the storm really hit—with such force that I feared the windows would break—the men came inside, laughing and dripping wet. Mom gave them towels, calling them silly, loving every minute of it.

I went upstairs and noticed light flickering inside the open door of my grandmother's room, something besides the charges of lightning that were filling windows with brilliant white. My father and grandfather, cheerful and wet, passed me in the hallway as they went into their rooms to change into dry clothes.

After hesitating for a few minutes because something was frightening me, I stepped into her room. Clothed in a lace nightgown and her customary long robe of beige, apricot, and green, her hair down to her shoulders, she stood at her bureau lighting a candle. Several were already burning. She was saying something I couldn't understand. Repeating the words. Perhaps it's Latin, I thought. It sounded like an incantation.

She didn't seem to see me. I noticed that my grandfather, dry now, was sitting in his chair by the window. He was watching her. We both watched her. "Lily's saying a prayer," he whispered, barely audible above the rain and thunder. "For the storm. Protection, you know." He smiled at me. He inhabited warmth and safety. She was in a spooky zone, and the sight of her made me shiver. I stood absolutely still. I wondered if our safety could possibly be entwined with her prayer.

CHAPTER FIVE

Since my grandfather had moved to Amherst, he had made a remarkable friend. Robert Frost, the Simpson Lecturer in Literature at the college, was a fixture in Amherst in the fall and spring, when he came for several weeks at a time to teach. He was a local celebrity, treasured for his poetry, but not made a fuss over, both because of his own crusty reserve and the inclination of New Englanders not to be impressed.

My grandfather was a more visible personage because wherever he went, he was followed by children. *Uncle Wiggily* books were still selling in the hundreds of thousands and syndicated all over the country, and the local papers had announced his arrival in town. His celebrity was of the acceptable, homespun, childlike variety. He was a picturesque sight, trudging up Spring Street to the center of town on an errand for Lilian, surrounded by children begging him to tell them a story or just walking quietly in his wake, happy to be near him. From a distance you could see the square, white-haired man with his tanned face, gesturing to the children, laughing with them, or holding them in silent thrall to one of his cliff-hanging stories.

Mr. Frost had stopped my mother in town one day and asked to meet Howard. She invited him for tea, although the men preferred sherry, and after that they began to spend time together. Frost was one year older, considerably taller, and—from a child's point of view—not nearly as nice. The few times I tried to sit on his lap, he obviously sensed my purpose as I approached him, because he brushed his legs with his hard hand, as if casting me off in advance, so I steered a path away from him. He had a deep, quavery voice and the kind of New England accent that turned "hear" into "hee-ah," while at the same time he sounded gravely patrician.

Once, I took Frost's big green-jacketed collection of poetry, which had recently been issued, and casually strolled across the hall in full view of the two men in the living room. I pretended to be reading the poems, as if I had no idea that Mr. Frost was near. I earned nothing from that pantomime.

They were a remarkable pair, the misanthropic poet and the benevolent children's writer. Frost rarely smiled, whereas my grandfather could hardly stop. Age was a running joke between them. Frost, pretending to be the younger one, teased Grampy, saying that the one good thing about the San Francisco fire was that his birth certificate burned up. My grandfather, on the other hand, liked to boast about his longevity. At seventy-nine, he said he was in his eightieth year. Each birthday was another triumph for him.

They took long walks together deep in conversation, Frost in his trademark sneakers. Grampy told me they spoke of harvests and weather, both men having a wide, specific knowledge of country ways. Perhaps in old age they were nostalgic for the tough simplicity of rural life. I don't think they talked much about each other's work, but I could be wrong. I know Howard would have admired Frost's strong-fibered, unadorned poetry, and perhaps Frost was drawn to the singularly American flavor of my grandfather's books. I don't imagine that the author of "The Death of the Hired

Man" would have cared much for the cozy world of Uncle Wiggily. But who knows? Frost wrote some gentle stories for his own children. A powerful bond developed between the two men, which shut out the rest of the world. The heart of their friendship was both mysterious to me and entirely natural. Something seemed inevitable about their coming together late in life. The elderly pair became a familiar sight, walking along country roads in Amherst.

Even though Frost was an aloof, flinty presence to me, I yearned to know him. I was seduced by the paradox that this austere man produced something as soulful as poetry. Unlike my grandparents, he didn't make plotted books for young people; he worked in the most sophisticated and elusive form of all. I tried to impose myself on his afternoons with Grampy, but I never succeeded. Neither did my father, whose presence was clearly not welcomed by the two old men. They seemed locked away together in their age and their wintry heads.

Meanwhile the author of *The Bobbsey Twins in the Country* and *Let's Pretend We're at the Circus* stayed in her room, "resting." She said she had a "bad heart" and her nerves were "too close to the surface" and her throat was "too small" and her blood was "too thick." It was said she suffered from "hardening of the arteries." In my mind she was changing from a romantic figure into someone I genuinely feared. I remember one day stumbling out of her room sobbing and disoriented. What had I said? What had I done? She was vociferously displeased with me. I'd gone into her room for a visit, and to my stunned surprise she'd called me "not a good person," a "bad spirit," and said that she hoped I was "ashamed" of myself. It was like having the wind kicked out of me. Mom said, "She does that to people. She makes them feel guilty. It's something she does."

I was astounded. The attack had happened so quickly that her ability to demoralize and confuse me so thoroughly felt like black magic. Maybe she reproached my motive for coming into her room, or my behavior as a daughter or granddaughter, or possibly my appearance. Maybe I'd said something rude that she'd overheard; I certainly never spoke rudely to her. I was shattered by her attack.

There was another scene around that time. I came home from school and ran upstairs to write something down in my diary. My father was standing in his mother's doorway, facing into the room, his hands raised in front of him.

"You don't know what you're talking about!" he said ferociously, but then he saw me and stopped speaking.

"It's nothing, Les," he said, and quickly walked down the hallway toward his own room.

"Mabel!" Granny called.

When my mother came, I could hear Lilian say, "I listened to Madeleine Carroll in a radio play last night, and I can tell you she would never, ever have anything to do with one of Roger's plays! That woman is a professional! The idea that he would ask a woman of that caliber to be in one of his plays is ridiculous!"

My mother disappeared into the room and closed the door after her.

I was shaken. Why wouldn't someone professional want to work with Dad? What was wrong with him? What did Granny mean?

Madeleine Carroll was in fact about to work with Dad in one of his TV plays—as were David Niven and Nina Foch. These were the days when Sid Caesar did live comedy and original television was at its zenith. Dad's plays had straightforward titles: *Fog Station*, *Way of Courage*, *One Hundred Red Convertibles*, *A Corporal's Christmas*, *The Key* . . . They were well-crafted thrillers and comedies with a heavy overlay of cliff-hanging romance. It was a great source of pride to my parents that one of Dad's pieces, *The Inn*, was published as a chapter called "The Hour-Long Television Play" in the book *Television Writing and Selling*, the current bible for TV writers.

After the death of *The Pioneer*, he was making money again. With live television he had found a good professional niche, although he hinted broadly that TV was only a stepping-stone for him in his quest for success on the New York stage.

We came together in the living room on Dad's TV nights. He sat in his tall armchair and crossed his slim tweed-clad legs. One long hand, wearing his onyx ring, rested on his knee. I sprawled on the floor by his side, his ankles inches from my face.

As I watched each play, I thought, This is so good! My father's so talented! He's met those people in the cast—they *know* him! My father is part of that exalted theatrical world. Oh, bliss. Dad was quite still, radiating modesty and contentment, a thin smile on his face.

Mom sat in her own favorite chair, which was upholstered with chintz. She looked stately and ready to pounce on anyone who spoke during Dad's dialogue. Grampy, in another armchair, said, "Here we go, Roger!" while the opening credits rolled. My two brothers nudged each other but kept the holy silence.

Why wasn't Lilian there? As if Dad's shows were as unimportant as our dinners, she never deigned to come down for them. Except once, when she sat bolt upright on the couch, then left during the first commercial, never to return. No one in my family said anything about it—then or ever in my hearing. It was simply assumed that Granny had no interest in anything on television, including work by her son.

Sometimes, when we were all together watching his plays, I looked at Dad, trying to find a sign on his face that he was bothered by his mother's absence, but I never found anything I recognized as distress. So I forgot about her and gave myself over to the general feeling of celebration among us.

As soon as Mom switched off the TV at the end of the telecast, Grampy said something unspecific and boosterish, like "Good job, son!" And I tried to say something specific and incisive, like "That was a great line you wrote at the moment when he realized he would never see her again."

The phone would ring.

"Oh, thank you!" Dad said into the receiver, smiling broadly now. "Yes, we'll get together soon. Thanks again."

Those nights were wholly sweet. My father was successful, my mother was beautiful, my grandfather was lovable, my brothers were adorable, my grandmother was . . . well, we didn't have to think about her. And I was the beloved daughter, the precocious girl whose future was full of bright promise. I was intoxicated by life.

In school, I looked two years younger than everyone else in my class. I was, in fact, one year younger than the others and looked a year younger than my age. My best friend was a foot taller than I, but none of this made much difference to me since The Dell was the axis around which everything important revolved.

After school I usually went right to Valentine Hall, the Amherst College dining center, which was a block from our house. There I sat at the soda counter, ogling the college boys. I always had a vanilla milk shake and an egg salad sandwich on toast. This was at about 4:00 p.m. After that I went home and ate a head of iceberg lettuce with oil and vinegar. At six o'clock, when we sat down for dinner, I still had a voracious appetite. And yet I was rail thin, my wrists as narrow as batons. My metabolism was incinerating calories. I couldn't sit still. If I crossed my legs, I was compelled to jiggle my foot up and down or sideways, so I twisted one foot behind the other ankle to stop moving. I had loose joints and virtually no body fat, so my legs wound around each other as if my bones were made of rubber. To my growing mystification, I was beginning to develop a strange rage whose source I couldn't divine. It was as if my frantic movements were in reaction to this new emotion, as if it were always behind me and I had to race to keep ahead of it. Feeling somewhat possessed, I walked the streets near our house, making loops through the neighborhood, up Spring Street, turning right on Seelye, past the Congregational church and down Main, where I lingered in front of Emily Dickinson's house trying to feel what it must have been like to be her, staying inside for a lifetime, choosing extreme quiet.

Back at home, in the afternoons before dinner, my father sat in the living room reading the paper and eating an apple. Grampy would sit upstairs by Granny in his Sleepy Hollow chair. That's what he called it. Looking like a Norman Rockwell illustration, it had large, dark red wooden armrests that curved all the way to the ground, and a back that could recline to a comfortable angle. "I'll go keep Lily company in my Sleepy Hollow chair," he'd say. My mother would be in her room writing letters or changing before dinner. I'd come downstairs, knowing Dad would put down his paper and smile at me. A smile that invited me to speak. "How are you, Les?" he'd say. My youngest brother, Buddy, might be climbing on Grampy's lap just then in his big chair. Brooks, sensing that I'd left my room, would follow me downstairs, but by that time, I already had Dad's attention, and Brooks would have to wait.

Dad took me for rides in our car or walks around the grounds. We spoke much more of his thoughts than of my own. My memory is that I was more interested in what he was thinking than in my own small life, but I realize now that couldn't have been right, because I was always reading or writing something in my diary. I had a lot of ideas and I liked to talk, so I think my attentiveness was partly because I sensed a desperate need in him to unburden himself, and I felt that my role was to react with as much sensitivity and intelligence as I could muster. I was vain enough to believe that I was a better listener than my mother and that I could more brilliantly assess a complicated situation. For all I know, he told her the same things he told me, but—like a mistress jealous of the wife—it was my secret pride that I shared his innermost thoughts. He was my first intellectual companion.

He told me about books. Camus, T. S. Eliot, Santayana were favorites. He was interested in Santayana's idea that the perception of beauty is a basic, primitive instinct embedded in the human personality. I wasn't old enough to understand what he was telling me, and I was certainly too young to read these books, but I had the overall impression that he was trying to discover what it meant to be a human being—and that beauty was essential to everything. Sometimes he asked my "advice" on a scene he was writing. Would a girl carry a comb around in her pocket? Was "don't be a drag" the right phrase? He listened solemnly to my answers and smiled at me with love. "Great, Les, thanks. You're a big help." Walking beside him, half as tall, I allowed myself to believe I was his equal.

One of his abiding preoccupations was sin. His face reddened with emotion as he told me that Catholics had it all wrong: there was no such thing as sin. His religious upbringing had been strict. I felt that I was witnessing the results of an agonizing journey through the wilds of dogma and harsh strictures. I thought he was like a soldier back from the front who had narrowly escaped death. And I was there with him, sharing his private deliverance. There was a trembling urgency in the way he spoke of the debilitating guilt of Catholics, who were frightened that they would commit a sin at every turn. It seemed to be a life-and-death matter to him. He made me feel that if I didn't abandon the concept of sin, my life would be wrecked. What a heady thought. I nodded sagely. No such thing as sin . . .

Literature, aesthetics, philosophy, sin—these were large concerns for a little girl. I carried them around with me as if they were the alchemy that turned me into a superhero whose weapon was a hidden knowledge of the soul.

On the afternoon of April 26, 1953, we had a small party for my grandfather's eightieth birthday. My parents' friends were drawn more from the Amherst College administration than from the faculty: Horace (Bud) and Mary Hewlett—he a former history instructor and current director of public relations, she a western beauty who wore heavy silver jewelry; Minot (Nat) Grose, the Amherst College assistant treasurer and soon-to-be business manager, and his wife, Ellie, who was wealthy, witty, and sad. All the couples who were members of my parents' circle were courteous, amiable, well-turned-out, well-spoken people, and they were serious cocktail drinkers who held their liquor and rarely raised their voices. Mr. Frost and Doris Abramson were both there, too. They were not natural chums. She was a theatrical, bohemian Provincetown lesbian; his curmudgeonly seriousness set him apart as a rural loner. They both had well-developed airs and suspicions, and they both probably felt superior to my parents' less intellectual friends. But to us, those friends were comforting, with their elegant manners and stable marriages, and easy to be with. My parents were entirely relaxed in their company.

Grampy, dressed in his usual white suit, shorter and bulkier than most of the guests, was oblivious to the subtle social currents around him. Radiating joy, he sipped sherry and basked in the high-ceilinged room filled with spring light. He was not a man without ego, and like a child, he loved being the center of attention. There were toasts. He made people laugh. Granny stayed upstairs.

For days the journalists had been phoning Grampy for interviews. Here's what appeared in the *Newark Evening News*:

"It was easier when I lived in East Orange," he confided via telephone. "You could talk to those bunnies in New Jersey. Up

here in New England the rabbits are less talkative. You meet one and make an opening comment like 'Nice day' and all he'll say is, 'I'll tell you tomorrow if it was.' "

There was a chuckle in Garis's voice. His caller told him he sounded chipper as ever.

"I am," he said. "I feel fine and I still get a kick out of the bedtime stories. The publisher has just brought out the 75th book on Uncle Wiggily. The first printing is 500,000 copies, so I guess people still like them."

Howard takes a daily stroll to get ideas for his Uncle Wiggily stories, which still appear in The News five days a week.

After the party, Grampy went upstairs to sit with Granny. The next thing we knew, he was heading for the front door.

"Where are you going?" my mother asked. "Dinner's ready."

"Back in a jiffy. Got to get something for Lily."

"Can't it wait?"

"She wants it now."

"I'll drive you."

She wanted skin cream for her arms, which she said were getting dry.

Later that night, suddenly awake from a frightening nightmare, I lay in the dark calming myself down. I'm here, I'm safe. Moonlight shone in brightly enough so that I could just make out the lines on my wallpaper. The swinging woman and the gesturing man were unfazed by the night's dark spirits.

I went into the hallway, about to make the long trek to the bathroom, when I heard a sustained sound coming from my grandmother's bedroom. I pressed my ear against her closed door. Had she been screaming hysterically, I wouldn't have been more surprised at what I heard. She was singing in a soprano voice that sounded like a child's.

" *'Petrum, Partrum, Paradisi, Temporie . . .'* "

What was this?

" *'How can there be a chicken without e'er a bone? Perrie, Merrie, Dixie, Dominie; How can there be a cherry without e'er a stone? Petrum, Partrum, Paradisi, Temporie, Perrie, Merrie, Dixie, Dominie.'* "

Who was she in her imagination? A child in Cleveland? Little Lilian, daughter of John McNamara and Winifred Noon from County Roscommon? Is this before or after her sister Annie died of tuberculosis and Granny wrote her a letter addressed to heaven?

Her voice was high and barely quavering, remarkable in someone so old. " *'How can there be a book which no man can read? . . . How can there be a blanket without e'er a thread? Petrum, Partrum . . .'* "

Maybe she's remembering being a young woman of energy and ambition, sitting at the city desk on the *Newark Evening News*, pounding out, on the stiff keys of her black typewriter, copy for the women's pages and impassioned suffragette screeds. Tall, proud, her hair bobbed daringly, eyeing Howard Garis, two years her junior, the new cub reporter, sitting nearby.

" *'When the chicken's in the egg-shell there is no bone, Perrie, Merrie, Dixie, Dominie; When the cherry's in the bud, there is no stone . . .'* "

"How do you spell 'postpone'?" Lilian asked Howard that day in 1896. She leaned across a table. They hadn't even met, so it was a bold move on her part. He answered, "P-o-s-p-o-n-e." "That's not how you spell it!" she declared. "It's how *I* spell it," he said, laughing.

Or is she singing to Roger, her baby son, in Newark? Before they moved into the big house in East Orange, before she began to be afraid for him, before she . . .

" *'When the blanket's in the fleece there is no thread . . .'* "

Before illness, before anger . . .

Then there was silence. I was dumbfounded. I had overheard another Granny, the pre-Granny Lilian. A vulnerable woman with no real worries, just the soft sadness that is woven into the fabric of a feeling life at any time past earliest childhood. I decided that during that song she wasn't revisiting her so-called prime, when she wrote her books. I had already heard her anguish at their deal with Stratemeyer, and I knew she was unhappy that Grampy's work outsold hers. No, this was a time when she was wholly her original being, free of jealousy and worldly disappointment. What I heard in her voice was purity—a purity compressed from an amalgam of her Irish heritage, her femininity, her comeliness, her talent and hope. Her singing seemed of a piece with her listening to those romantic soap operas on the radio. I never believed she was listening only to "see how they worked out the plot." She was doing the same thing I did when I listened—imagining other possibilities, other destinies, allowing herself to pretend for a few minutes during the day that she was living out a comprehensible life story that turned out well.

CHAPTER SIX

An Amherst Christmas in the 1950s banished for a few weeks the boredom, fear, and regret of ordinary days. When the life-size crèche was set up on the town green, the outdoor tree was illuminated in a cookie-cutter shape. The stationery store, Hastings, outlined its windows with colored lights, women began to wear lots of red, and reality gave way to a Technicolor ideal. I remember no menorahs, no alternative ceremonies. Snowy late-December Amherst was simply and fully the season of Christmas. In school, forgiveness, charity, and faith were recommended, as if we had it within ourselves to embody these exalted virtues. Which made us almost believe that we were indeed excellent human beings.

Soon after arriving in Amherst from Westchester, my parents, both Catholic at the time, became Congregationalists. When I was old enough to ask why, they told me it was because of the "Index." This was a list, they explained to me, of books Catholics were not allowed to read. My father had resigned from the Manursing Island country club in Westchester a few years earlier when they wouldn't serve lunch to the great statesman Ralph Bunche, founder of the United Nations and future winner of the Nobel Peace Prize. He was refused simply because he was a black man, which infuriated my parents. In the same spirit, they declared they couldn't be part of a religion that censored reading. I don't know why the Index became an issue only when we moved to Amherst; presumably it had been in force all along. Perhaps taking on the big house was the kind of life change that put them in the mood to make others.

Whatever burdens of grief my grandmother carried, one of them must have been her son's defection from the fold. No doubt she considered him damned. In fact, our whole family must have been joined in her eyes by our eventual punishment. She'd converted Howard to Catholicism from the Baptist faith when he married her, but although his belief in God was rock solid, he was never much of a churchgoer. Roger and his sister, Cleo, had been brought up as "good Catholics," though, and Dad went to Saint Benedict's Preparatory School in Newark, where he studied Latin and Greek, retaining a surprising amount of both languages for the rest of his life.

With a mixture of mysticism, belief, and pure American exuberance, we celebrated Christmas in our house with the intensity of primitive revelers. My mother festooned The Dell with holly, draped pine branches on the mantels, set tinkling gold angels chasing each other around diminutive candles. My favorite decoration was a miniature bower of heavy silver leaves surrounding blue lights, which threw murky, lacy shadows. I would stare at it and lose myself, as if entering Ali Baba's cave. Our house exuded smells of baked cinnamon and pine boughs and was resolutely atmospheric with the silken voices of the Robert Shaw Chorale rising from our "console" record player, singing of a magic child, a star in the night, and the kindness of kings. The songs made deep and thrilling emotional sense to me because I'd been listening to these enchanting stories in Sunday school.

Our Christmas tree, which I adored to the point of worship, was a massive monument to cheer. My father's taste ran to something so wide you could build a fort under it. From a fifteen-foot Fraser fir, he had the straggly top lopped off and the trunk winnowed until it fitted into an iron stand. Gingerly, he perched on a stool and placed the angel on top; then Mother wove strings of colored lights around the branches, all the way into the dark trunk and out again to the tips of the branches. She might sing the "Coventry Carol," which in her transparent soprano was haunting and shimmery. Several ornaments had survived from my maternal great-grandmother's English childhood, like the blue glass swan, the most delicately blown glass object I'd ever seen, which hung from a white string, so still in its pine space.

We covered the whole confection with silver icicles—thin metallic strips, some saved from the previous year, but most lifted carefully out of new red cardboard boxes. My mother monitored the icicle ritual. We were forbidden to throw them up onto the tree. With utmost deliberation we draped no more than two or three together, so that the overall effect was like a frosting of glittering silver tassels hanging straight down.

In the season of my eleventh Christmas, in 1953, my father was in a very good mood. Confident in the midst of his television career, he'd had five live plays produced in the last year. Now that so much was going his way, he took more time to sit after dinner, playing his mandolin and singing old songs. One evening, listening to him, I came up with an idea. On Christmas Eve, ever since our grandparents had come to live with us, our ritual was to surround my grandfather near the tree, a fire in the hearth and cups of hot cocoa in our hands, while he read the Nativity story from his over-

size family Bible. To my continued mystification, Granny didn't
come down even then, but it seemed a complete family gathering
nevertheless. A few days before, I'd had in mind commanding another family gathering.

In school we'd learned "The Twelve Days of Christmas" as a
memory game. Anyone who couldn't remember the list of presents
in this old English song was eliminated. I might tie for the winner,
but no one could beat me. I wanted to make everyone at home sit
around *me* while I challenged them to sing "The Twelve Days of
Christmas" so that I could show off my memory and win the game.
My pretext was getting my father to play Christmas carols on his
mandolin. Then at the right moment I would suggest the game.

All came to pass as planned. First we sang "O Little Town of
Bethlehem," which sounded glorious in the special tremor of mandolin picking. Then I explained the game. I'd written out each
verse on a slip of paper, but as soon as the person sang it once, I
would take the paper back.

I started: " *'On the first day of Christmas my true love gave to me a
partridge in a pear tree.'* "

Then Dad, in his light baritone: " *'On the second day of Christmas my true love gave to me two turtle doves and a partridge in a pear
tree.'* " He winked at me. He knew the song.

Mom continued with imposing assurance and fluting tones.
" *'On the third day of Christmas my true love gave to me three French
hens, two . . .'* " and so forth, building to a wavy partridge and re-
sounding tree.

My grandfather looked irrepressibly anticipatory. Five-year-old
Buddy sat on his lap, leaning against the red vest that fitted nicely
over Grampy's round stomach. Brooks was cross-legged on the
floor, and both boys were looking up at their grandfather's face,
which was rosy from many sherries.

" *'On the fourth day of Christmas my true love gave to me . . .'* "

He paused for effect. *"Four screaming roosters, three little pigs, two windup chickens, and a large dish from the pan-try!"*

"Not fair, Grampy!" I shouted.

Everyone was laughing and talking at once.

Suddenly my father went quiet, his eyes fixed at a distant point. His face paled. I had the strange idea that he had seen a ghost. Following his gaze, I saw what he saw. Standing across the hall at the bottom of the stairs was the silent figure of his mother. Sourly, quizzically, she was staring at us.

"Mother!" my father said, almost in a whisper.

My grandfather turned. "Lily," he said. He lifted Buddy off his lap and stood, his legs unsteady from age and wine. No one had asked her to join us, because we knew it was out of the question. Except for a brief moment, she hadn't been downstairs with the family in the nearly three years since she'd moved in.

She continued to stare at us, but now she turned her head from side to side, as if to say no to whatever might be asked. She was wearing her Japanese robe and brocade slippers. Her thick gray hair was gathered at the back of her neck.

"Mother," my father said again, approaching her. "Do you need anything?"

She put up her hands, almost like warding him off.

"What's all the ruckus?" she asked sharply.

"Singing," my father answered simply, something heavy in his voice.

"I need to sleep."

"Wouldn't you like to come sit by the tree?" my mother asked gently.

"I want to sleep."

I was protesting furiously in my head: We weren't making much noise, we were often *much* noisier, we were in the middle of an important song, why did you have to come down and spoil everything? Then I looked at my father and realized with a shock that he wasn't disappointed; he was desolate.

Days later, after Christmas dinner, my father called us into the library to listen to a recording of Dylan Thomas reading *A Child's Christmas in Wales*. Thomas had died that year, which made the occasion especially important for my father, who admired his poetry so much that the hard-drinking Welshman had become an unseen presence in our household, his soft, round face, babyishly high forehead, and curly hair familiar to me from book jackets. Through the room Thomas's wobbly voice rumbled. And when he came to the line about how it took someone as brilliant as Leonardo to put together model airplanes and Erector sets, we thought, Yes, we understand, instructions are *that* hard; and we privately congratulated ourselves for knowing *exactly* what he meant. My father's eyes were fixed on a frosty darkened window, his legs crossed, his lanky body relaxed. I thought how much this Welsh world we're hearing about belonged to boys and men—the boys running out into the snow, the uncles sleeping by the fire. And I wondered when my father had experienced the easy joy of young, unencumbered masculine energy. As I looked around at my family, all soothed by the rolling bass voice, they seemed to be momentarily freed from unexplained tensions that were creeping into our lives. There was something confusing happening, but right now we were happy.

CHAPTER SEVEN

The following spring, on Easter Sunday, my parents went out to spend the evening with their friend Mary Day in Northampton. The graduate student wife put us to bed and went back to her apartment on the second floor. After I said good night and closed my door, I tiptoed into the narrow linen closet that connected my room with the apartment. Thin moonlight spilled through the tall window at the end of the room. I crouched by the couple's locked door and tried to hear something from them. Nothing. Then I heard a sound that was all wrong. It wasn't coming from the apartment. Quietly I crept out of the linen closet and went out to the hall. Someone—it must be Granny—was moaning in Granny's room. At that moment Grampy rushed across the hall toward my parents' room.

"I'm calling Dr. Hogan," he said. "Your grandmother needs a doctor."

I looked in Granny's door. She was on the bed, holding her head and making horrible cries of pain. I didn't dare enter.

When he came back, he rushed to her. "Lily," he kept saying. "Lily. Hold on. The ambulance is coming."

"I saw a white light, Howard. I saw a white light. There's a terrible clamoring in my head."

"It's all right, Lily."

"My rosary."

"Here it is, Lily."

I remember the siren and the intense light beam sweeping back and forth into the front of the house. Men came upstairs with a stretcher. I moved aside for them.

When they were taking her down the stairs, Grampy stayed by her side, holding her hand.

"Am I going to die?"

"No, Lily. Hold on. You'll be all right."

At that moment my parents came in. There was much commotion while it was decided that my mother would ride in the ambulance with Lilian and Howard. My father would follow in the car. I was impressed with Dad. He was very calm.

That night, I lay down in a great turbulence of excitement. I looked at the sampling of Granny's books that I kept on the shelf at the head of my bed: *Judy Jordan's Discovery, Connie Loring's Dilemma, Barbara Hale's Mystery Friend, The Ghost of Melody Lane, Nancy Brandon's Mystery, The Girl Scout Pioneers* . . .

So long ago! She wrote most of them in the 1920s. Thirty years had passed. She must have been entirely different then. Her books were a dream of life, a dream that must have been her own, where young girls of bravery and intelligence were admired, a dream where daughters shared the burdens of their parents—although their burdens were little more than hard work or thrift—and the big cities were safe for girls if they lived in women's boardinghouses, and where each day overflowed with endeavor and exhilaration. Her characters were the opposite of how she was with us. In the 1880s, she had made her way from a family of working-class

Irish immigrants in Cleveland to a life of great accomplishment, a feat that would have been impossible if she hadn't possessed the drive of her heroines. But I had only known her as so worn-out that she had to lie down all the time. I wondered when her energy had deserted her, and if that was the reason for her unrelenting gloom—although Mom had told me recently that Granny admitted to having always looked darkly on her surroundings, and that her sister Mary had understood her well. "Lilian," Mary apparently said when they were young, "if the sky was perfectly blue from one end to the other, you would try all day long to find a cloud."

I wondered what kind of mood she'd been in when she wrote her early books for children. I was no longer seduced by the world of the Bobbsey Twins, with those two "adorable" sets of twins and the perfect parents and the picket fence. Trying to see ourselves in that picture was jarring to me now. As an eleven-year-old sixth grader, I identified with Judy Jordan, who at seventeen moved from her home in Pennsylvania to New York to become a reporter. Was this a version of Lilian's own story? I opened the book:

New York again, but no novelty to Judy this time . . . She had learned to travel alone, learned her way around the big city, learned self-reliance and the composure that stamps one as having had some experience. She looked about at the endless traffic and noted the murmurous hum it all consolidated into . . . all its noise running like a stream, rhythmic and melodious. "I love New York." She threw her head up proudly and really looked the part.

I began to drift off. What was going to happen to her? I tried to be sad, but I couldn't come close. There was so much going on—and all of it new.

In the morning the grown-ups went to the hospital, and when they came home around noon, Grampy was crying. Not sobbing, just quietly wiping tears away.

"She's gone," he said to my questioning look.

My mother looked weary. She put her hand on her father-in-law's arm. "Can I make you some lunch, Grampy?" (Like the children, she always called him that.)

"No thank you, Mabs. I think I'll go upstairs and rest." He trudged up the stairs, his head bowed, his hand gripping the banister.

I couldn't read my father's expression except that it seemed as if something were settling into him. I tried to imagine having your mother die, but of course, I had no experience to draw from. I couldn't even figure out what it meant to me to lose my grandmother. I wanted to cry—just to let out steam—but it wasn't going to happen. Without realizing it, I had begun my lifelong habit of trying to steel myself against being overwhelmed by emotion. He took me in his arms. "It's okay, Les," he said, as if reading my thoughts. "She'd been sick a long time. She was ready."

My brothers were standing with us. Brooks was crying, although I wasn't sure he knew why. Buddy looked mystified. Dad hugged them, too.

With somber urgency, but not the tragic demeanor my melodramatic imagination was looking for, my parents discussed plans for the funeral. Dad went into the library to start making calls. I heard him tell someone it was a stroke. To my amazement, he seemed fine.

Sometime in that period I remember overhearing my parents laughing together—in what they thought was a private moment—that Grampy no longer had to worry about Granny marking his Christian Brothers sherry bottle. Worried that he would drink too much, she'd kept his bottle, marked it, and checked how much was gone each day. My mother had seen him top it off with water—or sometimes with sherry from another bottle. Mom and Dad had a good laugh about that. In the spirit of rebelliousness, a spirit into which I seemed to have been born, I heartily approved. Here was one way at least in which Grampy had asserted his independence from his difficult wife.

In the next few days, obituaries appeared.

I knew most of what was in them, but I learned that she had gone to college and that she was a national Girl Scout counselor.

A national Girl Scout counselor! That revelation put me to shame. I'd been kicked out of the Brownies in second grade. I watched my friends become Girl Scouts, but I was not deemed fit to be one. No doubt I was hyperactive, but it was more than that. There was an ungovernable urgency in me to plead a different case—whatever it was—than everyone else, and I refused to assume my place in a regiment of well-behaved children. I simply couldn't shut up and stay still until I got older.

I read that Granny had campaigned for the installation of public playgrounds for Newark children, and during World War I she was "in charge of Women's Work," whatever that meant. She had sponsored a bill in Congress to establish the country's first service flag. What was a service flag? I was amazed at how much I hadn't known about her. Why hadn't I talked to her more? And yet I had tried. But somehow she never allowed it. If only I'd had all this information before she died, I could have asked her direct questions.

All the notices mentioned (often in the headline) that she wrote *The Bobbsey Twins* "under the pseudonym Laura Lee Hope." That wasn't news to me, but it occasioned an alarming telephone call.

I was in the butler's pantry helping my mother cut flowers when the phone rang.

"Hello," Mom said brightly. And then, more seriously, "Oh . . . hello." Followed by a long silence. "But . . . how can you *say* that?" Her small face collapsed, as if pulled from within.

"But Harriet, we didn't mean . . ." She sank onto a stool. "I don't see what's so wrong with the truth . . . Surely it's well-known by now . . . I can't understand . . . How can you speak to me this way?"

Who is Harriet? What is she saying to my mother?

"Get your father," she whispered to me, and I was off like a shot, racing into the library.

"Pick up the phone!"

He did. He stood between the desk and the bay window. Through the glass, the terrace wall gleamed in the sun. The April light was so bright behind him that Dad's head looked dark and indistinct. "Calm down, Harriet. Mabs, you get off. What's the problem here?"

He shooed me out with his hand, and I ran to my mother, who was now openly crying.

"She actually threatened me," she said in wonder. "The woman threatened me."

"Who, Mom? Who *was* that?"

"Harriet Adams. Stratemeyer's daughter."

Stratemeyer's daughter! Calling here after all these years!

"But why would she threaten you?"

"Because the newspapers said that Granny wrote *The Bobbsey Twins.*"

"What's the matter with that?"

"It's supposed to be a secret. The way that woman spoke to me! She said we had damaged her."

"Mom, it's okay. She can't do anything to us."

"How could *we* possibly damage *her*?"

The question was unanswerable—at least by me.

"She's crazy," my mother said, shaking her head. "I don't know how I can let her upset me like this. It's just so . . ."

"So what, Mom?"

"Unpleasant."

My mother's curse!

Later, my parents and grandfather gathered in the living room and agreed that there was nothing to worry about. Harriet was a hysteric who exaggerated the importance of hiding the identities of the Stratemeyer ghostwriters. She couldn't do anything to us. Their empire was hardly threatened by revealing that Laura Lee Hope was a pseudonym.

My father was furious that Harriet would try to bully the household of the man who had been Edward Stratemeyer's "right-hand man," creating series with him, making him a fortune, and never asking for more money. They called each other Mr. Stratemeyer and Mr. Garis, although they were very fond of each other. Howard was a witness to Stratemeyer's will and was at his deathbed. Grampy told us that in Stratemeyer's last hours he thought he was in a Baseball Joe book—a series that they had developed together.

According to Howard, Stratemeyer's ravings went something like this:

"Two down! Play for all you're worth, Joe! We've got 'em going! Come on now, bring us all in! Make him give you a pretty one, Joe! There's his glass arm showing! Oh, no, he's going to pieces! One more and we'll have him down! Out! Retire the side!"

Howard had been upset and saddened to see his old friend so disconnected from reality—not that Grampy was exactly a realist. Despite their differences in bank accounts and temperaments, they had been collaborators and friends, but Harriet's harsh call had unearthed a depth of bitterness surrounding the syndicate books that my grandmother's complaints had failed to reveal. Like a hypochondriac whining about pain, the woes of a neurasthenic were easily dismissed.

Fearfully, I asked about *Uncle Wiggily*. Was it okay to talk about those books? They assured me that it was. Grampy hadn't written them for the syndicate; they were his own.

I thought about the days at school when the principal announced an assembly because my grandfather was coming to tell Uncle Wiggily stories. The excitement I'd always felt, sitting on a metal chair, seeing how he made the children adore him, talking to them so confidingly. Once, he handed out handkerchiefs. He said he was going to tell such a sad story that it would make them cry. And then they laughed instead when he came to the "painful" part: Uncle Wiggily tied a string to a boy's rotten tooth, attached the string to a cork, then threw the cork out the window when the cat walked by, so the cat pounced on the cork, pulled the string, which pulled the tooth . . .

Clearly there were puzzles about my grandparents' writing. I'd always thought, in the simplistic way of children, that it had conferred on Howard and Lilian the unalloyed pleasure of recognition and accomplishment. But this Bobbsey Twins situation was twisted in some way.

"Don't bother about that woman," Grampy said angrily. "She has no claim on us. We've given them more than they deserved."

That was the only time I ever heard my grandfather say something critical about anyone.

As murky as the Stratemeyer shadow was that fell on us suddenly, the position my grandmother had held in the lives of our family was truly baffling. She was cranky and undermining. From what Mom told me, I gathered she'd been telling her son that he was unfit for life since she forbade him to play football as a boy and continued to urge him not to compete in any arena, telling him that he would only fail. Whatever successes he had were at the cost of fighting his mother's expectations for him.

Why did she do those things? Was she really afraid for him? Her overprotectiveness ran the danger of being permanently hobbling, but it was also ridiculous. When Dad was a young man still living at home, he used to go out drinking with his friends. The next morning he'd suffer from the usual array of hangover symptoms. His mother, fully aware of his drinking habits, would call his friends in the morning, asking them not to phone Roger because the ringing would bother his headache. She told them that he had drunk too much malted milk and it had upset his stomach. Malted milk! How ludicrous. But it was also extraordinary that she felt she had to go to such lengths to protect her son's reputation instead of dragging him out of bed and making him face the results of his behavior.

Yet, for all that, I'd been taught to respect her and was imbued with a sense of her importance. She had arrived on our doorstep with a pedigree that was part of our family's history, so I couldn't dismiss her as a crazy old lady of whom I should steer clear. She was a locus of imaginative energy, wherever that energy was coming from—from all around her or from her own personality. She was like a famous person traveling with an entourage, only in her case the entourage was incorporeal, a mist of reputed experiences she may or may not have had, in the middle of which she stood stubbornly silent. So even though she'd been a frightening presence across the hall, she held deep fascination for me. I could see how difficult it was for my father to deal with her and how egocentrically demanding she was, yet some part of me thought I should be like her, or more precisely, I should be like the person I'd been told she was but had never seen.

How to explain Grampy's steadfast devotion to her? He seemed nearly broken by her death. Well, they'd been married since 1900—fifty-four years. They came up together as journalists and then as "young adult" novelists. He had outstripped her in fame and earning power, and she'd been jealous of him, but surely that wasn't enough to turn her into the harridan who moved in with us. Nothing about her was clear.

Physically, what was wrong with her, anyway? I never understood. Perhaps her "thick blood" meant that her veins were blocked. She was also diabetic. The problem was that she was such a hypochondriac that after a while no one took her complaints seriously. In the end, she lived to be eighty-one, which in those years was a considerable age.

As spring matured into early summer, her death seemed to have opened a swath of space in our house. The air was different. With her room cleared out, the second floor felt positively expansive compared with before. Grampy still occasionally sat by her window in his Sleepy Hollow chair, but more often than not he'd take a nap in his own room before dinner. What had they talked about on those long afternoons? I wondered. Often they were silent together; he'd read or stare out the window. Her bad temper never seemed to bother him, as if he had the special protection of living in his own imagination. Now that she was gone, I would walk into her room just to feel the difference. It must take a long time for the dead to disappear, I thought, because something of her remained. The Virgin pictures and dark drapes were still up, but there was also an ineffable presence, as if her spirit were near, and I began to shun her room because it was spooky.

That was the spring of the Army-McCarthy hearings on television, to which my parents were glued virtually all day. After school I joined them and felt very grown-up assuming the righteous indignation of my family.

"Look at that bunch of no-goodniks," my mother said about McCarthy, Roy Cohn, and their colleagues. Watching our twenty-four-inch Zenith, we felt elevated by the notion that we were participating in our country's history by speaking to the screen. It was a lively scene. Sometimes my parents' friends came over and watched with them. Cocktails, loud talk, laughter, birds on the terrace, apple blossoms and violets . . . and the hope, as each day Senator Joseph McCarthy's character was exposed on national TV, that one of our country's true devils was being defeated. Without making the direct connection, part of me felt as if our own recent loss was reflected in the news. A darkness was clearing from the land.

With May came azaleas, cobalt blue forget-me-nots around the fountain near the bud-covered rose arbor, bearded irises and Manchurian red poppies in the garden, pansies by the driveway, and grape hyacinths in a crystal vase on my bureau. In the morning before breakfast I would slide my bare feet through the heavy dew to the oak tree so I could swing on the branch and think about my emerging self. I listened to the brook moving, and I found that I could concentrate on nothing but the sensation of being alive in the spring and looking forward to everything.

At the end of May, when Amherst College held its prom, we were one of the families that invited dates of the college boys to stay during the weekend. We had two, often from Smith or Mount Holyoke, but sometimes from farther away, like Vassar or Bryn Mawr or even the Deep South, who would share our guest room. I loved having the girls with us. At that time Amherst College was only for males—males who were to my eyes unparalleled exemplars of sophistication and beauty.

And the girls! There wasn't an inch of the fitted quilted bedspreads to be seen for the pocketbooks and clothing and all the mysterious female accoutrements scattered around. They would invite me in, and I'd watch these exotic creatures get dressed. The Friday outfit might be a pleated skirt with a cotton blouse or a sheath dress with pearls, and the girls were in high spirits, talking about their dates and where they were going for dinner. Are you going to the Lord Jeffery Inn? Oh, dinner at the fraternity?

But Saturday night, prom night, the outfits were beyond even my fevered imagination. Ruffled organza or taffeta dresses with layers of crinolines underneath. I would watch them first pull up their seamed stockings and fasten them with garters, then lower the dresses over their heads and step into silk pumps. Then came the perfume, which made the room smell like a flower shop. The girls in their dresses rustled when they walked. Crossing the hallway, making their way downstairs, the noise they made was like hissing steam escaping from a radiator. Sssssh . . . Sssssssh . . . Sssssh . . .

Downstairs, the young men waited in the living room or hall, rosy cheeked, polite, and tall. Each brought a gardenia corsage. During the precious few hours when the girls were dressing and the boys were waiting, I could hardly stand making the choice between being upstairs or down.

One early evening I had a tennis ball I was bouncing flamboyantly, unsure how to engage the pacing young man in conversation. He flashed me a wide smile and asked if I'd like to go outside and play catch. We went to the front lawn and tossed the ball. Dad had been teaching me vocabulary words. The latest one was "vapid." Concentrate, concentrate—how could I work in "vapid"? I was jolted by my eager dishonesty as I said that my friends were just so *vapid* compared with him and his friends. He laughed in astonishment that a girl the size of an elf had just said "vapid." He told me he wanted to marry me. He'd wait until I grew up. Okay? We were both laughing. I caught the ball and passed it from one hand to the other behind my back. The soft air, the romantic house, but mostly Dad's clever word had made this golden youth say these things.

"Okay? I'm going to wait for you. How old are you now? That's not so bad. In only seven years you'll be eighteen. I'll be twenty-eight."

Was there ever a girl happier than I?

A FEW WEEKS LATER, on a bright Saturday, my mother told me that Grampy wished to see me in the library. What did I hear in her voice? Some hint of importance. Her tone was mild but serious, as if speaking of highly consequential matters. I suspected that was her way of being part of something that was mine. I was starting to be jealously protective of my turf.

My grandfather, with his shirtsleeves rolled above the elbows, was seated at the desk, his white hair and clothes glowing from the morning light behind him.

"Sit down, Les."

It took a few minutes before he said anything else, which was so unusual that I became alarmed. Obviously he was in distress.

"You know . . . since Lily died . . ."

He took out a handkerchief the size of a dinner mat—like the kind he took out at my school to be funny for the children—and blew his nose with a loud honk. After fluttering it around in trembling hands, he balled it up and put it back in his pocket.

"You know . . . she used to write the endings . . ."

He looked down and drew out his handkerchief again, but the need passed.

"She wrote the endings to my Uncle Wiggily stories."

"I didn't know that! I never knew that!"

I was amazed. The endings were odd little flourishes that set those stories apart from all others because they were so nonsensical, so utterly . . . Howard Garis. "And so, if the cat doesn't spill the sugar bowl, so the ants come running and forget to make lunches for their little ant children, I'll tell you tomorrow about . . ." It was always a humorous chain of events in the nonhuman world, and it was a trademark of the stories.

"Well, you see, ever since she died . . ." He covered his face with the handkerchief, and his shoulders heaved. Eventually he made that trumpeting sound again while he blew his nose.

I was awed at his emotion. Crying while standing by her body was quite different from going to pieces in front of me on a sunny morning at home. Ours was a household of modulated expressiveness. It was believed that low voices and measured responses were the embodiment of civilization. When the telephone rang, we were instructed never to yell, but to seek the person out, draw near, and say in a soft voice, "Telephone for you." I, of course, had been railing against these constrictions since early sentience.

"I've tried to write the endings since she died," he said, "but I haven't the heart . . . I don't seem to be able to do them."

He looked at me, his face pale and swollen. "So, how would you like a job?"

"A job?"

"Do you think you could write those endings for me?"

"I could! I think I could!"

"Try a few. I'll see how they are." He sounded chipper again. "If I like them, I'll pay you two dollars an ending. I need six a week, so that would be twelve dollars a week. What do you say?"

"Oh, Grampy . . . Let me try. I think I can do it. I could help you, I really could, you'll see . . ."

"Why don't you look at the stories and study the endings. Think up a few and show them to me."

"But what about Dad? Did you ask him? He's the other writer in our family."

"He suggested you, Les," said Grampy. "He said he thought you were old enough to do them."

I walked out of there like a person with the most momentous

assignment in the world, which, it was certain, I would accomplish without fail.

Grabbing a pad and pencil, I ran out the living-room French doors, across the side terrace, and climbed quickly into the thick-limbed beech tree. But I couldn't think, because Grampy's head was visible in the library windows and my view away from the house was too sumptuous. A massive hedge of rhododendrons had recently burst into bloom, edging one end of the lawn with a soaring pink-and-white wall. Down the beech I went, across the grass, through the greenery opening into the clearing by the brook. I got on the oak branch and settled in. Too restless, I jumped off the branch and walked to the brook, where I could smell skunk cabbage. I picked a jack-in-the-pulpit and brought it back to the branch. I put it beside me on the bark, then picked it up. When I raised the top of the curved flower, there was a little stamen person in a—well, it's called a pulpit, and so it seemed. So if the . . . if the . . .

Up and down I moved the little person's canopy. Now you see him, now you don't. I swung the branch back and forth, back and forth.

So if the eggbeater doesn't . . . So if the milk doesn't spill all over . . . So if it turns out I can't do this and Dad is wrong about me . . . So if the robin . . .

CHAPTER EIGHT

I sent the endings home from camp in Vermont that summer and received money by return mail. Making me, I figured, a professional writer, which was a great source of comfort, since I was passionately unhappy. I was at a French camp that sprawled on prime acreage bordering Lake Champlain; it was run like a first-class prison. I can't remember ever seeing my endings in print, although I must have, and I would have been thrilled. What I do remember is the sense of honor implied in pleasing my grandfather with my words and relishing the idea that I had a place in his imaginative world. I also can't remember when I stopped helping him, but it was probably not long after that summer.

In mid-August, I joined my family in Kennebunkport, Maine, just in time for Hurricane Carol, one of the most vicious storms in New England history. We'd rented a fieldstone and shingled place called Rockledge, across a narrow road from the beach, and I remember the experience as a gleeful adventure with weather, even though this tropical cyclone, which made landfall in Old Saybrook, Connecticut, on the morning of August 31, was the most destructive storm since the Great New England Hurricane of 1938. In the end, 4,000 homes, 3,500 automobiles, 3,000 boats, and 71 people were lost. The full force passed west of us; what we got were colossal waves that hurled foamy tendrils across the road, and a roaring wind that blew porch furniture away if someone was stupid enough to have left it out.

Nothing could penetrate the bubble of good cheer that we floated in at that moment. My father's lifelong dream was about to come true. The off-Broadway theater that had presented *The Threepenny Opera* last season was beginning its 1954–55 season with a play by Roger Garis! In a matter of weeks, September 14 to be exact, *The Pony Cart*, his play, would open in New York. My mother put newspapers on the living-room coffee table with paragraphs encircled in black ink:

July 27, 1954

I. B. Joselow will present Roger Garis's drama "The Pony Cart" at the Theatre de Lys, 121 Christopher St., beginning Sept. 14. Mr. Joselow has leased the playhouse for four weeks with an option for two more weeks. David Pressman, of The Actor's Studio, will stage the play. Edwin Gifford will be the assistant producer.

August 16, 1954

Louisa Horton will return to the stage this season as the star of "The Pony Cart," the Roger Garis play which I. B. Joselow will present Sept 14 at the Theatre de Lys. Miss Horton, who was last seen on Broadway in Elmer Rice's "The Grand Tour" in 1951, will also be remembered as having played one season in John van Druten's "The Voice of the Turtle."

Mon, Aug 23, 1954

I. B. Joselow has signed Lamont Johnson for his production of "The Pony Cart" which goes into rehearsal today at the Theatre

de Lys. Mr. Johnson will co-star with Louisa Horton in the
Roger Garis play.

And my favorite, simply a headline: "PONY CART" ROLLS
SEPT 14.

Among those clippings was also a press release:

From Marian Graham, 341 Madison Ave

"The Pony Cart" is a drama which tells the story of a family's
fight against people in a small town who over-value their re-
spectability and put personal pride before their duty to society.
The time is the present and the locale is a fictional town in the
eastern part of the United States.

Prices: Tuesday, Wednesday, Thursday evenings $2.88, $2.30,
* $1.73*
Saturday and Sunday matinees $2.30, $1.73, $1.15
Friday, Saturday and Sunday evenings $3.45, $2.88, $2.30, $1.73

If you didn't want to pay as much as $3.45 on Saturday night,
you could pay $2.88, and if that was too much, you could get a seat
for 58 cents less than that, or 57 cents less than *that*.

My parents were trying to pretend to themselves that having a
play in New York was lovely, but really no big deal. This, after all,
was just the beginning of Dad's career as a playwright for the legit-
imate stage. He had many more plays in him.

"So, Dad, tell me about your play," I asked him. Carefully, Dad
explained that it was about a man who preyed sexually on little
girls. The parents of one victim try to stop him, but he's a prominent citizen, and the town closes ranks around him. The parents
and the town have a big fight.

Well! How embarrassing. Sex and little girls? I knew where he got the idea. A year ago I was walking home with a friend who said she had to stop in for a second to see a man who gave her candy. I waited a long time outside in the cold for her, almost an hour. It was dark when she came out. Why was she in there so long? "Because he likes to look at me with my clothes off; then he gives me the candy." I couldn't believe that this girl—who was younger than I, but not *that* much—really didn't understand that she shouldn't be undressing in front of this man. I told my parents, who told her parents, and sure enough, the police chief knew about him but considered him harmless. He was rich. Eventually the police made a deal with him: Move away and we won't arrest you. So he left our area. And now Dad had written a play about it. All right. I would be grown-up. I would take it in stride. Embarrassed? Me?

CHAPTER NINE

Coming home to Amherst from Maine, I could see that Dad felt more at home than ever in The Dell. He wore it like a second skin, strolling through the rooms whistling, playing his mandolin at night. He often played a song his Irish grandmother taught him. It sounded like a lullaby, but the words had a haunted twist:

Macushla! Macushla! Your sweet voice is calling
Calling me softly again and again

. . .

Macushla! Macushla! Your red lips are saying
That death is a dream and love is for aye
Then awaken Macushla, awake from your dreaming
My blue eyed Macushla, awaken to stay

Dinners were all about *The Pony Cart*. Who should play the mother when it moved to Broadway? Louisa Horton was an accomplished actress but not a star. Cathleen Nesbitt was a possibility. She was dazzling in *Sabrina Fair* last season. As was Jo Van Fleet in *The Trip to Bountiful.* What about her? The best would be Deborah Kerr, who was such a big hit in *Tea and Sympathy* at the moment, but that play might run so long that she wouldn't be free. Dad loved *Tea and Sympathy.* Robert Anderson's play was about an effeminate high school student who's afraid he's a homosexual. In the last moment of the third act, Deborah Kerr unselfishly offers her body to make him a man. As she unbuttons her sweater, she gives that now-famous line: "When you speak of me, and you will, be kind." According to Dad, Anderson had written a perfectly crafted play, with a neat twist to polish off the evening. That's exactly the kind of play Dad would be delivering in the future. As a matter of fact, it was possible that *The Pony Cart* might turn out to be just such a play.

My father went into New York for rehearsals and came back excited. Pretending to let me help her, my mother picked out her New York outfits. When it came time for them to leave for the opening, Mom looked spectacularly sophisticated in a tan suit and a jaunty hat perched on her black curls. Dad was debonair with his fedora and tweeds, smelling of bay rum aftershave. When he bent down to kiss me, I whispered that I was proud to be his daughter.

Their homecoming a few afternoons later was of another order. Dad came through the door with a vacant look in his eyes and went straight up to bed.

I didn't have to ask what happened. Defeat lay heavy in the air.

Mom kissed us and held us to her, saying the critics liked Dad's play—all except one. Later she talked to me in private. She was in a rage, the angriest person I had ever seen in my short life. She was elemental, volcanic. The object of her fury was Brooks Atkinson, the *New York Times* critic, whose pan was going to close the show, despite the fact that Walter Kerr of the *Herald Tribune* liked it. But the power of the *Times*, she told me, was absolute.

"I'm going to write that Atkinson a letter!" she said. "He has no idea how destructive his words can be on a life." Her voice was too high. "He writes irresponsibly and destroys a writer—a sensitive, talented writer. How dare he!"

Destroys? Actually destroys? My thoughts were in a whirl. I respected my mother's force. I loved her for it. She went into the library to write her letter and closed the door.

I walked upstairs slowly. Should I go to Dad? Would he want me to? Does he need to be alone? I asked myself these questions as I continued in the direction of his room. No amount of reasoning could stop me.

I entered my parents' bedroom. He was on Mom's bed, which was closest to the door, as if he had walked in there and couldn't get any farther. A cotton quilt covered him from his neck down, but I saw that underneath the quilt his hands were folded on his chest. He stared at the ceiling, motionless, except for the tears that rolled down his cheeks into his ears. His profile cut the air in the darkened room. His stillness was so unearthly that I couldn't even hear his breathing.

"It's all right," I said feebly. "It will be all right."

No response. For a sickening moment I thought that just after that last tear started on its way, he must have died. But no, there was another one emerging. How could one person's criticism do this to a man? It's so unfair! Part of me had a different, even more disturbing thought: Don't writers need to be a little tough? Where were my father's defenses?

Leaving his room, I passed Grampy, who was on his way in. Then I heard Grampy's voice through the door. "Don't worry, son. You're a fine writer. Buck up, son."

Some days later Dad rallied enough to take me to see his play before it closed. It was going to run for only two of its originally scheduled four weeks. The train ride was bracing because he confided in me how disappointed he was about the play. His candor made me feel the equal of any grown-up as I comforted him with words of hope for his future. I could see that he took heart from what I said. It was exhilarating to be in an adult world, discussing mature, sophisticated subjects like the New York theater and traveling with an elegant, handsome male companion. Whatever grave implications my father's discouragement might have had were lost on me. I was only present for the romance of the journey.

When we arrived at Grand Central Station, we took a cab to West Fifty-seventh Street to meet Dad's agent, a woman named Audrey Wood. She was also Tennessee Williams's agent, Dad told me proudly. His *Camino Real* ran last season, and a new play, called *Cat on a Hot Tin Roof* and rumored to be brilliant, would open soon. Audrey Wood was tiny, even smaller than my mother. She wore her blond hair pulled back, but teased up so high on top of her head that it looked like a tall golden dome-shaped hat perched on her pale, flat face. Without being maternal or even particularly feminine, she extended to us a kindness that felt like love. She let me pick up the tiny turtle that she kept in a glass aquarium on her desk. "Your father has written a very good play," she said, gently putting her hand on his arm. "You should be proud of him."

"Oh, I am."

At the Theatre de Lys, there were few in the audience. I studied the program and saw a long bio of Dad, telling all the things he'd done before I was born. I was impressed. It also talked about his parents' books, which surprised me, because I didn't think it was entirely appropriate to talk about your parents in your own biography. Well, we had an unusual family, and I could hardly believe my luck in being born into it. When the curtain came up, the stage had a reddish glow. The child was played by a dark-haired girl with high coloring—Rhoda Lewis (née Farkas). She was a lot larger than I was, and her speech didn't seem real. But it was artificial in a professional way, I thought, and I decided she was a brilliant actress. When the curtain fell at the end, a woman in front of me said to her husband, "This was an excellent play. I didn't expect it to be this good." I tapped her on the shoulder. She turned around to me. With great emotion I said, "My father wrote this play."

After *The Pony Cart,* my father spent many afternoons in his bedroom under his remarkable mercury-vapor sunlamp. From a sleek, sinuous six-foot shaft, a heavy silver dome extended improbably, floating over my father like a space-age cobra. He'd been sunning under a lamp for decades, having been taught by his mother that it promoted sound teeth, resistance to disease, straight limbs, and glowing health. Even Fibber McGee used one, Dad used to say with a grin.

Around four in the afternoon, the acrid smell of this lamp drifted through the upstairs. It was an ozone scent combined with the witch hazel in which he soaked cotton balls. He would squeeze the wet balls into flat disks and place them on his closed eyelids.

There was an unearthly quality to the scene of the wide metal dome above him radiating blue light while my father, wearing swimming trunks, turned a honey hue. He lay stock-still, the white cotton making his eye sockets look eerily empty, while he received whatever boon he imagined the rays could bestow.

CHAPTER TEN

At the beginning of 1955, our household, like most in that era, was regulated by routine. Dinner at 6:30, prayers before bed, clothes laid out for the next day, Saturday morning skating at the college rink, Sunday school at the Congregational church. All three children attended Smith College Day School in Northampton— Buddy, six, in first grade; Brooks, nine, in fourth; and I, at eleven, in seventh.

For the seven-mile trip from Amherst we had an intense bunch of kids in our car pool: shy, awkward Marcia Madeira, later to become a theatrical lighting designer; bossy Anne and gentle Stevie Brown, both two-instrument musicians whose father was the Amherst College physician; and gangly egghead Dick Schotte, whose father, an Amherst College biology professor, had a delight-fully grisly specialty. He amputated frogs' legs in order to grow them back with his soon-to-be-patented technique. His frogs produced stumpy protuberances with suggestions of toes at the end. His was a noble mission, and we believed he would change the world, since one day, with Dr. Schotte's secret serum, anyone with a severed limb could grow it back. He was a short European with a dark mustache and an accent that was all consonants. When he drove, we never came to the end of devising amputation questions for the professor.

After the disappointment of *The Pony Cart*'s failure, life gradually regained the lineaments of normalcy. Mom and Dad often went to the theater in New York. Dad's favorite play that year was William Inge's *Bus Stop*, about a few unsophisticated travelers looking for love, stuck in a rural bus stop on a snowy night. Inge had had another hit a few years before with *Picnic*, but *Bus Stop* was the one my father wished he had written. "A perfectly made play," Dad pronounced it.

He walked every day to his room at Jones Library to work on a new play called *Amusement Park*. No longer focusing primarily on TV, his main obsession became *Amusement Park*. Audrey Wood was encouraging. Dad was sure it would "go." He was also working on a new comedy during this period called *The Blue Balloon*. How did he write so much? By working almost every day.

As the years progressed, we continued to go away to the seashore each summer, although the vacations were shorter and the houses smaller. New worries crept into our lives. By the fall of 1956, Brooks, eleven, and Buddy, eight, were manifesting serious problems with reading, spelling, and concentration; we didn't know why. It was during this time that I began to realize how cut off Dad was from his sons' lives. He had plenty of time for me, but when my brothers appealed to him for help, he referred them to Mom. Whether he was unwilling or unable to relate to them I had no idea, but I could see they were hurt by his remoteness. Brooks, unable to handle sixth-grade work at Smith College Day School, was in grave difficulty. Mom would seat him at the desk in the library with his math homework and close the door. A half hour later she'd walk in and he'd be sobbing, having been unable to finish a single problem. During the Thanksgiving holiday, Brooks was taken out of the Day School and put into fifth grade at Eagle-brook, a school with special help for faltering students. Buddy, in third grade, was just holding on, and showing the strain.

In September 1956, Dad had a television play produced on *Matinee Theater*, starring Constance Bennett. It was a comedy called *One Hundred Red Convertibles.*

At the same time, we suddenly needed a new furnace and there was a great disturbance about money, although Dad's television play must have brought in something. The furnace had to be hotel-size in order to heat The Dell, but Dad hadn't sold anything except that one teleplay in more than a year, and Grampy said his resources were dwindling.

My grandfather's relationship to money had always been romantic. In the 1920s, when a piano salesman told him he worked on commission and desperately needed the money, Grampy bought two Steinways instead of one. Granny, in a fit of outrage, canceled the extra one. The fact is, he never earned what his enormous sales should have brought in. His royalty was below 5 percent, and his agent, unscrupulously manipulating his client's dreaminess, kept 50 percent of that. After Grampy came to Amherst, his support of our household depleted him further, so that as income dropped with sales, an increasingly large percentage of his savings went to shoring up his son's life. Grampy's money, which had seemed so solid, was in danger of evaporating. He paid for our furnace, and our house stayed warm.

During that crisis I remember walking down the hallway on the way to my parents' room after school. While I was approaching their door, I heard Dad say bitterly to Mom, "I find myself standing still in Grand Central Station, trying to figure out whom I could call next to try to sell a story or a play." His voice was quavering. I stopped in my tracks, wishing I hadn't heard him—or my mother's response, which upset me almost as much.

"I have faith in you, Roger. You're Broadway-bound, I know it. You'll make a killing and solve all our financial problems."

Dad groaned, and I moved away quickly, heading out to Valentine Hall. I would have a vanilla milk shake among the young men and feel the comfort of all that boisterous life.

Outside on Spring Street, walking up the hill toward the corner where I'd turn for Valentine, I took deep breaths and considered my life. At thirteen, I had recently started ninth grade at Northampton School for Girls, which I detested for its primness and lack of boys. My desire to break free had a shade of mutiny about it, because it wasn't just that stultifying school I wished to shed. I wanted life at home to reshape its outlines. I had heard my father admit to a desperate powerlessness. Was this because of who he was, or because of the nature of what he was trying to do? He seemed to have recovered from Brooks Atkinson's review of *The Pony Cart*, so I had assumed that his profession, although emotionally difficult, wasn't enough to sink a man. But now, two years later, his mood was dark again. Why? If he was powerless, what would happen to us, his family?

A sense of unease began to take hold at home; the atmosphere was changing. Our sturdy grandfather seemed frail for the first time. After his morning stint at the typewriter, he shuffled about the house in the afternoons and spent more time resting than he ever had before, although he still took the occasional walk with Robert Frost. After school, Buddy went directly to Grampy's room to tell about his young day. He would sit on the big red wing chair opposite the bed. From the hallway I could see down into the room, which was set back at the end of a short corridor. Buddy's small feet, swinging away, were visible below the seat, but the chair obscured the rest of him, and I never heard what they discussed. By dinnertime the old man was uncertain on his feet, his face was flushed, and his voice was unnaturally loud.

Sometimes, too, Dad was strange at dinner. He would act restless, tapping his fingers on the table, looking around as if there were something behind him. He might leave the table and go up to his room, claiming he couldn't sit still. If I saw him later, he'd be changed—eerily quiet, moving and talking slowly.

My parents had a friend named Denis Johnston, an Irish playwright currently teaching at Smith College, who occasionally came over in the evening. One night he declared that Mom would be perfect for the lead in a play he was directing at Amherst's Kirby Theater. Mom, who had acted in many amateur productions, was nervous about the challenge, but over the moon to be asked. She accepted immediately. Dad said nothing.

After Mr. Johnston left, my parents' argument blasted through the upstairs rooms. Dad said, "If you do that play, I'll go out every night and no one will be here to take care of the children!"

"What do you mean?"

"I mean you'd better not take that part! I'll be out, and you'll be deserting the children!"

"But . . . you never go out in the evenings without me . . . I don't understand . . . Why are you saying these things?"

"You just think it over! You just think how you will be affecting this family if you're in that play!"

"Roger, why are you doing this?"

"Stay home with your children like a good wife and mother, that's all I'm saying!"

"I *am* a good wife and mother!"

Eventually my mother began to cry. The next day she told Denis Johnston that she couldn't do the play. There was a tight truce between my parents, and I don't remember my mother ever bringing up the subject again. Years later, when I asked her about it, she said she thought Dad was frightened of being alone and wanted nothing that would take her away from him. He must have also been afraid that this play would lead to others, and eventually she might overshadow him. At the time, I was furious with him for curtailing Mom's life, and Mom, in her own measured words, was "very cross." None of us recognized what was happening to him.

CHAPTER ELEVEN

March 1957

Pushing lima beans and Salisbury steak around on my plate, wondering why my father looked so unexpectedly animated at dinner tonight, I asked him how his trip to New York went. "As a matter of fact, it couldn't have gone better," he answered, to which my mother perked up in several of her little ways. She might have jutted her chin a centimeter higher, or squared her shoulders, or raised an eyebrow; it was clear she was about to take hold of the conversation.

"Your father has a very exciting prospect," she said, with the gravity of a presidential announcement.

Carved into the mantel of the dining-room fireplace were two urns that reminded me of Aladdin's lamp. I used to gaze at them and imagine that I could lift one out of the wall. It would become three-dimensional in my hands, and I would rub it until the genie loomed before me. What do you wish for? he would ask. I wish for my father to be happy, I would answer.

"What happened in New York, Dad?" asked Brooks.

"What happened?" I echoed.

"Tell us, son," said Grampy.

"It may be premature," he said, smiling.

Mom put her hand on his arm. "I think there's no harm in telling. Do you, Roger?"

He shrugged.

Mom took a breath, which expanded her buxom chest, and said, "Your father has a new play called *Amusement Park*, which he's been working on for some time now. There's a producer named Elliot Martin who read it and liked it enough to ask for rewrites. And of course your father did those, and now Mr. Martin wants to produce it. And he has asked a very famous director named José Quintero to direct it. He directed Eugene O'Neill's *Long Day's Journey into Night*, which is currently running on Broadway." She took another proud breath. "And a marvelous actress named Jo Van Fleet is going to star in your father's play."

"I met with the three of them yesterday in New York," said Dad. "It was a great meeting. They all want to go ahead."

The table erupted. After my exclamation of joy, I stood solemnly and walked to his place, then leaned down and hugged him. "I'm so proud of you."

His eyes filled with tears. Be strong, I thought with a pang. Be strong.

My mother rang the dinner bell that signaled Jean to come in and clear. I sat back down, and we all stopped talking for a few minutes, but our thoughts were so full that it seemed as if words were still flying.

"Now, what were those rewrites you did, Roger?" Grampy asked over dessert.

"Oh, this and that."

"But what particularly?"

"The usual: strengthen the characters, clarify the action, make the denouement more surprising and dramatic. That sort of thing."

"And I bet you did a bang-up job, son." It occurred to me that he'd had a few drinks before dinner.

"Roger did a wonderful job," Mom answered.

"I always said to Lily that you were a skilled writer, and you got a good start with us, laying pipes, as we used to say, to make the plot go smoothly." His voice was booming. "That training when you were writing for Mr. Stratemeyer paid off for you, as I knew it would. You can tell a good yarn, son. I always said so. There's nothing to it if you know what you're doing. Not so different from building an engine."

Dad's face drained of color. He leaned back in his chair, one hand holding his napkin, the other on his forehead.

"But that was . . . This is . . . You can't . . . ," he mumbled. "Excuse me."

He pushed back his chair and left the room. We fell silent. I could hear him trudging upstairs.

"Well, I don't know what I said." Grampy looked confused and crushed. "I know he's always been sensitive, but Lord a'mercy . . ."

Dad's not going to make it, I thought with sudden despair. Something bad's going to happen.

The next day when I came home from school, I could smell the sunlamp upstairs. Softly, I walked a little way into his room and watched him, clad only in his plaid swimming trunks, lying under the blue light with those wet cotton balls over his eyes. The lamp made a soft metallic hum, so I don't think he heard me enter. I left without speaking, feeling a curious embarrassment for him.

Later, while he ate his apple in the living room before dinner, I asked if I could read his play. Above his faded yellow oxford shirt and light brown tweed jacket, his face was as ruddy as a fisherman's. He said he'd be delighted to give me his play, and there was a faint iridescence behind his eyes, hinting at worlds of happiness. He almost always had that potential about him—flickers of wild hope that would sometimes escape from his sober demeanor. As if he carried a dream with him of brilliant possibilities.

I read *Amusement Park* with the avidity of an explorer poring over a map. I was only fourteen, a young age to make reliable judgments, but the story gripped and amazed me. It was stranger—and much darker—than I had imagined. The first thing that struck me was the triptych of the Virgin Mary on the wall of the living-room set. It reminded me, of course, of Granny's pictures, and I wondered how Dad had been affected by seeing those images continuously as he came of age.

The play starts with a thirteen-year-old girl talking to the audience. (She reminded me of myself, which, although flattering, was disconcerting. Did he watch me when I was unaware?) She is a flutist, and at the moment we meet her, she's in the process of making her father a tape of her playing. I often played the piano for my father, who was usually willing to sit down and listen to my progress. Her name is Linda, not unlike Leslie. She is beginning to mature physically—as I was. We're both late bloomers in that department. She is a reader and a thinker. Just as I was getting to know her, she says she's going to die soon from heart disease—which floored me. Why would Dad kill off the girl? The atmosphere in the play is heightened with the paradox that Linda doesn't seem to mind that she's about to die. She has no self-pity. It was hard for me to accept her attitude, since I would be apoplectic if my time on earth were to be cut short.

Linda's mother left the family five years ago; when she didn't return, Linda's father divorced her. He works in the amusement park across the street; we can see the neon sign and the Ferris wheel through the back of the living room, making the park an eerie presence. The father takes in boarders to make ends meet, and he has hired a housekeeper to cook and be with Linda, since she has no mother. Linda seems perfectly happy without a future. She's a brave, appealing child who lives in her imagination. In a funny scene, she fantasizes about her mother coming back, which she is sure will happen.

A new boarder arrives: a young, pretty Irishwoman named Kathy, whose opinions are straight from hidebound Catholic dogma ("There's judgment, there's purgatory, there's hell"), although her secular, ambitious side sizes up Linda's father as a handsome homeowner who might one day take over the park. She immediately sets her cap for him. And then the mother comes back, which ruins everything. She is an alcoholic who has been thrown out by the man she left the family for. Now she has nowhere to go. First you think she only needs a room for a few days; then you realize that she wants it all back—the husband, the house, the daughter.

The boarders all accept the fact that Linda is going to die, but the mother, full of lifelong delusions, prefers to think it's a lie. Nevertheless, she plots to use this "lie" to persuade a judge that a mother's place is with her dying daughter and that therefore she should be allowed to move back in and take over. There was something familiar about the mother, but I couldn't put my finger on it. She wasn't like Mom or Granny. She reminded me a little of Dad. Damaged somehow, she is at the mercy of her fears and her unrealistic perceptions. At one point she says, "I've been taken over," meaning she has no control over her behavior. Also meaning that the person she "really" is can't be found anymore. Linda tells her that she should leave and start a new life, but despite Linda's belief in her mother's possibilities, we know she is probably incapable of pulling herself together.

During this act I had a moment of recognition that made me shudder: Linda spies on the household in order to understand the adults in her world. Linda's father, when he realizes she has spied on him, is taken aback and disapproving. What would Dad say if he knew I did the same thing? Maybe he already did. Maybe we were watching each other.

Then comes the shocking scene. Linda has concluded from her eavesdropping that her father would be happy with the Irishwoman. In order to thwart her mother's plan to move back, Linda decides to commit suicide—an act she minimizes in importance by comparing it to merely getting off a train one stop before the end, since she knows she has almost finished her journey. She turns her back to the audience, faces the park, and skips rope, singing a rhythmic jumping song. Her heart goes into arrest as the curtain falls.

That was the end of the second act. One act to go. Why didn't the play end there? I'd been sitting on my bed without noticing that the light of this early March afternoon was failing. Walking to my windows to look out on the thinning snow, I felt a lurch into grief. The girl dies? To help her parents? Children are supposed to be taken care of by their parents, not the other way around. The mother was so sad and the girl so happy; what a twisted situation. When I looked outside, I saw Buddy near the apple tree, trying to make a snowman from the paltry remnants of winter. As he rolled his ball of snow, he would come to patches of brown grass, so he'd move around to the other side of the ball and go back the way he came. His progress was slow. It was getting dark. From downstairs I heard faint strains of *My Fair Lady* coming from the library phonograph. *"I have often walked on this street before . . ."* We had the album of the musical, which was still playing on Broadway. My parents loved it. Buddy was giving up on the snowman. He walked a short distance away from his work, then stopped and looked back, as if trying to make up his mind. The air was dark gray now; there were no shadows on the snow. Buddy walked toward the house. It was cold today, below freezing. I really didn't know my father. So much was hidden.

I switched on the lamps in my room and picked up the next batch of pages.

It's a week later. Some business with the boarders—one is singing because Linda wouldn't want him to be unhappy about "a little thing like death." Is death a little thing? The father is sad and bitter. He talks about needing to hear the truth for once. He's concentrating on the amusement park and all those make-believe entertainments, and he's wondering what it means to have his daughter gone, and why all this has happened. "Can't we have . . . just one quick glimpse of the truth?" It's as if his loss has stemmed from living and working in a world of make-believe. And now the Irishwoman comes into the room. She wants to make sure that the mother leaves as promised. The plan is that the mother will take a bus in an hour, but she's still upstairs in her room. The father can think only about his daughter. The Irishwoman begins to say that according to the Church, suicide is a sin, but the father gets so upset that she backtracks and adds piously that the Church also says "there is no blame if due to a temporary state of mental strain, the mind gives way." Before I have time to think through my anger at these religious inanities, the mother enters. She's drunk, but dressed and packed.

Now the play takes a strange turn. The mother talks uneasily about moving on. It doesn't sound as if she means moving to another town. She says a lot of self-loathing things, including, "What should a mother do when her daughter kills herself to force her to leave so her father can marry another woman?" Suddenly she takes a gun out of her purse. She's going to kill herself, too! Mother and daughter! The father embraces and kisses her in an effort to relieve her despair and defuse the situation; the Irishwoman grabs the gun and . . . kills the mother! I didn't expect that. For one thing, it seemed clumsily melodramatic. I tried to banish that thought. The dying mother says that she will finally find herself again and be reborn.

My world was tilting on its side. Do I understand from this play that my father has a familiar, almost friendly connection with death? That he imagines death as a warm release? A path to a happier state? When I see a distant look in his eye, when he seems to retreat into the shadows of whatever room he's in, perhaps he's thinking about death. Or, if I really listen to what this play is saying, perhaps at those moments he's communing with death, taking it into himself, seducing away its cold threat.

In the play's last scene, after darkness has engulfed the stage, we see Linda in a spotlight with Johnny, the boy she liked. We know that she's dead and he's asleep, but for now they're on the Ferris wheel—represented by chairs onstage. The boy tells Linda that she got everything wrong. Linda, in a hopeful mood, says maybe it was right for her mother to die, since now she can get away and be free. They look over their chairs, as if they're at the top of the wheel, and Linda says, "Johnny! We'll fall out!" That's the last line of the play.

I was confused. Where would she fall? Back into life? Apparently, even after death, carnival rides are dangerous.

I had enough analytic acuity at fourteen not to miss the glaring link between life in an amusement park and growing up in the fantasy-factory household of Tom Swift, the Bobbsey Twins, and Uncle Wiggily. But did Dad see it? And even if he saw it, I wondered if he had analyzed the meaning it had for his own life.

I thought about my mother's belief that fairy tales could bring you closer to the truth. To her, Uncle Wiggily's world was a model of how people should live. The conviviality and kindness in Grampy's books demonstrated, in her mind, the verities of a moral life. Whereas in *Amusement Park*, Dad seemed to be saying that make-believe kept you from the truth, and that without truth, life falls apart.

I heard a knock on my bedroom door. "Dinner, Les," Grampy called cheerfully.

"Coming!"

I was deeply affected by my father's play. To my fourteen-year-old mind, the dialogue sounded sophisticated, witty, and rhythmically upbeat. It was a gripping story, which surely boded well for his career. My mind was spinning with these appreciative ideas, but I didn't know if they were sincere. I wondered about the taste and honesty of killing off the mother. I was disturbed by the daughter's role in her family. Was it her place to sacrifice herself for them? The play never seemed to question the morality of her decision. But I loved this play. I thought I loved this play. I gave up trying for critical honesty. Anyway, I was too young to be a theater critic. My job, if I understood it correctly, was to help make Dad proud of himself.

A few days after reading *Amusement Park*, I paid a visit to the dumbwaiter. Although I hadn't grown out of spying, and never would, the dumbwaiter was a feature of my younger life. Under the influence of Dad's girl character at the end of the play, watching the living from her invisible netherworld, I wanted to be alone in a dark space and recapture the absolute secrecy of hovering behind walls. I still fitted in the box. It felt like home. The rope was smaller in my hand and harder to pull than I remembered. I went all the way up and all the way down, but I heard nothing from the house.

I'd had a good conversation with Dad about his play. He'd listened seriously to everything I said, as if he were hearing an oracle. I was awed by the degree to which my opinion seemed to matter to him. It came over me in waves how powerful my presence was in his life. I wasn't sure I was entirely comfortable with the responsibility such influence implied. While he waited for *Amusement Park* to take shape in New York, he worked on his comedy, *The Blue Balloon*. He had two new plays now, one with a pending production, but instead of becoming steadier, he was increasingly agitated. I saw it in little things, like ranting when he misplaced his glasses.

In the basement, as I sat in the dumbwaiter behind the laundry-room wall, I heard footsteps come down the stairs. Nothing. And then singing. My mother's voice was becoming more and more beautiful since she had begun studying with a new teacher. She stopped to clear her throat, then began again. I had accompanied her several times on the piano while she practiced this aria from *Madame Butterfly*. Ah . . . how lovely . . .

"Vogliatemi bene,
un ben piccolino,
un bene da bambino,
quale a me si conviene."

Love me, just a little, like a baby, that will be enough. It was a plea from a woman who existed only for her man, desiring no other life.

" *'Noi siamo gente avvezza . . .'* " I pulled my knees closer to my chest. In my dusty wooden hideaway her voice floated around me, pure and clear, and except for a subtle, tremulous plaintiveness, her singing exalted a world outside our day-to-day lives. After a while I pulled on the rope and slowly rose up through the house again.

CHAPTER TWELVE

It started snowing in the afternoon. I was skating at Orr Rink, owned by Amherst College and next to the Cage, their athletic building. Three or four times a week I met regularly with a group of kids my age when the outdoor rink was open to the public. We chased each other and raced and showed off moves, skating backward as fast as possible or squatting down on one leg and holding the other straight out in front as we coasted down the center. The boys wore hockey skates that made a masculine cutting sound on the ice as they glided around confidently. When they came to their decisive stops, they would lean away hard from the edges of their skates and cast up showers of ice chips—sometimes inches away from a girl. The girls' figure skates were quieter and not as fast, but much better with curves and turns. The snowflakes that day were the size of small daisies. If you raised your face up to the sky, you could catch them on your eyelashes, and your face was soon covered by soft splotches of moisture. The snow was coming down so thickly that eventually we headed home, our skates over our shoulders, hanging from the ends of our tied-together laces, each of us excited to be visited once more by snow, since in a few days it would be April.

At home, my father was laying a fire in the living room, whistling. Through the French doors I could see the snow blowing in swirls over the side terrace. Already the ground was smooth and pale, holding the thin afternoon light in its crystals, with no more patches of grass to be seen.

At dinner Grampy told us once more about the blizzard of '88, when he was fifteen, in which he and Edna van Allen were the only two students who came to school in Binghamton, New York. He had walked a mile through the snow to get to school, and he had to walk back around drifts higher than his head. Dad's eyes were oddly flat, and when he spoke, his words came slowly. He sipped his water with tiny slurps, ate very little, and while Jean put dessert before us—sliced Del Monte peaches with thick syrup—he said he had to leave the table.

"Will you be down for *Perry Mason*?" my mother asked.

"Maybe."

Later I slipped out alone and walked up Spring Street toward town. It was snowing harder than ever, covering everything gently, relentlessly. At the second crossroads I looked down Seelye Street toward the Congregational church, which loomed gray and dark against the white that had by now swathed its sloping roofs. The spindly steeple, set apart by outdoor lights, merged with the sky as it disappeared upward into snowflakes. This was the domain presided over by Thayer Greene, our minister, the man who brought me through his convocation class and patiently dealt with my incessant questions—especially about Jesus' contradictory and confusing parables. I was drawn to this exceedingly tall New Englander with a deep voice and close-cropped beard who responded carefully to all questions, answering in slow, resonant tones. He was a third-generation minister from New Hampshire who had

gone to Amherst College on the G.I. Bill after the war. I learned—
not from him—that he had graduated summa cum laude. When I
joined the church as an "adult," at thirteen, meaning that I would
henceforth attend the regular Sunday services instead of Sunday
school, I told him I couldn't in good conscience say that I believed
Jesus was the actual son of God. If there really was a God, and he
sent a human down, why would he send only one? And why then,
and why for such a brief period of time? It didn't make sense that
miracles could happen in the first century and not now. Therefore
the miracles couldn't be real. To my thinking, they had to be some
kind of metaphor written down by early Christians to tell a story.
Thus went my hyper-serious adolescent reasoning. Mr. Greene allowed me to stay quiet when the others chanted about the Trinity
in our convocation ritual. He made an exception for me, and I
loved him for it.

At the top of Spring Street, Amherst spread before me in a
pristine version of winter, like a village in a snow globe. Snow
fell around the few streetlights like shifting white veils, as if to remind me to cover myself against the cold. On the Common, the
branches of the old maples were actively accumulating soft mantles
of snow against the dark skeletons of the trees.

When I walked onto the Common, I spoiled the snow with my
tracks. All the stores were closed except College Drug on the far
corner. The window of Hastings' store was softly outlined by a dim
interior light. I seemed to be the only person in town. No, there
was a man trudging up the sidewalk of Main Street, past Aubuchon Hardware and Bolles Shoes. He went into the drugstore. I
thought about the very fat man who worked in there who was
friendly to my father but rude to my brothers and me.

I watched my breath puff before me. Along the east border of
the green, the trees were planted in two rows, making an arched
walkway that tonight looked altogether magical.

I started back home. I'd heard it said that snow was like a shroud, but it never seemed so to me. How could something with the power to transform an ordinary landscape into unearthly beauty be anything but a blessing?

In the vestibule I stamped my feet to get them warm, pulled off my boots, and hung up my jacket. As soon as I was in the hallway, I heard voices from the library. Something was wrong.

"Jesus, Mabel! That's your answer?"

"I only said . . ."

"That I walk like my *mother*?"

"Well, you said you were worried because . . ."

"I said I was afraid I *might* be taking too many pills. And you . . . my God . . ."

"I was only agreeing with you. Lately I've noticed your walking is unsteady, and it reminded me . . ."

"That may be one of the worst things you've ever said to me! Sometimes I think you're a witch! How am I supposed to live in this house?"

At which point he strode furiously out of the library and right into me.

"Oh, Les . . ."

He stopped for a moment and glanced at me wildly before rushing upstairs. I could hear Mom crying.

ON A SUNDAY NIGHT in late April, Mom's dark green dress with the wide belt and her beige shantung dress with its bolero jacket were laid out on the bed, ready to go into the suitcase. A blue satin quilted lingerie bag overflowed with stockings folded carefully along the seams. Presumably, her underpants and bras were tucked discreetly beneath them. Her miniature high-heeled shoes stood in a row next to the suitcase, like sentinels guarding her escape. Already packed were her skirts and sweaters. Dad sat in an armchair with his head in his hands.

"It's such a short time," Mom said soothingly, moving between bed and suitcase. "Catherine Sage is coming every day, and she'll stay for dinner and see to the children's homework. Maggie will make breakfasts and do the grocery shopping. Mary Koslowsky will come in on Wednesday to clean and do laundry. I'll be home Sunday."

Dad said nothing. I was perched on the bed, excited for Mom and happy about living without a mother for a week. Much as I liked Catherine Sage, a clever, good-looking lawyer from Peterborough, New Hampshire, whose husband had left her, I didn't know why she had to take care of us; but then, Catherine was too much the career woman to make a fuss over children, and too much of a freethinker to impose her will on others. She came into our lives through Grampy, who mysteriously began meeting this young woman for lunch at the Lord Jeff. Was he hoping for more? I liked her and thought she might be good company during Mom's absence.

"I don't know why you do this League stuff, anyway," Dad muttered miserably.

Mom had been selected by the Amherst League of Women Voters to represent them at the national convention in Chicago. The League was active in social issues such as racism and, of course, women's rights, and my mother was a vocal, hardworking member. It was an honor to be chosen to go to Chicago, and she was not going to be deterred by her needy husband, as she had been a few years earlier when she gave up the lead in Denis Johnston's play. Besides, this was different. She believed the League did important work and that her contributions mattered to the world. So she was going.

The depth of my father's need for my mother was a mystery to me. I knew they spent a lot of time talking together in the bed-room, sometimes even in the middle of the night. But generally I didn't see signs of his dependency. They moved through the house separately, he usually lost in thought, she always busy and often singing or talking to one of the children. She didn't lean on him to do chores, since Maggie and John, the young couple in the back apartment, did jobs in exchange for their rooms. I knew that Mom read his work and discussed it with him, and that was an enormous bond that they had, but surely he could do without her comments for a week. I didn't see a lot of physical affection between them. There was no hugging or kissing on view; they were both too for-mal for public displays. But every now and then one of them would touch the other's arm or face, and it was clear that they were phys-ically close. But his panic at losing her for less than a week made no sense to me. What was the big deal? Besides, *I* was here. *I* could handle whatever serious discussions he wished to have.

CHAPTER THIRTEEN

Amherst in April is a time of suspension. The snow has melted; the air is heavy with moisture and still blows a cold edge. Daffodils are out, tree buds are tight knobs on their branches, forsythia blooms, the ground is damp and soft. Robins are busy pulling worms, but the sun has only a few days to warm the trees and flowers between bouts of frigid rain. Everything is waiting for the next season.

With Mom away, Dad began to call his agent, Audrey Wood, day and night for news about *Amusement Park*. What were the next steps? When would it be announced? He was a man possessed by his future and unable to resist his need to push anyone in New York who might secure it for him. I don't know if it was Mom's absence that made me notice his behavior more, or if she normally had a calming effect on him, so that without her he lost his impulse control. Who was he calling besides Miss Wood? Several times I saw him slam down the phone.

He was also having arguments with his father, something I had never seen before.

"It's too much fuss!" Grampy said to Dad in his booming voice. "Besides, it's dangerous. Better let sleeping dogs lie."

"Why can't you see how important this is?" Dad shouted. He was furious.

"Oh, do what you want!"

"I'm doing it for you! Why can't you see that?"

"I know, son," Grampy said steadily. "Do what you want."

Then there would be the sound of Dad loudly leaving the scene, stamping his feet on the floor, slamming a door.

Later I would see Grampy, his large white-capped head bowed forward as he shuffled around. He hummed to himself through his despondency. What was this all about?

In the late afternoon Catherine Sage would sit upstairs with Grampy in Granny's old room and talk about her divorce. Once, I heard her let out several loud, gasping sobs, then fall silent. It was a primitive sound, shockingly unguarded. She had formed a bond with Grampy that excluded Dad, who would walk by the open door on the way to his room and leave them alone. I was surprised that Catherine would choose Grampy over Dad as the person she wished to pour out her heart to. I couldn't understand it, since it seemed perfectly clear that besides being closer to her age, Dad had the more-developed sensibility. Catherine's visits made me wonder what depths of understanding my grandfather possessed.

Dad was turning into a wanderer. He walked through the rooms of the house, paced the terrace back and forth outside the living room, his hands in his jacket pockets or clasped behind his back. He often mumbled to himself and shook his head. His appearance didn't invite company, so I stayed back. His face was florid with emotion. At dinner he was distracted and heavy-voiced. He spoke slowly and would leave before dessert, climbing slowly up to his room only to come downstairs a few hours later to make a cup of tea or watch a little television or go outside for another walk. He was unreachable.

On Saturday, the day before Mom was to come back, the sun came out and Dad was in a good mood. He invited me to his study at Jones Library in the afternoon. I'd never been to his room there and considered this a precious invitation. He had to secure permission from the staff for a visitor, as those writers' rooms were treated by the library as sacrosanct.

My route took me up Spring Street, diagonally across the Common, then onto Amity Street to the stately brick-and-flagstone library. On the Common I beheld a scene that never failed to send pulses through me. A clump of children surrounded my grandfather, who was sitting on a bench telling Uncle Wiggily stories. His splendid head, with its prominent nose, dark-circled eyes, and silky hair, moved with the story, nodding to the children, cocking to one side as he pretended to figure something out, and his sturdy hands fluttered in the air, embellishing his words. There must have been about twenty children, some on the ground, some standing behind him leaning over his shoulder, some piled on the bench beside him. Even from a distance they radiated a rapture of concentration—storyteller and listeners mutually spellbound in the midst of a busy afternoon, oblivious to everything but the woodland adventures of a rabbit.

I felt a sudden pang of isolation, realizing all at once what it must have been like for my father when he was a child, watching his father charm other children while he had little time for his own. Grampy was a professional enchanter but a remote father, and the resentment I felt at that moment, passing him on the Common, was bitter, and shocked me. Giving the group a wide berth, I ran the rest of the way.

Moving through Jones Library's ornate arched doorway, then

up two flights of wide, dark wooden stairs with carved banisters, I reached the hushed third floor, where a few rooms were loaned to local writers. Ray Stannard Baker (aka David Grayson) had written his eight-volume biography of Woodrow Wilson there, and the poet Robert Francis came every day.

Dad gave me that loving smile of his as he opened his door. "Welcome," he said. He pointed to the room that housed the Frost collection. "I'm across from Robert Frost," he said proudly, then told me that the poet had been there the previous day and had greeted him, asked after Grampy, and said he'd walk down the street to see us soon.

I was a little surprised at this talk, since Frost's visits had been a steady feature of my life. I hadn't realized how impressed my father was by knowing him, and that perception made something in me shrink. "Well, come on in and see my room," he said.

The room was plainly appointed, with heavy wooden furniture—a large desk in front of a high window, a wide armchair, a few old lamps. It was a pleasant and serious room. Amidst this sturdy furniture, Dad's thinness made him look eerily insubstantial. Had I realized before how his bony shoulders made peaks under his shirt? I became conscious for the first time that his slenderness was crossing the line into emaciation.

I asked him if he was working on a new play and he said yes, a comedy called *The Blue Balloon*. Audrey Wood seemed to like it; they were looking for a producer.

"Mostly, though," he said, "I'm trying to get the ending right for *Amusement Park*. Elliot Martin, the producer, doesn't think it works, so I'm giving it another go."

I thought of Dad's characters at the play's end: Linda, the daughter, has killed herself; Linda's mother, divorced years ago, is set to take a bus away from the house into an uncertain future as an alcoholic with no money; Linda's father is going to marry the pretty Irish girl.

I sat on the chair and crossed my legs, ready to tackle the problem.

"Let's see," I began, feeling needed. "You have Linda's mother and father and the Irish girl in the same room. Linda is dead. What would really happen?"

"If I knew, I'd write it."

Trying to sound tender instead of critical, I ventured, "I think the shooting seems a little melodramatic."

He said nothing for several minutes. I began to feel I'd crossed a line.

At last he said, "When you get older, you'll understand that life is much more dramatic than you think—melodramatic, if you want to call it that. I would say heightened beyond what we think is seemly. But you can't turn away from the truth because it's lurid or jarring."

I looked at him with his Brooks Brothers shirt and his perfectly trimmed blond mustache and his long, sad face, and I thought that one thing he had for sure was style, the style of a man in control of his world, the calm, conventional style of privilege. The style of a man who knows how to bewitch women. I remembered the early *Liberty* magazine stories I'd seen: "No Rules for Women—A tingling tale of hearts adrift and that queer thing called love," and "A Woman's Riddle at the Sphinx," and those long stories he wrote for *Redbook* magazine's annual "complete novel" issue. One was called *Nobody Else—Ever*, pure romance and adventure. He wrote dozens like that. He couldn't have thought those stories were depictions of real life, of actual truth. They were the dream life of readers who wished to be romantic heroes. But he was older now, trying to be a different kind of writer.

This was the year I'd read every novel by Erich Maria Remarque translated into English, and I felt I had experienced firsthand the muscle of language used to describe lurid truth. Although how Remarque did it, I had no idea. In my passionate adolescent mind I had decided that truth, the principle of pure truth, should be the aim of writing.

I had a suggestion for his play. What if the mother takes the bus just as Linda's father realizes that he'll never be happy with the Irish girl? So the audience thinks that if the mother hadn't gone away, the father might have been happy with her again. It's kind of a big mix-up—everybody has made the wrong decision.

"That's terrible, Les. How do I show that? You can't predict the future in a play; you can only show the present. And who's to say the mother could ever stop drinking and get a grip on herself? Besides it's chaotic, soft, and open-ended. Audiences don't want that."

He was backing up on himself.

I said, "I still think that if Linda's mother pulls out a gun and then the Irishwoman grabs it and shoots the mother . . . well, . . . it feels as if the writer is manipulating the action to fit the story. I'm not sure it's believable."

"Do you think you know enough about life to say what's believable and what's not? Life is a series of stories, one after the other, and sometimes those stories are tragic. God is a storyteller. We're his characters; he makes up the plot."

"But we have some say in it!"

"Of course. Each time we make a decision, the story changes and God adjusts the narrative. But we don't realize how each decision has been determined by the circumstances we've already lived, the hand God has given us. Our choices are fewer than we think."

Another silence. He stood by the window, looking out.

"People don't see what's going on around them—the dramas everywhere. Most of us don't . . . we're not smart enough or brave enough to perceive life as it actually is. We live in the shadow of reality."

I flashed on the dumbwaiter, myself in the dark, listening. Guilt spread through me. I shouldn't have lurked behind the walls like that.

I changed the subject and told him I didn't want to go to Northampton School for Girls anymore. Did he have any idea how old-fashioned it was? Before our dances with the boys from Williston Academy, our teachers inspected our necklines for modesty and our stocking seams for straightness. Did he know we were forbidden to chew gum or eat on the street because these habits were "unladylike"? I wanted his permission to go to the public school in Amherst. I lived in this town but had never gone to school here. What about it?

I didn't know at the time how scarce money was. Years later I wondered if he had asked me to his office that day to tell me I would have to leave private school.

Sure, he said. Amherst High School was fine, whatever I wanted.

I was shocked by how easily he acquiesced.

In my memory of this encounter, the air in my father's office was stale, almost fetid. Perhaps the library kept the heat pumping even though the April day was mild.

When I entered the room, Dad had been expansive and pleased with his surroundings. But by the middle of our conversation, he was closed into the space like a prisoner who needed an escape plan but couldn't devise one to save his life.

And then my mind played a terrifying trick on me. I half imagined, half saw, his mother standing behind him, smirking. She appeared between his back and the window, as if she had come in that way. She had the hyper-reality of dreams; I had no idea why I had suddenly conjured her. I must have registered alarm, because he swung his head around to look behind him, and of course there was nothing there.

When our eyes met, we were each aware of secrets in the other never to be revealed. It was a profoundly destabilizing moment.

"Why don't you scoot along so I can work."

He tried to smile, but it twisted into something else. Oh, my dear dad.

WHEN OUR MOTHER RETURNED, she walked into a household subtly changed. Dad was grateful to have his wife restored to him, but his attitude was petulant ("I don't know if you expected me to do all the shopping, but we're out of a great many things") and alarmed, as if his missing her to that degree exposed to his sight the menacing beast his terror had become. He did his best to cover these emotions with his genuine love for her and curiosity about her trip, but he was raw with affront. Catherine Sage took Mom aside and told her that this household needed "a strong woman's hand." I overheard her say that everything fell apart when she was gone, and I was full of resentment at her characterization, even though I could plainly see that while his wife was away, Dad's strength was embarrassingly diminished. An adult person should be able to stand alone, I thought, squaring my own shoulders. Grampy, whose routine had not wavered even though he'd had that mysterious argument with his son, told Mom she was a sight for sore eyes, and I thanked God for the male rock in our household.

Mom shook her little head at Catherine Sage's words, like a dog shaking water off its coat, and said something like "Fiddlesticks."

The following Saturday was typical of April. The air was slate-colored and so heavy with moisture that your face felt wet even though technically it wasn't raining. Distant hints of sun edged the clouds. Mom got out her hand pruner and lopping shears, which were kept in a musty pantry off the back porch, pulled on leather gardening gloves, and headed for the rose arbor. I followed along, ready to gather up the thorny canes and start our spring brush pile. We went down the stone back steps to a narrow wooded path that opened to the main back meadow. Another path snaked left through tall greenery. It was set with large flat rocks, so that walking it felt ceremonious; it anticipated the gardens, the square stone fountain, and the long rose arbor to which it led. Heirloom roses grew up and over this arbor, roses that bloomed only once a summer and had a lusty fragrance.

Even though I was past the age, the first thing I did at the arbor was to jump in a hopscotch pattern to the other end. The slate slabs with tufts of grass and weeds between them, set in a design made uneven by the frost heaves of harsh New England winters, suggested the one, two, one, two, of hopscotch, and I'd been hopping it like that since I was five. At the bottom of the arbor, someone before our time had hung a wooden swing from braided, moss-slimed rope, and I usually took a high-flying ride when I reached it. Today was no different, although I did feel guilty as I looked back and saw my mother on her knees, pushing the pruner into the woody mass at a column's base.

Soon we were working together in silence, except for the chirping of birds. "Look, so many goldfinches," Mom said contentedly, and after a while Grampy wandered down. He asked if Mom needed a hand. I could see how much he wanted to pitch in, but he was eighty-four and Mom didn't want him to exert himself.

"Like to do something about the greenhouse one of these days," he said, sweeping an arm in the direction of the wooden building that housed a two-car garage, a room under the eaves, and a ruined greenhouse.

"I could start vegetables in there," he said. "Just needs a little work."

We looked at the rusting frame, the cracked and missing glass, the cobwebs draping corners. Mom's eyebrows shot up. "I don't know, Grampy. It looks like a pretty big job."

"Never hurts to try, Mabs. Nothing ventured, nothing gained." He trudged up the driveway, his shoulders dipping sideways with each step.

I told Mom that while she was away, Dad and Grampy had been arguing, and I asked her if she knew why. Her answer astounded me with its implications of epic foolishness on the part of the man who wrote four hundred books and fifteen thousand Uncle Wiggily stories, the man whose imagination had been compared to an open tap.

When *Uncle Wiggily* was at the height of its popularity, Howard had been approached by an agent named William Erskine, who promised Howard lucrative deals all over the world. Howard would profit beyond his wildest imaginings and forevermore could leave all business to Mr. Erskine. What a load off Howard's back! Erskine had apparently snowed Howard into agreeing, even though he would take 50 percent of Howard's earnings. This wily businessman must have spun a heady tale, because Howard agreed on the spot with a handshake and days later signed a contract that held him to these terms in perpetuity—up to and including his heirs.

"Your father is trying to break this contract," Mom said. "It's very complicated because Grampy's lawyer is your uncle John, and John is against making any changes in Grampy's situation. He thinks Erskine has done well for your grandfather. So Dad's attempts to free Grampy from this dreadful agreement are causing a lot of trouble in the family, since John is dead set against it."

John Clancy was married to Dad's sister, Cleo. They had one

daughter, Carroll, whose long, elegant legs and glamorous job for *Life* magazine filled me with awe. She was unfailingly nice to me, and I liked her very much. Her mother, Cleo, was, in Mom's words, "a cool customer." She was four years younger than Dad and had never been on easy terms with him. While they were growing up, she ridiculed his sensitivity. When she was twenty-three, she married a successful, strong, stable man—in stark contrast to her brother—and set up a prosperous household not far from her parents. She maintained a self-protective detachment from her mother, which, according to what she'd told Mom, she had seen the need for while still in her teens. John served on the boards of several prominent banks and companies, and was a commissioner of the Port Authority of New York and New Jersey. He was a powerful figure.

It made no sense that Uncle John would be against breaking the contract.

"John doesn't want to make trouble for his father-in-law this late in life. He's just trying to protect Grampy."

We let these words sit in the air.

"I don't think that's the way to do it," I said.

"No."

I asked her about overhearing Grampy use the word "dangerous" in connection with all this. Apparently, Uncle John told Grampy that if he tried to break his contract, Erskine would persuade Milton Bradley to stop publishing the Uncle Wiggily Game. Erskine would threaten to pull Johnny Gruelle's Raggedy Ann—which Erskine represented with very different terms from his deal with Grampy—from Milton Bradley. The toy company would have to choose and would drop Uncle Wiggily. I was aghast. Could Erskine really do that? Dad didn't think so, but Grampy was scared.

Mom also told me that Granny used to say—and here she

imitated Granny by using a high-pitched, shaky, fretful voice—
"William Erskine could ruin us."

"I don't know if you're aware of this, but Dad is also quietly
having meetings about getting Uncle Wiggily on television. He
wants to separate from Erskine before any deal is in place."

I began to speak. I had so much to say, but Mom put her finger
up to silence me.

"Listen to that!" she said, turning toward the wooded path.

It sounded like three short whistles.

To my surprise, Mom whistled back in the same tones. I hadn't
known she could do that.

"It's a cardinal," she whispered.

Then the cardinal answered her. They conversed like that for a
good five minutes. Human conversation was over.

THERE IS A MOMENT that spring that I recall with the undefined
clarity of a distant glimmer across a field. It was after school. I was
in the dining room; the top of the Dutch door to the terrace was
open, and I became aware of voices beyond the door.

". . . guess those city people don't have much use for a country
rabbit . . ." This was my grandfather.

"I was so close . . ." My father, forlorn.

I moved closer to the door. ". . . almost signed," Dad said. And
I remember also that he said, more than once, "I'm going to keep
trying." That stayed with me. "I'm going to keep trying."

"It's not your fault, son," the old man said in his loud voice.
"Business doesn't fetch out the best in human nature."

"It was all set . . ." Dad sounded stunned and puzzled.

"Well now, well now . . . Uncle Wiggily's not an up-to-date fel-
low, you know," Grampy said pleasantly.

"I'm sorry, Dad," I heard my father say. "I'm so sorry."

The front door slammed, and I got out of there, through the kitchen—Jean was just arriving. I said something to her as I rushed out the back door. In a moment I was down at the oak tree on my branch, looking up at the sky through the new leaves. The conversation I overheard wafted around me—was this the TV deal?—but I kept it diffuse and apart. I listened to the brook purl over its rocks.

That evening before dinner I heard Grampy singing in his room. There was a hint of melancholy in his voice; he sounded like a boy trying to cheer himself up. It was a ditty from his childhood:

"My bonnet lies over the ocean,
My Scotch cap to Glasgow has gone,
My old Tam O'Shanter
Has taken a canter—
I think it will end up in Bonn."

A week or so later, in May, Mom announced at dinner that Eugene O'Neill's *Long Day's Journey into Night* had won the Pulitzer Prize for drama, which, she said, is good news for Dad because that play was directed by José Quintero, the very man who would be directing *Amusement Park*.

Brooks and Buddy clapped their hands. Grampy gave a little laugh. Dad looked pained.

"These are the people who want to work with your father," Mom was saying. "In fact, didn't Elliot Martin produce *Long Day's Journey?*"

"I don't think so, Mabs," Dad said.

"No, I'm sure I'm right."

"You're wrong!" he snapped.

"All right, all right." But you could see she was reserving her opinion for later verification. "Anyway, José Quintero is the main one. The director runs the show, as it were."

Dad heaved a loud sigh. "I don't know why the hell they don't get back to me."

"There's no need for that language, Roger," Mom said.

"Oh, for God's sake! What a prig you are."

As if she'd been slapped, red blotches sprang to her cheeks. First I thought she was going to fight back, then she seemed about to cry, but instead she bit her lip and rang the bell for Jean.

Jean came in. Mom started to say something, but Brooks interrupted. "Dad, this is great!" The kindest of us, Brooks continued, "Your new director helped that playwright win the prize. And now he'll help you!"

Before Dad could answer, Jean, not knowing what we were talking about but following Brooks's lead, said, "Congratulations, Mr. Garis."

"This is not my achievement, Jean," Dad said stiffly. "It's Eugene O'Neill's. And he's dead."

Or perhaps he said "not my achievement, Mrs. Bosworth," because around this time Mom had decided, in the interest of social equality, that since Mom was called Mrs. Garis, Jean should be called Mrs. Bosworth, which actually hurt Jean's feelings because she thought that by this formality, my mother was trying to distance her from the family.

As Jean cleared the table, I thought about Dad's saying "hell," and his childhood Catholicism and more recent Protestantism. Do we Congregationalists believe in hell? I didn't think so. Granny certainly did, though. She was scared to death of it. Her fear of damnation was her most defining characteristic. Dad had been making frequent trips to the Congregational church around the corner at odd hours during the day, and the minister came here often to visit Dad. Mr. Greene and my father would go into our library for long sessions. Whenever I could, I pressed my ear to the closed door and tried to hear them, but all that came through were Mr. Greene's rumbling bass tones and occasional sharp sounds from my father. Despite my straining to hear, the words remained unintelligible. I would have given a lot to know what passed between them, especially what Dad said. You don't call a minister unless you need help. I wished I knew why he needed so much help.

Later that evening, in the starry dark, Grampy took Buddy, in his blue pajamas, onto the terrace to point out the moon. It was the merest sliver of a crescent. The old man said, "Horns to the east, soon be increased; horns to the west, soon be at rest." He explained that the side of the moon the crescent appeared on told you whether the moon was waxing or waning. In this case it was waxing; it would get bigger and bigger as the days went by. Buddy took his grandfather's hand. I watched them stand like that in silence, the plump man with his feet planted sturdily apart and the wispy boy, both of them looking up at the moon as if it were about to increase for their pleasure.

WITHIN A WEEK it was as if a tornado had hit my father.

He went to New York to meet with José Quintero. Apparently, in Quintero's apartment, Dad read the rewrites Quintero had asked for, and the director declared it a "magnificent play." He asked to come to Amherst to work on the next two acts. On the appointed day, I was told I couldn't have friends visit. Mom cooked lunch, but no one arrived. Dad called Audrey in confusion. Audrey said the production was off. She told him that she had just had a meeting with Quintero and Elliot Martin during which the two men withdrew. Dad began yelling during the call and didn't stop, it seemed to me, for days or weeks. This became a time of slammed doors, stamping feet, and loud curses for Audrey Wood, the woman who had smashed his life. They were set to go! She ruined everything! He worked himself into a frenzy, passing through the rooms with the startled velocity of a chased animal, hurling himself into the car for wild drives through the countryside. Eventually he couldn't stop himself from picking up the phone and firing her. He left the best theatrical agent in New York, the woman who represented Tennessee Williams, because Dad was absolutely convinced that Quintero and Martin were "one hundred percent on board" until they talked to Audrey. Audrey had turned them against him and destroyed him. I heard Dad say many times that Elliot Martin, Jo Van Fleet, and José Quintero were all clients of MCA, the agency for which Audrey worked. He figured that for nefarious reasons of their own, Audrey, in cahoots with MCA, had killed his play. Which of us had the knowledge or power to dissuade him? We could only watch. (What actually happened was that Quintero was offered Carson McCullers's new play, *The Square Root of Wonderful*, which he left *Amusement Park* to direct. He quit *Square Root* in rehearsal, and George Keathley was credited as the director in the program. The play opened in October, got unfavorable reviews, and closed after forty-five performances. Did MCA dictate Quintero's decisions? Unlikely, but there is no way to know.)

During Dad's storms, we three children shrank into our corners. Bud was having a lot of trouble with third grade at Smith College Day School, so Mom helped him with his homework in the afternoons, when she wasn't trying to calm her husband. I went off on my bicycle after school every day, headed for Woodside Avenue, where a group of friends lived in Amherst College faculty houses. Grampy, as a kind of work-therapy scheme, proposed to his son that the two of them fix up the greenhouse together. It would be a father-son project. Surprisingly, Dad seemed grateful for the idea. He borrowed how-to books from the library, made lists, walked the captivatingly stocked aisles of Aubuchon Hardware. He appeared in old khaki pants, a tape measure or a yardstick or a paint scraper in his hands.

And then, just as suddenly, that was over, too. Without consulting his son, Grampy hired a glazier, a carpenter, and a painter. Once again, Dad was furious, but this time with less steam. We heard him mutter the words "sidelined" and "useless." And then he began to shut down. He stayed in bed until the afternoon, had headaches, took naps, lay under the sunlamp, came to dinner in a fog.

At the end of May, our parents told nine-year-old Buddy that he had failed third grade and would have to leave the Day School. In the fall he would attend fourth grade in the public school. He cried hard. He took it as if it were punishment for inadequacy, and no one talked him out of that idea. Never mind that he had an encyclopedic knowledge of whales, knew a dozen poems by heart, and asked startlingly penetrating questions at dinner. Like his brother, who was also struggling academically, he couldn't spell. Written language was a code he couldn't crack. During that spring, before his academic crash, he sat in a crook of the beech tree, his back against the trunk, legs stretched out on the path-wide branch, a pad and pencil in his willowy hands, devising a phonetic spelling system that worked for him. But his teachers weren't interested, or worse: they thought he was contrarian and subversive. It was with a shock that he realized life could be painfully simple: he didn't meet their academic standards, so he was banished from their school.

As spring matured and we felt the first heat of the season, The Dell was ripening into its lush summer beauty. A wall of heavy-petaled rhododendrons in emerging blossom limned the back lawn. Peonies and irises bloomed in the garden. The deep-silled house windows were left open day and night. I liked to be the first downstairs so I could open the French doors from the living room to the covered side terrace and walk into the morning, pretending I was a newly born nymph emerging into the sun.

On a close, humid day, Mom gave a singing recital in our living room. I played the piano—not for the opera arias, for which her teacher accompanied her, but for Gershwin's "Summertime," the last piece on the program. Her voice was pure, expressive, and vulnerable. Friends sat on chairs borrowed for the occasion. Grampy beamed; Dad looked serious. When it was over, I sensed a strained politeness in their friends, none of whom, as far as I know, had ever given a private music recital. But all had gone well, and Mom's emotions were so stirred that she accepted compliments as in a dream. Mrs. Madeira said, "Good for you, Mabel! Good for you for doing this! And you have such a lovely voice!" Hypersensitive as I was on Mom's behalf, I heard no condescension from Mrs. Madeira. It was a fine moment.

AS THE SUMMER WORE ON, sounds of hammering and laughing wafted up from the hired men at the greenhouse, which, pane by pane, was taking form while my father resumed his daily stints at Jones Library. I don't remember much about him just then. He kept to himself.

About this time each year, one of our ginkgo trees began to exude an unpleasant odor. My mother, who hated the smell, said it was the female. I was impressed by the tree's forceful nature. It had the redolent power to send out a scent like an urgent message. I stood beneath it and wondered what it was trying to say. But the message was short-lived. The scent died away in a matter of days. I pressed the leaves, which looked like pale green fans, between pieces of waxed paper and kept them in one of my books at the head of my bed. Those were mysterious trees from far away.

What I didn't know then was that Austin Dickinson, Emily's brother, had planted them for another Mabel, the love of his life, Mabel Loomis Todd.

Austin was Amherst's first citizen in the late 1800s. Treasurer of Amherst College and an avid horticulturist, he created—with advice from his friends Frederick Law Olmsted and Calvert Vaux, who designed New York City's Central Park—the Amherst Common, which until then was a swampy hayfield. He and his wife, Susan, had three children. They lived next door to his two sisters, Emily and Lavinia. But in middle age his private life exploded when he fell headlong in love with Mabel, twenty-seven years his junior, married to Amherst astronomy professor David Todd. Austin and Mabel had a passionate thirteen-year affair that ended in 1895 with his death. In 1886 Austin had deeded a corner of the Dickinson Meadow to Mabel and David and helped them build a Queen Anne house, which he sited and landscaped. She named it The Dell, inspired by the sloping land by the brook. Mabel had a trained voice, and she must have sung some of the arias that my mother, my own Mabel, had been singing throughout my childhood. And there would have been private recitals.

In 1898, three years after Austin's death, they sold the house to the Churchill family. Nine years later Mrs. Churchill moved the house to a lot across the street and, on the original property, built the house we bought in 1948. Mrs. Churchill retained not only Mabel Todd's poetic designation, The Dell—since it described the site more than the house—but also Austin's plantings, which included hemlocks, birches, forsythias, hydrangeas, magnolias, beeches, apple and chestnut trees, and, yes, the ginkgoes.

This landscape, which never ceased to move me, had been created by an inspired naturalist for the joy of spending romantic hours in a natural paradise. Standing under the ginkgoes, I didn't understand then that I was under the spell of an extraordinary love.

"After so much wandering, then . . . ," Austin wrote to Mabel on March 1, 1884, "we have found each other . . . was I in dreamland— or in the world of the real! I thought it must be dreamland . . ." And that is what he made of The Dell—a dreamland.

THAT SUMMER is a blur to me, except for the sound track to it, which was a crooner singing "Besame Mucho." I played it on a little square record player in my room, pretending to be in love. As I danced around in my room, I knew that outside my door a creeping incoherence was making itself felt.

Something was happening to Dad. On the most obvious level, he was losing an alarming amount of weight. His shoulders sagged, his chest was concave, his walk was becoming a shuffle. He was only in his fifties, but suddenly my attractive father looked haggard and twenty years older. Every day he walked to Jones Library and worked on something—a novel, I think—and every afternoon he returned like a beaten man. At dinner he said his food was too hot to eat, or too bland—*Why is there no taste?* he would ask. One night he looked down at his plate and his head bobbed, remaining inclined toward his food. I thought he was falling asleep, and I became enormously upset. Wake up, Dad! Wake up! He looked up at me with wet, red-veined eyes. He said nothing, pushed his chair out, and left the table.

"Well . . . well . . . ," said Grampy. "Well . . . well . . . He's fretful tonight."

Other nights he was possessed by frantic energy.

"Do you have summer reading for school? Leslie? Brooks? Buddy? Even Buddy's not too young. I want you to settle down with your books right after dinner. And you must take notes. Don't rely on your memory. You can show your notes to your mother tomorrow.

"Mabs, did you buy the typing paper? And the carbon paper? I'm nearly out of carbon paper.

"I should call Toby Dakin about that infernal Erskine. Don't let me forget."

"Not at night, Roger, not a business call at night," Mom pleaded.

"He won't mind! Don't you think I know my own friends well enough to know whether or not they mind being called in the evening? You think he's just my lawyer? He's my good friend. I know what I'm doing, Mabs. Do you think I'm a savage?"

"Of course not, dear."

Around this time—August, I think, just after Brooks's twelfth birthday—my parents called him into the library and closed the door. Soon after, Brooks emerged with tears pouring down his face. He went up to his room, then came running down, slammed the front door, and took off on his bike. When he wasn't back by dinner, we were all worried; by 8:00 p.m., my parents were frantic.

"This isn't my fault!" Dad ranted. "A man can do just so much!"

"I know, Roger. No one is blaming you," Mom said soothingly. "We'll find Brooks, don't worry . . . don't worry . . ."

To give Buddy (and himself) courage, Grampy sat in the living room with the boy. The old fantasist told him a Mary Bobbs story, a series he never wrote down, created only for our family, about an old woman who lived near the Erie Canal in Pennsylvania. There was a bullfrog in her pond, and she had a tall Indian man for a friend.

"She brought him soup on her porch, you know she was very thoughty . . ."

For the third or fourth time, my parents went out in the car to look for Brooks. Long after dark they returned with their son, who went up to his room without a word.

Over the next few days Brooks wouldn't tell me what had happened. Throughout his childhood his reticence about himself bordered on secrecy. But eventually I found out.

Dad had been counting on *Amusement Park*'s opening in New York that coming season, and he was also hoping for a production of his comedy *The Blue Balloon*. Betsy von Furstenberg, a young actress of some renown, wanted to star, and various producers were interested. He'd gotten many encouraging letters. But that production fell through, also. So he was left with no known future income. Once again, he was entirely financially dependent on his by now financially strained father. Dad wrote to Brooks's school, Eaglebrook, asking them to understand his situation and reduce their fees, but they said no. Brooks, therefore, couldn't go back to the only school where he had ever been happy. He would be going to public school, which, with his severe but undiagnosed dyslexia, frightened him desperately. Just the sight of each other reminded Brooks and Dad of their inadequacies, so they kept apart as much as possible, and dinners were somber.

CHAPTER FOURTEEN

In September all three of us started public school. It may have been upsetting for the boys, but for me it was a great adventure. The social mix was heady; children of Polish farmers sat next to children of university professors. There was a distinction made between vocational students and college-track students, but, even so . . . I'd never had such a wide range of peers to stare at, go out with, be in clubs with, become enamored of. What I remember of those first weeks was the inebriation of variety.

When I came home from school, the upstairs was enveloped in a heavy hush. Occasionally I would wander into my parents' room. In my father's far corner there was a Chinese screen around his bed, which he'd put there in the last year. Strange how dark his corner was even on the brightest days.

A regal mahogany bureau stood tall against the wall opposite his bed. Intricately curved brass handles drooped from shapely drawers. Next to the bureau, his closet held all those good shirts and suits, his silk Sulka robes and burgundy leather slippers.

On this day, as I often did, I planned to filch some change from the top of his bureau and go to Valentine Hall for the milk shake and the boys. But when I put my hand up for the money, I heard his voice, faint and thin.

"Les?"

I moved around the screen and saw him lying there with his face turned up stiffly, perfectly in line with his stretched-out body. The blue blanket his mother had brought years ago covered him to his neck. On his bedside table, next to the rose-glass lamp, he had a pile of books. I noticed *The Psalms*, something by Camus, and a book on top that looked brand-new, with a charming cover: a white flower pattern on lavender, like an embroidered bureau scarf. It was *Memories of a Catholic Girlhood*, by Mary McCarthy.

"I didn't know you were here."

"Yes."

"I wasn't really stealing your money. I would have put it back." My face burned with my lie.

"It's all right. I know you would."

"What's the matter?"

"I have a headache—a lulu."

"I'm so sorry."

"Sit here by me. Pull up a chair."

This I did.

"Tell me about your day."

This I did, too, keeping my voice low, mindful of his headache. His white, bony hand reached out to his bedside table for a hand-kerchief. How much weight had he lost? His wrist was like a heron's neck. He turned away from me, blew his nose, and turned back, facing up again. His hand, still clutching the handkerchief, slipped under the blanket.

"Tell me what you're reading, Dad." Asking each other about our reading was a well-worn conversation between us.

"That Mary McCarthy there might be the best book I have ever read."

I picked it up.

"Perseverance wins the crown," he said heavily. "A priest told her that."

"Do you believe it?"

"Absolutely."

"Would I like this book?"

"I don't know. You would if you're interested in Catholic upbringing. It's rather far from your experience, luckily. But I'm still reading it. I'll let you see it when I'm through."

"What's your favorite part? So far."

"There's a section—I think she's describing her grandmother— where she says religion is only good for good people . . . because for some . . . some who are . . . or can be . . . destructive . . . the temptation is great toward pride . . . and anger . . . and even sloth . . . deadly sins . . . and judgment of others. Though maybe she talks of judgment somewhere else. I never thought of that. That religion is only good for good people. It's an astounding idea."

He said all this slowly, dreamily, as if I were disembodied and floating before his unmoving eyes. It seemed as if he were creating each word from the air as he spoke, as if that word had never existed before he gave it voice.

I put the book back on the table without opening it. "I'll read it when you're through," I said, although I was being insincere. The book didn't appeal to me then; my mind was too jumpy for philosophical nonfiction.

CHAPTER FIFTEEN

At the beginning of October, Mom drove Dad up to a hospital in Cooperstown, New York. Mary Imogene Bassett, it was called. Dad said it was for the bursitis in his shoulders, but it seemed to me we had good hospitals nearby that could have given him the cortisone shots he wanted. A doctor who lived up the street, after many consultations with my mother, had suggested Mary Bassett, so I had an idea that there might be more to it than bursitis.

While they were gone, Grampy gathered us on the terrace after dinner to watch Sputnik, earth's first satellite—made by the Russians—track across the starry sky in a stately arc. We stared up in wonder, gripped together in silence for the quarter hour it took to progress above us and drop out of sight. When it was over, Grampy said, "Man has touched the heavens."

DURING THE ABSENCE OF OUR PARENTS, I wandered into the library to a startling scene. All around the desk on the floor were open magazines—oversize magazines, much larger than the ones available at Hastings. The wood swivel chair I'd so often seen my father and grandfather occupy was pushed against the window, and I could see no person. I walked around the sturdy oak desk, and on the floor, in place of the chair, my brother Buddy sat with one of the magazines open on his lap, almost covering his legs, so that his little leather shoes popped up below the heavy pages like two brown bookends. "What's all this?" I asked him. He was frightened, as if he'd been caught in a crime. "It's okay, it's okay," I assured him. "But what *is* this?"

"I thought everyone was out," he said.

"Where did these magazines come from?"

"In here." He motioned to an open drawer at the bottom of the desk. "Dad keeps his old magazines here."

I had never known. I sat down on the floor with him. I studied Buddy curiously. He was looking at an ad for a large automobile that stood in front of a white clapboard house with bright blue shutters. Standing by the car, a young woman in a fitted skirt that reached almost to her ankles waved with one hand and with the other clutched the hand of a pretty child. They were both laughing. The car door was open. It seemed they were going on a trip, but not too far, because they were so happy at home.

I lifted the magazine off his lap and looked at the cover. *Liberty*, February 25, 1939.

"Why does Dad have this?" In a moment I understood, as I flipped to the table of contents and saw his story "Gorillas Aren't People—Romance in the circus! A thrill-a-minute tale of laughter and peril and love. Reading time 29 minutes, 40 seconds."

"I like the pictures," Buddy said.

I gave him back the magazine and turned to others. I picked up a copy of *Redbook*. On the cover was an announcement of *Nobody Else—Ever*, by Roger Garis, *Redbook*'s complete March 1948 novel. Here was a 1944 magazine called *Country Gentleman*, where I found Dad's "Fixed Star—On leave from the Pacific front, an Army flier must head the attack on a ruthless undercover band at home. The first of four installments." Here was a handsome publication called *American Magazine*, in which he had a story called "The Lady Dreams of Tigers." And another *Redbook* annual complete novel, this one for 1947, called *Women and Houses Have Secrets*.

In a 1940 issue of *Collier's* was another story, with a drawing of a mother in a jaunty hat with a feather. She wore a body-hugging plaid suit with an ankle-length skirt and was being scolded at the dinner table by a chiseled-jawed father as an adolescent boy looks on in confusion. It was called "Little Refugee—The tribulations of Professor Paxton, who knew much about science, little about girls and nothing at all about small boys."

There were dozens of Dad's stories here, all with lines meant to seize a busy reader's attention ("This was the beginning of as brilliant and crooked a plot as ever led to murder"). These yarns didn't seem much different from the work his parents (and he, too) did for the Stratemeyer Syndicate, except for the age and supposed sophistication of the audience.

Dad's work for the magazine market, which I'd never seen before, was obviously and unapologetically disposable entertainment. Yet for his own pleasure he read Camus and Mary McCarthy. What kind of writer was he? Had he changed over the years? How permanently were the rules of structure and tone embedded in his mind? I suddenly feared that he might never be able to write originally and honestly.

Bending toward the pictures, Buddy said, "It's a whole world."

I was so occupied with my own thoughts that I didn't answer him. But he caught my attention when he said, "I want to go back there, but it doesn't exist anymore. I don't exactly know what they did then; I only know what they didn't do."

"What's that?"

"I can't explain."

We turned pages together for a long time. I thought, So many plots, so much romance, such innocent suspense, so different from what was being written now. And Buddy, presumably, dreamed about the cars and families and unguents for pain and proud steel mills and fail-safe fishing tackle and Ol' Judge Robbins, who put crimp-cut Prince Albert tobacco, the National Joy Smoke, in his dashing pipe.

Soon after starting public school, Buddy was told he was not up to fourth grade and was put back to third.

CHAPTER SIXTEEN

Things will get better soon. Leave me alone."

"But Roger . . ."

"I don't need a psychiatrist. Things will get better."

This conversation between my parents followed a particularly strident blowup between my father and me, his sallow cheeks flapping with the fury of his accusation that I made a mess everywhere I went. "Look at these records on the floor! Look at the potato chips on the couch! Look at that book facedown! At least I thought I taught you how to treat books! This disorder is shameful! Pick everything up! And do it now! This minute! Don't you ever powder your nose? You look terrible. What is that horrible music? Turn it off!"

When I protested that there was only one record on the floor and the potato chips weren't mine, he told me savagely that I had the manners of a monkey.

As he stomped out, he stumbled, regained his footing, and burst into tears.

About a week later, the day before Thanksgiving, Mom called a doctor on Spring Street, the same one who had recommended

Mary Bassett Hospital. I heard her begging him to come and talk to Roger. "Things are getting out of hand," she said. "He's so excitable . . . he's rude to the children . . . he won't calm down . . . he talks incessantly about getting his play on, his agent, his father's contract . . . like a broken record . . . He's really way off . . ."

I remember vividly what happened next, because it happened in the front hallway and several of us were there, drawn by the raised voices. My father, my mother, and the doctor stood in a rough circle facing one another.

"How dare you!" my father yelled. "How dare you say this place is in emotional shambles! How dare you come in here and insult my home! And I suppose you think this is *my* fault."

He shouted the words "my fault" as if he were hurling poison at the doctor.

"This is not my fault!"

He ordered the doctor out of the house, but before he did that, he made my mother promise, in front of everyone, that she would never call that doctor, or any other psychiatrist, behind his back again. Her voice quavering, she promised. And the chastened doctor, a young, kindly man, left The Dell, never, as far as I remember, to return.

A month later, on a December night, I came home in the dark, walking with my skates draped on one shoulder, feeling in my face the bright tingling of the ice I had floated over, living again the smooth turns and the abandon of skating, recreating the rhythms with my stride.

As I stepped onto our drive, I suddenly saw a figure standing in darkness on the front lawn. I'd never seen a prowler around our house before, and I went hot with terror. I crouched down near the ginkgo.

What little moon there was glowed faintly across the roof from the other side of the house onto the thin snow. The man stood in the long shadow of a chimney, looking at an upstairs window. He wore a brimmed hat.

He stood absolutely still. I waited, I didn't know for what, heart pounding against my ribs. Should I try to leave silently and get the police? Slowly he began to raise his arms. The shadow that covered him was moving, too, as the moon traveled in the sky. All at once his arms were straight up and the moonlight shone on him. Stunned, I realized it was my father. His arms fell back to his sides, but he remained facing the same window. It was his mother's old room. He made a noise that sounded like a cough. The two of us stayed as we were perhaps five more minutes, although it felt as if time had rolled itself out into the depths of space. Finally he moved toward the front door. I stayed hidden. I was now, in a way I had never dreamed, a keeper of a secret. After a while I went inside and announced that I was home. Our cat, who was curled on the iron heating grate in the floor, barely raised his head. All was quiet.

DECEMBER 19 was my mother's forty-first birthday. Really, she looked amazingly young. Her skin had a fine, creamy whiteness; her black, curly hair was thick and lustrous. The only indication of her age and recent stress was her mouth, the ends of which at times twisted back into her cheeks as if pulled from inside. Dad appeared downstairs in the late afternoon, so groggy he seemed barely awake. But they went out anyway to visit the Hewletts. By the time they came home, I was asleep.

I was awakened by a horrifying scream. It was a deep, masculine, strangled cry. I sat up in confusion. Within seconds I realized that it wasn't just one scream. It was an extended, primitive series of howls. I jumped out of bed.

What I felt was beyond terror as I stood trembling in my flan-

Our first Amherst winter, 1948. A snowplow is heading our way down Spring Street,
past the Lord Jeffery Inn.

(BY PERMISSION OF THE JONES LIBRARY, INC. AMHERST, MASSACHUSETTS)

LEFT *Dad feeding me while I study the camera, June 1943.*

BELOW LEFT *Granny, holding her favorite pen and wearing a ring I now have, at her home on Evergreen Place in East Orange, New Jersey, about 1930.*

BELOW *Dad, too serious for his outfit, with his father in 1902.*

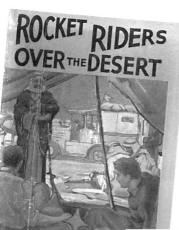

ROCKET RIDERS OVER THE DESERT

HOWARD R. GARIS

TOM SWIFT AND HIS AIRSHIP

VICTOR APPLETON

UNCLE WIGGILY and THE SLEDS

COPR. MCMXXXIX. THE PLATT & MUNK CO INC.

JUDY JORDAN

By LILIAN GARIS

THE BOBBSEY TWINS IN THE COUNTRY

LAURA LEE HOPE

TOP *The Dell in winter, 1950.*

ABOVE *Around the dining room table, Christmas 1955. From left to right: Buddy (with joke hand), Dad, John Burns (Mom's father), Joe Quinn (Doris Quinn's husband), Jamie Quinn (Doris's son), Grampy, Brooks, me, Mabel Burns (Mom's mother), Doris Quinn (Mom's sister), Mom.*

RIGHT *My newlywed parents boarding a plane at New York's LaGuardia airport, heading for their honeymoon in Washington, D.C., November 1, 1941.*

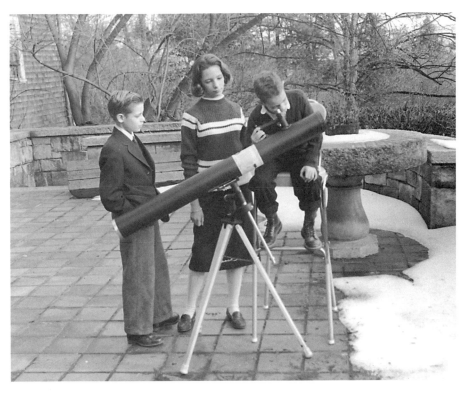

ABOVE *My brothers and me, trying to see something in the sky from our terrace, late winter 1956.*

LEFT *We pose by the apple tree behind our house, summer 1949.*

ABOVE *For Uncle Wiggily's fiftieth birthday and Grampy's eighty-eighth, April 25, 1961, Grampy tells stories in our backyard to children startled by a reporter's camera.*

RIGHT *Robert Frost and Grampy on our terrace, 1956.*

ABOVE *Dad at his desk on the third floor of The Dell, 1955.*

LEFT *My college graduation photo, 1964.*

Dad in 1966, a year before his death.

nel pajamas in the cold December dark. Like waking in the night to a fever, I was suddenly infected by the venomous possibility that nothing would ever be the same again, that life had lost its beautiful promise.

I ran into the hallway, toward the sound, which clearly emanated from my parents' bedroom. I stopped at their closed door. My mother's voice overlapped with my father's shouts.

"Mother! Mother!" he was yelling. And also, "Get away! Get away!"

Mom pleaded, "Roger, Roger . . ."

I huddled down against the door, wrapping my arms around my bent legs, knees hard against my shoulders. Granny is dead, I said to myself. She is dead. But she is in there. She is with Dad.

I heard banging. "Mother, where are you?"

"It's me, Roger. It's Mabel. I'm your wife. Come to bed. It's all right."

I pulled my legs harder against myself so that I was merely a sliver in the air. I began to cry.

"Where are you, Mother?" he moaned. "Where's Mother?"

"She's dead, Roger. She died. Don't you remember? She's dead."

"Oh, God, Dad's dead! He's dead!"

"No, your father's alive. He's nearby. He's asleep in our house."

"He's dead. My father's dead!"

"He's alive, Roger. Your mother's dead."

"Why did she have to die?"

"It was her time. She was ready."

"You're my mother. I see you."

"Your mother's dead, Roger. I'm alive. I'm your wife, Mabel."

"Why are you here? Get away!"

"I'm Mabel, your wife. Your mother's dead."

"Get away! Get away, Mother!"

"I'm Mabel, your wife . . ."

"Are you there, Mother? Where are you?"

My father's words were punctuated with sobs. He seemed to be a child who by some freak of nature had the voice of a man.

Long after Dad was still, my mother talked and talked. I heard her say he needed a doctor. He must have been protesting, maybe shaking his head, because she said it over and over.

I stayed crouched against their door until silence fell. Devastated, frightened, I had the surreal sense that if I moved away from them my parents might die of unhappiness during the night, but if I stayed vigilant I could keep them alive until morning, when they would revert to their normal selves. Unaccountably, no one else had emerged from bed. After a while the quiet darkness did its work, and I fell asleep at my post.

PART TWO

* * *

CHAPTER SEVENTEEN

It must have resonated with him that his dreaded hospitalization was to be in a place with the same name as his most successful television play.

The Inn, it was called—a white brick mansion of two hundred windows. On these windows sunlight filtered through birches, elms, and conifers, old-growth giants whose job it was to soften the impression of a hospital masquerading as a tycoon's residence.

This stately building was the residence hall of Austen Riggs Psychiatric Hospital in the town of Stockbridge, tucked into the Berkshire Mountains of western Massachusetts. The town itself, a favorite of wealthy New Yorkers during the Gilded Age, had been, a century before that, a Protestant mission for Native Americans. By the twentieth century, Stockbridge was so picturesque that the town's most famous resident, Norman Rockwell, painted Main Street, and it became the iconic image of a New England village.

But on that admission day in February 1958, Dad wouldn't have gone to the Inn first. He would have had to check into the Medical Office Building, another massive white structure with a more European aspect. It had bays like cut-off towers, in which were set windows with curved shutters, suggesting a world of ease and elegance, Persian carpets, and silver tea service.

He had arrived at this pass by a dramatic route. The morning after I listened at his door to his delirious combat with his mother's spirit, he was taken, reluctant but resigned, to a psychiatrist. Bud Hewlett had found the doctor, and he drove my shaken parents the seven miles to Northampton. By this time, still not convinced that he needed a doctor, my father, in a paranoid rage, managed to offend the psychiatrist, who said callously, "Let's talk turkey," and pronounced my father in such a state of psychosis that he could be committed against his will—that minute, from that office. The doctor needed only to make one phone call and Dad would be taken away.

My father fled not only from the office, but from the country. After calls to lawyers and threats to sue the doctor, he left for Bermuda with my mother.

I remember a terrible disorientation that engulfed all of us the day they left. Dad was in a sullen panic. Mom had everything organized, but she looked dazed nevertheless. This trip was clearly something more and less than a vacation.

Bermuda was cold. Dad couldn't stop shaking from the chill, even though he had no fever, so they went to Jamaica. There they encountered a workers' strike and riots in the streets. So they fled once more, this time to Miami.

In Miami they found two benevolent, helpful men: a minister and a psychiatrist. During those Miami days he broke down completely.

All night he sobbed while my mother held him in her arms, telling him he was a good person, a good father, a good husband, a good writer, a man whose life mattered. Already gaunt, he had lost forty pounds since May, and as he clutched her weakly, his face wet with tears against her neck, she had the impression that she was holding him back from an abyss. Without her, he might slip down forever. Nothing in her past had prepared her for coping with mental illness, and she was as mystified by the situation as she was determined to solve it.

At home in Amherst, a new psychiatrist, a young man named Dr. Michael Green, gently steered my father to Riggs. Warily, Dad hoped Riggs could save him.

I know of these events, even those I didn't witness, because in 2001 I obtained a legal document requiring Riggs and another hospital to release all their files on my father.

I found a universe in those papers. I found my father's past, both near and far, as related in his "history." I found his fears, his resentments, his tormented relation to his parents, the unraveling of his hopes, and I found his diagnosis, which, much as I studied it, shed merely the dimmest light on the man. I heard my mother speaking to doctors about life with her disintegrating husband, although she didn't understand what was happening and was sure these were passing moods that would clear up as soon as he had a success.

The most revealing, and most moving, portion of the file was written by the nurses who attended him. In their simple language they brought to life my father's passage among them.

STANDING INSIDE THE INN, he looked around and said that he would always be lost here: there were too many doors. On the way to his room, he peered down corridors whose multitude baffled him. The extended labyrinth they suggested was ominously impersonal; picturing those distances made him shiver. His room, although commodious, with a fireplace and a handsome mantel, didn't have its own bathroom and was perhaps not large enough to work in. The nurse assured him that they'd find a larger room with a private bath.

Before his disorientation became overwhelming, the nurse introduced him to his sponsor, a patient named "Mr. L." They talked in Mr. L.'s room until it was time for a cocktail party in "Mrs. G.'s" room.

A cocktail party in a psychiatric hospital. Of all the facts and opinions in these notes that fix this period in the 1950s, cocktail parties in patients' rooms is the most striking. Probably half the patients at Riggs had problems with alcohol or drugs, and yet, despite one of the best psychiatric staffs in the country—including the renowned Erik Erikson—patients were encouraged to carry on whatever private lives they wished. And since Riggs was expensive and psychiatric bills in that era were not covered by insurance, the patients were of the class that regularly attended cocktail parties.

Dad came to dinner with Mr. L. and later went alone to a movie shown in the building called Shop.

The next morning, he had a headache that developed during the day into a pain that went down the side of his face. To the nurses and doctors he claimed obsessively that he was in this hospital because of the perfidy of his agent and his father's agent. His own agent prevented his work from being seen, and his father's agent was trying to cheat the family out of money they needed to live on. At night doctors prescribed an extra dose of Sodium Amytal—on top of his regular one—to help him sleep.

It is clear from the records that for at least a year he had been taking Sodium Amytal regularly. This drug is a highly addictive barbiturate—what today would be called a hypnotic agent—with a tranquilizing effect. In those days it was the drug of choice for an array of mental illnesses from sleeplessness to psychosis. Its effect on the system is to slow it down. Everything decelerates: racing heartbeats as well as racing thoughts. An overdose brakes the body to a stop. The doctors at Riggs saw no problem in giving my father Sodium Amytal. And although they often spoke of a "possible toxic factor" to his illness, it doesn't seem as if it ever occurred to them to treat him for addiction.

ON THE THIRD DAY, he was so anxious that he asked for ten minutes in the morning with his doctor, Paul Emery, even though it wasn't his scheduled time. At lunch he was "exceptionally quiet." On the fourth day he went home for the weekend.

On his return to Riggs, he couldn't find his room. In rising panic, he walked by doors without recognizing the one meant for him. When at last a nurse helped him, he laughed it off, saying he was the same way in cities. He never knew which way to go.

During his days he moved slowly, tensely, from appointment to appointment. When he was asked to interpret a Rorschach inkblot, he said it was an animal struggling over something inconsequential, something a child might have discarded, like an empty can. From which the doctor concluded that his despair arose from believing he was a failure in his work and personal life and that he chased empty goals.

The report of his activities meeting said: "In his very distraught state, it was difficult for him to concentrate on . . . our activities program. He did tend to favor something in the greenhouse. He had one at home in which he had never been able to work because his father has taken it over." Despite visiting the Riggs greenhouses, he never went back to them.

In shop, which he attended distractedly, he began to whittle a "free-form" wood sculpture, but he gave it up, saying he had no manual creativity. He told Mr. Loveless, the artist in charge, "My father, now, he's great at doing that sort of thing." He undertook carving a little canoe for Buddy to float in the bathtub.

During one of his therapy sessions he told Dr. Emery that when he was a boy, his mother's mother, Irish-born Winifred Noon McNamara, came to live with his family. He remembered her as extremely devout, "full of little remarks," and, he thought, extremely fond of him. She was the one who taught him the lovely song called "Macushla." But one evening when the family sat together after dinner, she suddenly looked wildly at her grandson, who was twelve, and cried, "Get him out of here! He is bringing devils with him!" He felt confused and hurt, but he also had another emotion. He thought with horror that there "might be truth" in what she said.

Something else he told the doctor gave me pause. It turns out Dad thought his mother was addicted to drugs, probably from 1930, when she had had a gallbladder operation that turned into a yearlong life-threatening illness. At that time, pain medication consisted almost entirely of opiates. Dad reported that he remembered his father saying, long after the operation, "Lilian, are you taking that stuff again?" As I read this astounding piece of information, I remembered the day Dad had crashed into me as he practically ran from the library because Mom told him he walked like his mother. Maybe that was the first time he realized that he shared more than a depressive nature with her. They had addiction in common! Then I remembered that Granny had a sink installed in the music room in East Orange, New Jersey, so that the doctor didn't have to use the "lavatory" when he washed his hands. For her to go to such trouble, she must have seen him frequently and depended on him greatly. Was she still using drugs when she lived with us? A local doctor visited her every week. He could have written her prescriptions, which Grampy dutifully would have brought to the drugstore even if he objected. (He was so averse to confrontation that I once heard him say to Mom, "Mabs, I wouldn't argue with the Devil himself!") I can't know with any certainty whether she had a drug problem, and my cousin Carroll, whom I asked after the question was raised, said she never saw Granny behaving as if she were "out of it." But I can't discount the possibility, and I tend to believe it was true. It would help explain how she went from being a vibrant woman to a recumbent recluse.

At Riggs, Dad's loneliness led him to the occasional cocktail party, although he didn't drink. At one given by "Mrs. M.," the patients asked him if he would read his play to them sometime. He left that gathering buoyed by their interest, and a few nights later he read the play, which was received with many compliments. He couldn't know that the doctors began to hear from their patients that they had sat through a very disturbing play. By the end of the week, several doctors knew the story of *Amusement Park* from beginning to end, having listened to patients' detailed retelling. They began to notice this gentle, quiet patient who had written the play with a violent ending.

DESPITE HIS "EXTREME CAUTION," he told Dr. Emery more and more of his past. At six years old he started Saint Rose of Lima, a Catholic school, and began a "period of distress and frights with no release." He was frightened of the nuns and priests, especially Father Corcoran, the fire chaplain. He trembled when boys were physically thrown out of Sunday school. At home on school mornings he would hang on to the front door, unwilling to let go, trying with all his might to stay inside. His parents would pry him off the doorjamb to take him to school. He compared being at Riggs to hanging on to the door. As long as he was here, he was safe—if only temporarily.

During the day he was acutely aware of noise, and his head-aches worsened. At dinner one night he talked of his parents, of all they had achieved. However, he said, no one in his family was good with money; he was the only one who knew how to handle it. Considering how many times he told his doctors that he felt guilty about accepting his father's money, which, actually, was even now paying for his stay at Riggs, this was an extraordinary statement. After dinner he went straight to bed, and asked for pain medica-tion at midnight.

When he was eleven years old, he had such relentless insomnia that his father—no doubt with much reluctance—took him to a psychiatrist. This was 1912. The doctor, an advanced medical man, put the boy in a chair and applied an electrical current that pulsed through his body. After the shock, Howard came back into the room and the doctor declared proudly that the boy was cured. It's doubtful that there was any helpful effect from this primitive elec-troshock therapy, but Lilian, with her own depressive tendencies, must have taken note of her son's.

In his room at Riggs he had nightmares of people conspiring against him. They were distant visions of enemies in shifting com-binations—his mother, his father, his agent, his father's agent, his grandmother. He awoke with a heavy dread that they hadn't fin-ished with him yet.

"He tires easily," a nurse wrote. "Although he's only fifty-six he seems very old."

In his late twenties his short stories were selling well to maga-zines. He fulfilled a ten-story contract with *Liberty* magazine, and when he turned thirty-one, *Liberty* offered him another contract. But suddenly his mind became a wayward enemy. He stared at the page, unable to write. He couldn't keep a grasp on his focus, and he couldn't remember simple words. His misery increased swiftly un-til, in fear for his sanity, he arranged to check himself into a psychiatric hospital in White Plains, New York. However, his father had other ideas. Unable to conceive of any unhappiness that couldn't be cured with a dose of healthy living, Howard persuaded his son to forget the hospital and go instead to a "health camp" in northern New York State. His father made the travel plans and paid the bills. After a month, my father did, indeed, feel better, and he resumed his life, even though the experience left him demoralized and bewildered.

AT BREAKFAST IN THE INN, on Friday, February 28, he seemed "restless." After breakfast he went back to his room, but at 11:15 he came to the nurses with a headache. His eye was partly closed from the pain. He was afraid of the staff conference, which was to take place at 1:00 p.m. that day.

The staff conference was a tradition at Riggs. The doctors studied all the material gathered on the patient so far, which contained his "history," his psychiatrist's extensive reports (the combination of which was called "the abstract"), and the notes of the nurses and staff members who had had any contact with him. The conference would begin with the doctors speaking briefly among themselves. The patient was then invited to enter the room. Any doctor who wished had a chance to speak with the patient. After the patient left, the doctors conversed with the purpose of defining the diagnosis and recommending the course of treatment.

Presiding was Dr. Robert Knight, chief psychiatrist, famous for, among other achievements, redefining the "borderline" diagnosis for patients who fell between neurosis and psychosis. Also present was Dr. Erik Erikson, the renowned psychiatrist who coined the phrase "identity crisis."

My father was about to face a lineup of foremost experts on psychiatric maladies, celebrated scholars of the human condition.

They had the moral heft that accrues to large practices, devoted students, influential articles, and financial solidity. The meeting would be recorded; I have the transcript.

During World War II, my father worked for the Office of War Information in Washington, investigating which doctors were being sent to war and which "conspired" to stay home. This assignment ignited my father's already kindled wariness of doctors. As a reporter for the *Newark Evening News*, he covered local hospitals and came up against a great deal of medical arrogance. Add to this background his youth in the house of a hypochondriacal mother who was suspicious of all authority and his recent experience with the doctor who threatened to commit him, and it is easy to understand Dad's fanatical distrust of doctors. He saw them as people whose knowledge of suffering was theoretical, not empirical. In his opinion they hadn't experienced pain of their own, just observed it in others. It therefore cost them nothing to concern themselves with anguish.

These men with their fine perceptions would determine his fate. They would decide how sick he was and if or how he could be cured. Given his fragile sense of self, he would also have been deeply alarmed that they would be making another decision, however subtly stated. He must have felt that they would weigh in on how significant his life was, insofar as his life at that point was inseparable from his psychological turmoil. He was about to be reviewed.

Aware of my father's fears and prejudices, I identified with his helplessness as I prepared to read the transcript of this session. I was actually shaking as I held the pages, wishing my sympathy could affect the outcome but knowing that there was more darkness ahead for this blighted man.

Before my father was brought in, Dr. Knight opened the meeting with the immediate circumstances that had brought the patient to Riggs. He told of the patient's clash with the Northampton doctor and said that my father treated the man "with overt contempt in such a way that 'Dr. S.' got the impression that he was a very disturbed man and finally tried to bring him up short with, 'Do you know you're certifiable?' Then this scared the Hell out of him, and he had to get the lawyer and flee town for fear the doctor would pursue him."

Dr. Knight summarized subsequent events, ending with a report from Dr. Michael Green, who had guided him to Riggs. According to Dr. Knight, Dr. Green helped my father see "that he should try to separate in himself the frightened little boy who was now showing all of these symptoms from the craftsman, as writer, and to view himself as having certain problems in certain areas of himself, not to feel completely overwhelmed, and so on along these lines which helped to pull him together a little bit."

Dr. Robert White said that he had an "overall impression that some toxic factor could well have been a major ingredient in this acutely disturbed period. How much barbiturates was he taking?"

Dr. Paul Emery: "My understanding would be up to nine grains of Amytal at night."

"Understanding from whom?" asked Dr. White.

"From the patient," answered Dr. Emery.

Dr. White: "Do I remember correctly that he joined AA at one point?"

Dr. Emery: "Yes."

Dr. White: "So far as you know, he has not been drinking for these last six to twelve months?"

Dr. Emery: "Not for the past five or six years."

After further discussing possible substance abuse, they invited my father into the room. Polite greetings were offered and answered. Then Dr. Knight asked him, "How has your writing been going since you've been here?"

"Well," Dad answered softly, "I've finished the first act of a television play. It seems satisfactory."

"Of a three-act play?" asked Dr. Knight.

"Um . . . If the rest of it goes that well, I think it will sell."

"You do that on your own and try to sell it, rather than . . . You don't have any order for such a thing?"

"No, I don't have an order. However, I have sold to the program for which I am aiming this, *Matinee Theater*. They don't pay as much as the night shows, but there aren't very many night shows left. And, uh, it will help pay for Riggs."

"It looks as if you have gained a little weight since I saw you at first," Dr. Knight said kindly.

"Yes, about ten pounds."

He had achieved 120 pounds, up from 109 pounds when he was admitted. He was just short of six feet tall.

Dr. Knight asked, "What was the weight you carried most of your adult life when your health was best?"

"Well, uh, about a hundred and forty-five pounds. Between one forty-five and one fifty."

"That's where you'd like to be?"

"I'd like to be a little heavier, but I've resigned myself to that weight."

After that, Dr. Knight asked him about his moods at Riggs, and he reported that he was feeling better. He said that last weekend at home he was "able to answer all of the children's questions, and able to answer my father's questions, and able to answer my wife's questions, and some of my own."

"So things seem to be on the mend for you?"

"Oh, distinctly, yes. There is not the slightest doubt of that."

The next part of the meeting was entirely taken up with my father's recitation of his struggles to break the contract between his father and his father's agent.

"My father has been defrauded out of twenty-five thousand dollars by this agent, which means what they call a setoff claim in Massachusetts, and I doubt very much whether he'll dare to sue . . ."

On and on he went.

"Also, [the agent] circulated a letter, not scurrilous, but nevertheless very uncomplimentary to my father . . . an invasion of privacy direct, an invasion of privacy against the postal laws, and I believe close to a criminal offense."

There were details about the Milton Bradley Uncle Wiggily Game; the role his brother-in-law, my grandfather's then lawyer, played; exactly when William Erskine, the agent, came into the picture. It was an exhaustive narration, ending with his statement that at last things were on the mend.

"It looks as though my efforts have succeeded."

"You feel pretty good about that?" asked Dr. Knight.

"I will when the contract's completely nullified."

"How long do you think you ought to stay at Riggs? We are going to make up our minds from a professional standpoint. But how do you feel about it?"

After a moment of hesitation my father answered, "Well, I feel that the severity of this attack . . . is lessening greatly. It reached its peak in Miami, as I told Dr. Emery, when I was pretty much unable to function, and my wife literally had to hang on to me and tell me things were all right. It was a very bad time. It was then I sought Dr. Green and received a reply. That began the cure. Or the rehabilitation. It was not sufficiently firm to be lasting, but the door had been opened or the shade had been pulled up a little, and there was light. Now I feel that several more weeks here . . . will result in a healing process of the traumatic experiences which led to that breakdown. And at that time I will be able to go home, resume my work, and continue with, if not Dr. Emery as an outpatient, then with, perhaps, Dr. Green."

When asked if he wished to continue here with Dr. Emery, he said, "Yes . . . if it's at all possible. I feel that he and I, at least on my part, have established a bond . . . I feel completely at ease with him, and I feel it is a relationship which is very valuable to me."

Dr. White asked him about his nutrition and his barbiturate use. Dad answered fully but probably not entirely honestly. They discussed that together for a while, and then Dr. Knight asked if anyone else would like to ask a question. No one volunteered, so Dr. Knight said, "That's all, then. Thank you very much."

Dad answered, "Well, thank you very much."

I wonder how he felt when he left the room. It was Friday, so he was about to go home for the weekend. He'd be able to spend that night in his own bed behind his Chinese screen.

THE FIRST PERSON to speak after "the patient" left was Dr. James J. Hartford.

"Well, certainly the illness is manifested by a good deal of panic and fearfulness. I had one of my patients . . . give me a blow-by-blow description of his play. And it . . . has a good deal of violence in it. The central theme is a mother of a sick child leaving the home and husband, having another woman come into the house and sort of get the inside track with the husband and daughter, and then having the mother return. Then there's a lot of suspense built up as to which woman is going to get the husband and the little girl. The end result is that almost everybody dies. The little girl dies; the man's wife is shot."

"By whom?" asks Dr. Knight.

"By the intruding woman. But not before the husband accepts the original wife back. And this is the way the play ends. The intruding woman shoots the man's wife. It is obvious at the end of the play that the intruding woman is going to leave. This leaves the man without wife or child."

Dr. Joseph O. Chassell said, "This is called *Amusement Park?*"

Dr. Hartford: "This is called *Amusement Park*. It's a very violent thing. The child kills herself in the mistaken belief that it will help her father by ridding him of her mother and allowing him to marry the young woman. And it seems to me that the patient is both the child and the child's father, in the sense that the play seems to point out that the child is sort of the innocent bystander who has to stand the vagaries of circumstance. It would seem that these are the kinds of violent fears that the patient has regarding himself, and probably gives us some idea of what the patient expects from treatment. In a sense the child's death answers some of the questions for the father and mother, and it would seem, perhaps, that the patient's hospitalization here also has solved quite a number of questions, and it has taken something as violent as this. His illness has freed him from the pressure of his family, and the pressure of his discontentedness with his work. In the role of the little girl, he has freed his father from a good deal of pressure on him, too. I hope the end of the patient's hospitalization is a little happier than the ending of this play."

Dr. White, who understood something that no one else did, said, "I want to concentrate on one aspect of this case. There is no question but what this hassle he got into about the play and the mix-up, not only with his own agent but his father's agent, and the rejection and the hurt from those issues and his own play, were very important factors in precipitating this acute period of agitation. But I want to speak of certain aspects that I think have been overlooked. I think this is a serious shortcoming in the abstract. For a man to lose this much weight and to have been on, I suspect, more than nine grains of barbiturate a day, and to have been on some amount of Bromo-Seltzer as he went downhill, I think would be very ample grounds for there to have been a real toxic factor in all of this . . . I think this is important in making the diagnosis, because while you can say he has a poorly integrated narcissistic character that is now decompensated, up until this point in his life he's been a fairly—from the social point of view—organized and operating man. He's had a lot of difficulties, but he has made a going concern of his life under some fairly difficult conditions."

Dr. Chassell commented, "Well, I think a pretty good case could be made for a toxic complication, but he smells paranoid to me." The doctor explained that the patient's story about the contract and the play is swollen with a theatricality that doesn't gel with real life. In my father's version of events Dr. Chassell found "a paranoid touch." In the end, the solving of all these problems "makes very little financial difference in the picture. It sounds . . . as if he were feeling his creativity had given out and the thing to do now was . . . to make sure that he could hold on to all that there was in the family. His father's creativity has also given out, so they must hold on to everything possible. And he must guarantee that the last thing that he produces, which might be the last thing he will ever produce, makes a killing. This kind of anxiety of everything's gone out—we must hold on and make the most we can of it—seems to have been a pretty prominent thing. I question if his play doesn't go on, or if he doesn't get a wonderful big new idea of another killing—apparently in both senses of that word—he'll find himself in the same situation. I suppose the best help is to have this comfortable lifeline back here . . . His therapy would be a therapy of good health and solid achievement in TV, these would be the prescriptions, rather than any large doses of insight."

Dr. Knight commented that the patient had initially wanted to be thoroughly psychoanalyzed, sure that his troubles could be traced back to the beginning of his life. But in the course of his stay he had been contented with his supportive therapy and had given up his desire for deeper analysis.

And then Erik Erikson spoke. As I read through his remarks, I was struck by the force of his intuition and reasoning. I am going to quote them almost in their entirety because he seemed to have a special grasp of my father's character. Erikson's groundbreaking work on identity derived from theories of the German philosopher Martin Heidegger, who posited three stages of development: the *Umwelt*, or the biological self in nature; the *Mitwelt*, the self in a human environment, the world of social relation; and the *Eigenwelt*, the private world of the self, a sense of authenticity. Erik Erikson took those formulations and added others he thought necessary to development. He identified eight stages through which an individual must pass in order to have resources and strength and confidence. Erikson believed that if a person is prevented from completing any of these stages, he may be violent or fanatical or distorted in other ways. A student of Gandhi and Martin Luther, Erikson's great contributions were these stages and his ideas about what makes an individual.

Here is what he said about my father:

"I think, dynamically speaking, he's a very dependent person who after a while hates the person he's dependent on. It's the root of his paranoid reactions to people. I think he likes us at the moment because he knows he doesn't have to stay, and because by being here, he escapes the persons he really is dependent on at home. I don't know whether the prognosis that he will get over his trouble, how long-range a prediction this is. He undoubtedly will get over this particular problem, but what will happen after he has been home again is another question. Especially if the father goes on living.

"One of the main factors right now is that the father has become dependent on him, where he has been dependent on the father all this time. And he just doesn't feel old enough, or mature enough, or firm enough for that. It was obvious that even if he was quite rational about the actual business involved, the push with which he went right into that discussion of his father's agent certainly showed a paranoid pattern. Which again has to do with somebody on whom the patient has been dependent all these years. Now he has to protect the father against being exploited. Just as he has somebody in his own background he thinks has hurt him—his own agent, Mrs. Wood. Now it's the father's agent. Of course earlier in his life it was the father himself who threatened him. That means he's the father's boy to a quite, I would say, malignant degree.

"If you would just count how often the abstract says that at the suggestion of his father he did such and such, even in his adulthood. You can see that he has been living off his father—how his father helped with a few thousand dollars, instead of saying somewhere to this boy, 'Now you take care of yourself.' The father apparently never did that . . . and the boy has never recovered from it and now cannot quite stand the power he has over the aging father.

"I would say, if you want to allocate it to a particular life crisis, it's more than a generativity crisis, I mean as I formulate these things . . . his despair has to do with an integrity crisis. The generativity business has been going on for many years. He lives in a family of writers. Everybody writes something. And everybody suggests to him what he should write and what he should do. That's another reason why he's so glad to be here . . . It was interesting that he said, as an illustration of how much better he felt, that when he went home, he could answer all the questions—my wife's questions, my father's questions, my children's questions—"

Dr. Knight interjected, "And my own questions."

"And my own questions," Dr. Erikson continued. "I thought that was about the formula for him. That he has lived under such overstimulation all his life, and made himself passive to other people's demands. So that's a sign for him of having improved, which shows in turn that all the previous stages have been underdeveloped. He certainly cannot have a great deal of intimacy, he's obviously a very much closed-off, rigid, unintimate person.

"As for identity, it says here he was trying to be somebody he wasn't. That, undoubtedly, he has felt all his life. And even further back, one feels the mother is behind it all. The point being that he transferred the dependence on his mother onto his father. And his father was glad to take it over. Thus was created in this boy this whole jealous, passive, paranoid combination, which a continued dependence on the father, with a deep, inner hate of him, implies.

"It is interesting that he wanted to be hospitalized when he had the first depression, he wanted to sign himself in, and his father prevented him, sending him to a health camp instead. So he has been in search of a hospital ever since. And it may help him actually. He's probably very glad he has Riggs here so if anything happens again, or as he would put it, if he bleeds again . . . like a child holding on to a door, well, he can come here, hold on here for a while. That's probably what he intends to do."

AFTER THAT SPEECH, the doctors worked together for another half hour to produce a diagnosis. Here it is:

Depressive and paranoid psychosis now in remission as a decompensation in a narcissistic, obsessive, paranoid character disorder and characterized by weight loss and psychosomatic complaints (question of significant toxic factor).

How does that translate? "Decompensation" connotes symptoms that have surfaced that, until now, have been held in check. In other words, a patient's defenses, overwhelmed by the underlying illness, suddenly give way, and the result is decompensation. Even understanding the fulcrum of this cumbersome psychological equation, the diagnosis is confusing. If depression and paranoia are symptoms, how are they different, in psychiatric formulation, from the underlying illness, since paranoia is also identified as part of the root character disorder? As I understand the complicated disorder called—with mythic oversimplification—narcissism, his was a classic case. At the heart of narcissism is an undeveloped ego, so that a person has no solid sense of self and measures his worth from the reflection of himself he imagines the world is giving him. Many of the highest achievers of all time were narcissists, working tirelessly to prove themselves worthy. But those are the exceptions. Most go through life wondering who they are, looking for clues outside themselves, feeling uniquely superior when things go their way and plunged into the void when they sense failure. They are pathologically unable to turn inward for answers, because their secret is that there is nothing there. Authenticity, value, and image are septically entangled.

One of the best descriptions of narcissism I have found is not from psychoanalytic literature, but from James Baldwin, in an essay called "Down at the Cross":

The person who distrusts himself has no touchstone for reality— for this touchstone can be only oneself. Such a person interposes between himself and reality nothing less than a labyrinth of attitudes. And these attitudes, furthermore, though the person is usually unaware of it (is unaware of so much!) are historical and public attitudes. They do not relate to the present any more than they relate to the person.

The results of my father's standardized psychological testing were slightly different from the staff's: *Borderline psychotic state with depression being the most outstanding aspect, with conspicuous paranoid features also, and, in addition, some hypomanic potential.*

The verdict is more easily understood: he's depressed, occasionally psychotic; he is paranoid and potentially manic. Yet both of these diagnoses seem to me to miss the mark. He felt despair and hopelessness to a nearly unbearable degree. His dystopia made him fearful and suspicious. His narcissism prevented him from getting a foothold on his latent strength. But even with all this mental deciphering, the overarching truth of his condition was that he had a biological psychiatric illness, and on top of that he was addicted to barbiturates. These good and brilliant men, who went a long way toward untangling the knotted threads of my father's psychology, were unable to find certain crucial answers that would not be available for another thirty years.

ON RETURNING TO RIGGS on the Monday after the staff meeting, my father told the nurses that his weekend had been tough, but he coped by trying to keep busy. Over the next two weeks he had constant headaches, worked on Buddy's toy canoe, and wrote in his room. He complained to a nurse that he was extraordinarily low, but he said hopefully about his depressions, "I understand they do go away."

I was the only child to visit Dad; Mom thought Brooks and Buddy were too young to come. We sat on a stiff couch in a large reception area, our talk subdued but ordinary. A bald woman walked slowly down a staircase at the end of the room. She put each foot forward as if she were kicking a rock ahead of her and until it landed she didn't dare count on the direction of her progress. Only then did she put weight on that foot and toss the next one out. "A wet brain," my mother whispered to me. "Too much alcohol." Dad flinched. Overcome either by the sight of the woman or Mom's statement, he said he had to go back to his room, and a nurse took him away. It was a short visit. When I hugged him goodbye, his shoulder blades felt like knives. I looked to Mom for explanation, but she merely patted me on the back and headed for the car. "It's okay, Les. He'll be fine." We drove home in near silence.

RIGGS HAD A PATIENT whose career my father would have dearly liked to have: William Inge. The most prominent playwright of the 1950s, even more successful at the time than Tennessee Williams, he had written a string of hits, starting with *Come Back, Little Sheba* in 1950. *Picnic* won the 1953 Pulitzer Prize and became a hit movie with William Holden and Kim Novak. *Bus Stop*, which opened in 1955, ran for thirteen months on Broadway and, with a screenplay by George Axelrod, was made into a film starring Marilyn Monroe. In December 1957, *The Dark at the Top of the Stairs*, a veiled version of his midwestern childhood, opened to rave reviews.

Inge, a homosexual, was an alcoholic. Unlike Williams, whose florid personal style and coterie of young beautiful male followers announced his sexuality, Inge was a buttoned-up midwestern gentleman who favored tweeds and kept his sexual identity hidden all his life. As he aged, his alcoholism developed into a raging disease, despite intense psychoanalysis, which, for years, he had been getting at Riggs. By 1958 he had taken an apartment in Stockbridge and spent a good part of every day at the hospital as an outpatient.

He and my father, for whatever reasons—and I actually think their similar tweeds might have played a part—became friends. I've often wondered if Dad realized that they had something else in common: Audrey Wood. She was Inge's longtime agent. Dad and Inge often had dinner together, discussing theater and literature. Taking the great leap, my father worked up the courage to ask Inge if he would listen to him read *Amusement Park*. Inge agreed. The date was set for the afternoon of March 11, 1958.

At that time Inge, whom I met at Riggs, was a man who had changed dramatically from the figure he cut in his youth. The fine high forehead and wavy hair he displayed in photos from his twenties had transformed into a wide, pale globe topped with grizzled clumps of white. His classic Grecian nose, his finest feature, looked now, in his wrecked, spongy face, like the pinched nose of a scornful priest. His once-thin eyebrows had spread into unruly shrubs, and his lips, formerly shaded by a fashionable mustache, now, in the glare of day, looked tense and overwhelmed. His large, mournful eyes peered down over his bitter mouth as if judgment were imminent.

My father's physical form had been transformed by his illness in the opposite direction. He was skeletal rather than soft. His face was longer, not rounder, and his bleak eyes were forbearing, not challenging. In trepidation and hope, he prepared to read his play to the man who knew how to achieve what my father was trying for, the man who had the answers. With manuscript in hand, he walked to a small room in the Inn where he would meet Inge.

Contacted nurse at 5:50 p.m. Very tense and depressed. Spent some time in the sitting room with the nurses. Spoke of being depressed all the time. Wept a great deal. Told nurse that he had read one of his plays to Mr. Inge, and he, Mr. Inge, thought it "was just not right." Patient said that perhaps he should give up writing. Felt some better after talking. In for dinner.

Sodium Amytal grs.3 at 11:40 p.m. Very quiet, seemed quite depressed. Came to nurses' room at 3:30 a.m., crying and shaking. Very upset. Nurse let him lay on couch in living room and covered him with a blanket. Said he could not stay in his room, crying, asked about doctor-on-call. Nurse said she would call him, and he could then talk with him, maybe he would feel better. He was hesitant to awaken doctor, but agreed that he would probably feel better. "He will have to do something," patient said. Nurse took him to his room and put him to bed with extra blanket and hot water bottle. Shivering and shaking, asked nurse to stay with him. Nurse did for one half hour. Trembling, said that medicine was not working, unable to lay still. Sodium Amytal grs. 3 ³/₄ intramuscularly, repeat, as ordered at 4:24 a.m. Nurse sat with him. Said that he has gotten quite upset over the news that P.L. [a patient] was being sent to a closed hospital. This indicated to him that she was psychotic, no hope for her. Nurse explained that the doctors here felt some patients needed more structural care than we offered, and these people really did better in that kind of situation. Felt better after hearing that. Said what an awful mess his life is. Too much to cope with. Nurse left him quiet and practically asleep.

The next day at breakfast he was depressed and homesick. "I must go home," he told the nurses. "I cannot stay any longer."

Oddly, he longed for his mother. He said that even though she was "cold and unsympathetic," he felt "an unfathomable yearning for her."

At 10:30 that morning he had an appointment with Dr. Emery, from which he emerged sad and anxious. Apparently Dr. Emery had brought up the unthinkable. How would he feel about entering McLean Hospital? Yes, it was a "locked hospital," but McLean had resources to deal with the extremity of illness my father was beginning to exhibit. "Do you think I'm psychotic?" Dad asked in panic. I don't know what the doctor answered, but no doubt he tried to be gentle and calming. It was only a suggestion, Dr. Emery said. It was, of course, completely up to my father. But at Riggs, even with therapy five days a week, they weren't making him better. He was slipping out of their therapeutic hands.

By afternoon the nurses reported that Mr. Garis was "extremely frightened."

He called his illness a beast that was devouring him. "I will fight this thing," he said. "I will fight this thing."

A few days later my father looked lifeless, though he managed to shuffle to his appointments. He could barely talk, as if there had been a rupture in his speech. He had received news from Dr. Emery. It was the considered opinion of the doctors that my father should be transferred to McLean Hospital.

On March 17 he was discharged. The plan was that he would spend one full day at home and on March 19 travel to Belmont, Massachusetts, and check into McLean.

WHEN DAD CAME HOME, I studied him. I knew that he had to go to another hospital right away, so something dramatic must have happened at Riggs. Mom had told us he was getting better. By what fiendish alchemy had he been transformed into a man getting worse?

I think now that some part of me must have been relieved that he would be leaving again. During his absence—even with his weekends at home, in which he was so tentative that he trod a very light footstep on our lives—our family functioned almost normally. My mother had her periodic migraines, but she was singing more and better than ever. Arias accompanied her through her day. I heard them in the morning before I went to school while she was making my brothers' beds and in the afternoon when I came home and she might be upstairs sewing. Without Dad at dinner I had no fears that my grandfather and mother—both of whom were talkative and liked to guide the conversation—would overwhelm my father. With Dad away, their strong personalities were rather exciting. Dad's presence required them to pull back, even though it went against the grain of both their natures.

Dad trailed sadness like a long cloak. He evoked such pity in me that I could hardly bear it. I was sure there was something I could do to help, but what? My inability to answer this question didn't discourage me from believing that I would eventually find the solution to his inarticulate suffering. Naturally, it was easier to live my fifteen-year-old life without the pressure of my father's melancholy. And so, guiltily, I welcomed his hospitalizations. I dared to hope that he would come back cured.

And yet, even though a large part of me wanted him to go away again, I was intensely disturbed to learn he'd have only a day and a half at home before the next hospital. If the first one couldn't cure him, could the next? My mother told me he was too sick for that hospital. Too sick for a *hospital*?

As soon as he walked into the house with Mom and Mr. Hewlett, who was carrying his bags, I saw that he was in a state of terror. Brooks, sitting on the stairs, looked dolefully at his parents. Bewildered, too sad for his age, he seemed already resigned to troubles. I knew he could use comforting, but my thoughts were all with my father. I didn't have room to worry about my brothers.

Grampy came padding down the stairs. He was shocked at how his son looked, but he tried to hide his reaction. Since he was under the impression that Dad had been off at a "health farm," he asked how he was feeling.

"I'm fine, Dad. Just a little down, but I'll soon be well."

"Well, son, as the hymnbook says, doubts assail and oft prevail."

"Yes, that's true."

The old man looked confused. He hadn't actually meant to speak of sorrow; he was just reciting a mild childhood saying that came into his mind. Together that afternoon—the sturdy optimist absolutely bewildered by the diminishment of his son, and the reedy intellectual on the verge of utter collapse—it was hard to believe one was born of the other's seed. In terms of physical resemblance, they had in common only their deeply recessed blue eyes, but the world seen by one man would be as alien to the other as the earth from Pluto.

Mr. Hewlett's fine face wore its familiar generous smile. Although he tried to mask his incomprehension, it was clear that he, too, was stumped. Except for my father, all the adults had a substantiality that Dad's presence seemed to put under review. Their unthinking assumptions of causality, happiness, purpose, even of mass, were cast into dramatic relief by my father's mysterious attenuation. I could see that Mr. Hewlett was eager to leave so that he would feel himself again. He was such a true friend, though, that he stayed until he was sure there was no more need of him. I have never known a kinder man.

From the McLean notes, I learned something that happened at home that night. Around 2:30 a.m. my mother was awakened by my father's loud praying. It went on for several hours. He asked for strength and courage. Just to make it through.

CHAPTER EIGHTEEN

A dmission notes to McLean Hospital, March 19, 1958:

General Physical Examination reveals a thin, middle-aged male in no physical distress but who is trembling profusely in a manner consistent with shivering. Temperature 98.6

When my parents arrived in Belmont on a bleak March day, my father's impression of McLean Hospital was not of the commodious mansions whose elegance was a boost to the spirits, as he had been told to expect. It seemed to him instead that he had come upon a conclave of somber hulks rooted to their sites like castles of unforgiving conquerors. He told my mother that he was on the threshold of a vast fortress indifferent to the appalling suffering it contained.

In all, there were twenty-seven buildings on 240 acres. Built in the nineteenth century to house mentally ill members of Boston's wealthy families, it had undergone medical changes since then, but it still reflected the phenomenal prosperity of the American industrialists who had assembled McLean's baronial rooms. And it was still, as it had been from the beginning and remains today, a Harvard teaching hospital.

McLean brings to mind a great literary heritage. Sylvia Plath's *The Bell Jar*, Hannah Green's *I Never Promised You a Rose Garden*, and Susanna Kaysen's *Girl, Interrupted* were all written about McLean, as was Robert Lowell's famous poem "Waking in the Blue": "(This is the house for the 'mentally ill.')" James Taylor wrote his legendary song "Knockin' 'Round the Zoo" about his long stint there. But these works had yet to be created in March 1958. In my father's time the hospital didn't have poetic significance: it was a lockup for rich psychotics.

The chief psychiatrist in 1958 was Alfred Stanton, a controversial figure because of his cool manner and his unwavering belief that talk therapy could cure every mental illness, even schizophrenia. In his desire to make patients conscious of their conditions and ultimately responsible for their cures, Dr. Stanton banished many common procedures, from hot-water bottles to electroshock therapy.

Dr. Stanton's recent strictures—he had been at McLean for only three years—were partly the reason why my father's admittance turned into a drama that lasted for hours. My mother, having researched electroshock therapy over the past month, thought it might turn my father around. He was amenable to the idea, since nothing else was working. At the end of his stay at Riggs he brought it up to Dr. Emery as a possibility, and the doctor said that it might help, he wouldn't rule it out. But my mother was absolutely convinced. At McLean, as soon as papers were produced for my father to sign, my mother insisted that her husband would require ECT, that in fact he was coming there expressly for that treatment. McLean said they would not guarantee it. She became enraged.

His wife, a petite, dark-haired woman, very neatly dressed, was
very forceful and determined at the time of our encounter with
her. The interview was consumed by her making clear her hus-
band's need for immediate shock therapy, that this was his pri-
mary reason for wishing to be admitted to McLean Hospital.
[Because of] Mrs. Garis' need to control and direct the patient's
therapy . . . it has been necessary to help her realize that this will
be planned by the physicians.

My mother, in that meeting and subsequent ones, didn't make a
good impression. Elsewhere in their notes they called her an "aggressive, managerial woman." From her point of view, however, she
was a lioness protecting her own; she felt threatened to the core,
and nothing would stand in her way once she made up her mind
how to help.

The patient states that his problem is one of extreme panic and
fright, associated with depression.

Like putting flame to scorched skin, the tug-of-war between
his wife and the doctors, along with the prospect of mixing with
psychotic patients in a locked hospital, raised the level of my father's anguish to livid heights. He said he wouldn't stay, he was going back home, this was a terrible mistake. Back and forth it went
in the admitting room that afternoon. My father insisted on plac-
ing a call to Dr. Emery at Riggs. A McLean person reached Dr.
Emery and handed the phone to my father. They talked for a long
time. Dad got a little calmer. Dr. Emery managed to convince him
that admission to McLean would be helpful to him; it was what he
ought to do. Dad handed the phone back to the McLean man and
said, in a wavering voice, that he would stay.

After Dad had been shown his room in the building called Belknap, my mother held him in a long embrace. When she left the ward, a big door clanged shut and was audibly locked. It was then that she broke down sobbing.

LATER that day:

Afternoon nurse: Patient wants company of staff—states he has "the shakes"—trembling. Appears frightened of other patients.

Evening nurse: Responds to suggestion and is very coopera-tive—appears very tense and depressed—appears eager to talk to nurse concerning his depression and despair—trembling. Ate fairly well at supper. Very depressed—talking of religion—ap-pears frightened of others and of being "locked up." Requests sleeping medication.

The next day, the nurse reported that he was very depressed, restless, and tense. He paced the halls and complained that he couldn't get better there. He was described as "pleasant on ap-proach" but "shaking" and "seeking much reassurance."

As the days wore on, the reports stayed very much the same. He was up during the night, pacing, shaking, and "seeking reassur-ance." Sometimes he had good days and "much better spirits," but the depression soon descended again. It doesn't seem as if he ever had a full twenty-four hours of relief.

As his fear of other patients lessened, he began to listen to their troubles, offer advice, and then become severely disturbed when the patients didn't improve. This cycle repeated itself—as it had at Riggs, with the same results—so that the nurses finally told him not to become involved in other people's problems. He tried to heed their advice, but again found himself listening, responding, and then distraught at his inability to effect change.

My father had a quality that made people wish to confide in him. He listened with complete attention, possibly because he was momentarily relieved of being himself, and possibly because he thought that if he learned how others lived, he might teach himself how to do it, or how not to. Intensely sensitive to his surroundings, he was not personally defended in the way most people are; he didn't present a firm and polished self. He seemed to blend with the air around him, and anyone who came close to him felt folded into his aura. I can easily imagine other patients spotting a person who would take them seriously, meld with their sadness, and apply his acute intelligence to the problem.

He spent a lot of time in his room, resting and reading. He brought four books with him: *The Psalms*, *Prayers for Daily Use*, *Three Great Irishmen: Shaw, Yeats, Joyce*, by Arland Ussher, and C. S. Lewis's *The Screwtape Letters*, the last being a series of letters from a senior devil to his nephew, instructing him how to win the soul of a young man. Since C. S. Lewis was a devout Christian, his book is a kind of opposite game—playful, but deadly serious. It's an entertaining description of the behavior that casts a person out of God's embrace.

My father chose these books carefully; he hoped each in its own way would help him. The Arland Ussher book, with portraits by Augustus John, was the literary primer. These Irishmen, with whom he had a national affinity through his mother, had achieved my father's youthful but now abandoned dream. Even so, the opening paragraph about Shaw might have given him some comfort, since he thought that his own writing contained both color and mystery:

I write frankly as one who was never a Shavian . . . His mind lacked two things which I am still romantic enough to prize— color and mystery . . . I have met not a few persons—quiet natures, totally unknown to fame—with a far greater subtlety of thought and range of perceptions than ever Shaw had. That of course is not enough to make them "great," but it shows the difficulty of the concept of greatness . . .

I like to think this book began well for him. And perhaps he felt encouraged that God would eventually shelter him from demons in this passage from *The Screwtape Letters*:

When I see the temporal suffering of humans who finally escape us, I feel as if I had been allowed to taste the first course of a rich banquet and then denied the rest.

Dad never forgot that his grandmother said he was "bringing devils with him." It's likely that he thought he just might be in the grip of the Devil, and that he was fighting for the Devil's release.

He told his case psychiatrist: "I have a feeling of needing to be rescued from despondency and panic. I have made some strides in conquering this feeling, first of being accepted by God with all my panic and fears." The psychiatrist added that Dad "didn't feel his recovery was automatic. It was in the hands of God." His greatest desire was "only peace, most of all—he hopes for strength to endure until deliverance arrives."

Alone in his room, he read Psalm 69 over and over:

Save me, O God; for the waters are come in unto my soul. I sink in deep mire, where there is no standing: I am come into deep waters, where the floods overflow me. I am weary of my crying:

my throat is dried: mine eyes fail while I wait for my God . . .
Deliver me out of the mire, and let me not sink: let me be deliv-
ered . . . out of the deep waters . . . Let not the waterflood over-
flow me, neither let the deep swallow me up, and let not the pit
shut her mouth upon me. Hear me, O LORD; for thy loving
kindness is good: turn unto me according to the multitude of thy
tender mercies. And hide not thy face from thy servant; for I am
in trouble . . .

Meanwhile, my mother was making her own arrangements for
rescuing her husband. She had a plan.

3/26 Received call from wife in AM and appeared in much bet-
ter mood. Stated he had almost made up his mind to give up
writing. Suggest patient be observed for any depressed reactions
to conversation with wife today.

Hearing of a job opening editing agricultural pamphlets for the
University of Massachusetts, Mom decided he should take it. It
would bring in enough money to see them through until something better came along. (They were both in agreement that Mom
should be home with the family and not looking for a job herself.)
In any case, he should do no more writing. It was only making him
worse. He agreed to give it up.

The nurses watched him carefully, but his only immediate reaction was a bad cold. A week later the nurse wrote:

Up at 2 AM for repeat sedation. In the morning apparently feel-
ing better. Out for walks most of day. Quite pleasant in ap-
proach but however still appears depressed. In the evening rather
depressed. States he is anxious over prospect of visit home. Well
controlled, some pacing, quite tense.

After the weekend he said he'd felt panicky. Then, on April 10:

Patient did not sleep all night. In the day appears somewhat depressed, says he feels exhausted. Talking about his anxieties. Worried about going home. Says he knows he will not sleep at home and that he has a lot of problems to face. Quite a bit of pacing.

My mother's plan involved more than giving up writing, and when he went home for his visit, she laid it all out. As far as she was concerned, he had to get out of that hospital. He had to pull himself together, change his life, bring in some income, and all of that would make him better. She drove him to the hospital and demanded that he be discharged.

In the words of Marianne Sommerfeld, the social worker, "His wife felt that by this rather swift and dramatic action she had done more for patient than his doctors could and that he was now ready for discharge." He had been there four days shy of a month. They shrugged their collective shoulders, wished him well, and let him go.

CHAPTER NINETEEN

Dad came home from the hospital with the abashed spirit of a man forced to face his sins only to find that he is forgiven. He would give up writing, he told me, but that was okay because he needed to be realistic and make a living. His new realism would make him solid, and Lord knew he needed that. He would work for the University of Massachusetts, editing these agricultural pamphlets. "But Dad, what do you know about farming?" "Language is language. It's the one thing I'm good at," he answered. "And I'll be glad to get a paycheck."

I didn't know then about his charged relationship with universities. He'd told us he had gone to Princeton, but the truth was significantly more complicated. He hadn't done well enough on his College Boards to get into Princeton from high school, so he went to Georgetown for one semester, but—he told his doctor at Riggs—he was so homesick that he left. I think that he had internalized his mother's overprotectiveness to such a degree that he felt imperiled without her. He then went to Columbia while living at home. He accumulated enough credits and good grades to get into Princeton the following year, 1920, when he was nineteen, but he commuted from home, spending only a few nights a week at school—staying at Nassau Inn—did poorly, and left there, too. He went to NYU for two years, still commuting, then got a law degree at New Jersey Law School, but he never took the bar exam. Perhaps, like his sons, he had dyslexia, but he was also hampered by being fearful and lonely. His memory of those years must have weighed on him when he took this lowly university job.

I watched for signs that his resolve would be short-lived, and what I found was not exactly what I'd been looking for. He was always using his handkerchief. I could hear him all over the house, blowing his nose. I knew he was crying, and I couldn't stand it. My sympathy for him was continually being swamped by rage at his frailty. Rage was my constant companion, for which I hated myself. At one point I asked him an ordinary question—Is it okay if I go to the movies with Jim Guest on Friday night?—and his blue eyes, which actually seemed to have gotten paler over the last year, filled with tears. "What is it?" I asked in a challenging, not altogether kind way. "It's nothing, Les. Only a cold." "Oh, okay." I turned away as if taking his answer at face value. Amidst the pretense of normalcy in our house I was able to keep my own pretense of non-recognition, and no one was able to penetrate my defenses. To do so would have opened the floodgates.

While we were happy to have Dad home again, he was much frailer than we had hoped. What did the hospital do for him? There was a palpable sense of the entire household having to gear up for another bout of sadness when we all just wanted to get on with our lives. I especially felt as if I were being called by the future; I was in training for it, and it would take strength and focus. Everything in me was straining toward a larger life. I had just turned fifteen.

Mom was the only one who seemed energized by Dad's return. She darted among us like a hyperactive child, running from one task to another, talking all the time, baking pies, singing, gardening, taking Grampy for drives, making up for our father's deepening silence, taking up the parental slack. A few times she invited Charles Cole, the president of Amherst College, over for a visit. One day she showed him our whole house, upstairs and down, which I thought was silly, since he had certainly seen his share of large houses. Nat Grose was also coming over a lot. When he left, Mom would walk him to his car and stay talking for an inordinate amount of time. I could see they were attracted to each other, and I was just old enough and had read enough European novels to decide that they might be better off with each other than with their own needy spouses. But I also knew that Mom was too much a rule follower to betray her husband.

It turned out that Dad's giving up writing was just one part of Mom's plan. But she didn't reveal the centerpiece of her strategy until dinner one evening in May.

Before that dinner, however, something happened that thrilled and rattled me in almost equal measure. Amherst, a staid town that prided itself on standing above most popular culture—a typical library talk was on Horace—decided in a good-natured, tongue-in-cheek way to hold a contest for Miss Amherst. There had never been such a thing as Miss Amherst before. There would be no preliminaries, no semifinals, no names put forward, and no campaigning. The contest was open to all Amherst girls, and the vote was town-wide. Ballot boxes were placed in stores, and people laughed as they cast their votes for their daughters, sisters, and friends. It was a lark. The crowning would take place at a town fair.

Lo and behold, the winner was announced: it was Leslie Garis. I was absolutely mystified. How on earth did this happen? Then again, maybe I had an inkling. There was a rumor going around that one Amherst fraternity had stuffed the ballot box. It was possible that all those milk shakes and the flirtatious scoping at Valentine Hall had paid off. However I was chosen, as I walked in the village during the ensuing days, I had the notion that people were smiling at me and wishing me well. I found myself smiling at everyone I saw, smiling into my mirror at home. I felt like a fool in love, in love with my windfall of happiness.

My mother took me to Springfield to buy a dress for the crowning. It was tiered and embroidered chiffon with a lime green taffeta sash. I had a court of runners-up, and when I stood on the platform wearing my crown, I gazed down at my father's face, which looked, for the first time in years, relaxed and contented. So this is what it takes, I thought in a harsh instant. He's the father of the queen. That thought passed in a flash, and I was again, as before in those enchanted hours, newly overwhelmed with love for my tender, vulnerable family. My resentment of Dad's illness and Mom's willful sunniness were wiped away with one unexpected life turn. I could afford the emotional confusion at home; it wouldn't bring me down. I was Miss Amherst.

And now we come to that fateful dinner. It started on a high note. Grampy was pleased that several children rang the doorbell that afternoon looking for Uncle Wiggily. He took a short walk with them, told a story, and signed their *Uncle Wiggily* books. "After a spell they went on home," he said. "How about you, Roger? How's the new job?"

"I think you'd understand it better than I do," he said. "I'm editing something about the difference between the cost of milk bottles and cardboard cartons. It doesn't exactly take my fancy."

"Well, son, that could be an interesting topic. Let's see—"

Mom, suddenly reddening, and with a loud intake of breath, interrupted. "I have something to announce." We turned toward her as she cleared her throat, which she always did as quietly as possible, as if it were something to be ashamed of.

"I want to tell you all that I have been in negotiation with Mr.

Cole and Mr. Grose of Amherst College. The upshot of it is"—she looked straight ahead with level eyes—"I have sold our house to Amherst College. We will be moving—"

Before she finished her sentence, I was on my feet. With a wild voice that came from pure rage, I screamed, "You can't do that! This is our home! You can't sell our home! You have no right to do that! No! It can't be! You can't just do that! You have no right!"

I was dimly aware through my rant that Brooks—unable to hold in his feelings, unwilling to make accusations, sick at losing his home—had made the only statement he could: he vomited. Dad was crying. Grampy sat still and said nothing. Buddy also started to cry.

"Your father and I agreed it was best," she said in a faltering voice. "It was while he was in the hospital. We decided then—"

"How could Dad decide anything in the *hospital*? He was *ill*!"

At that point Dad stood so abruptly that his chair fell backward. He rushed upstairs, his hands covering his mouth. Mom reached an arm out in his direction, then dropped it and crumpled back into her chair, stricken.

Brooks went into the kitchen to find a cloth to clean up his vomit. Jean came out with him to help.

I sat back down in my chair and looked at my hands twisted together in my lap. I hated my mother. Hated her. She had manipulated Dad into this move. There must be something I could still do to turn this around. I determined I would never leave this house.

I could hear that she was beginning to weep. I stole a glance at her and saw that her bottom lip was trembling as she made soft gasps.

"You have no idea—no idea—what it has been like trying to keep this household together. Don't you understand, Les? Don't you see we can't afford to keep living like this?"

I wouldn't answer.

"Someone had to do something. It fell to me. Your father—"

I didn't want to hear any more. I ran up to my room.

IN THE MIDDLE OF THE NIGHT, I awoke in the darkness. I went to the window, hoping for a moon to illuminate the outdoors, but it was too pale. I would need a flashlight if I went outside.

I dressed and opened my bedroom door. Absolute silence. Downstairs, I got a flashlight from the butler's pantry. Now I had a choice. Would I go out the kitchen door, the terrace door, the French doors, or the front door? It mattered. Everything I did tonight mattered crucially.

I chose the terrace. Looking out over the low wall, I could see the apple tree holding the faint moonlight in its blossoms. It glowed.

I descended the stone steps leading down to the grass. On the lawn I turned off my flashlight to see if my eyes would adjust to the night.

What was my plan? Just stand still and wait. If I can see in the darkness, I'll think of something. I listened for animals but heard nothing. They must be lying low, having heard me. Too bad. It would have been nice to be accepted as a night creature.

Soon I was able to see, but just barely. My plan began to materialize. I realized at once that it was not an action plan. It was a mind plan. I would think myself forward. That was all there was to do.

I sat under the apple tree, blossoms overhead, and looked at our house. Not a single light was on. It loomed like an ocean liner, war-darkened against hostile planes.

Calamity. What else was it? My father's illness had won. His debilitation had brought us down. We had lost The Dell. But what was wrong with me that I thought our family needed such a huge place to live? Of course we didn't need all that space. I was beginning to feel steadier, but I shook suddenly as if from an electric shock. It wasn't the space, it was the magic. How could I give up the magic? The light through leaded windows, the secret rooms on the third floor, the panel under the stairs, the cupboards over my bedroom mantel, snowy days through the library windows, the wisteria ladder up to the balcony, the swinging oak branch? But even beyond all that, I was the person who inhabited those spaces. I was those spaces; they were part of my blood, my bones. I would be a different person somewhere else. Duller, less illuminated within.

But then I thought, as I moved away from the tree, perhaps we would all be less haunted. There would be no bedroom where Granny had lived. Maybe Dad would have a better chance somewhere else. Perhaps wrenching ourselves away from such a powerful force as The Dell would free us to be stronger on our own. I lay on the grass and looked up.

I was grateful for stars. When I was younger, I used to wish the stars could move in the sky like fish in water. I wanted to guess how they would change position, watch them chase each other, playing in the deep dark. Now I was grateful for their fixed positions. They had never seemed more magisterial than they did that night. Every one of them was somewhere right, but what determined their placement? I had thought The Dell was my site in the world, even though I always knew I would grow up and make my life elsewhere.

I felt a new calmness, as if I were falling into my own space and I would land just right. I knew that before this move was over, I would have more rage and despair, but for now I was hopeful.

INSIDE THE DUMBWAITER on a torpid August afternoon I could hear the voices of the moving men. Today was the day. I had crawled in here in a last attempt to hold it all close, to be lost inside the house. I might stay here while they left. But already the house was losing its soul. In whatever ways The Dell had become as familiar to me as my own skin, in fact seemed an extension of my skin, those ways were dematerializing, and the house, as it became emptied of rugs and furniture, books and pictures, was becoming more and more alien.

I was not even at home in the dumbwaiter. I hadn't been in it for such a long time that I was shocked how, in order to fit, I had to press my back up against the top of the box and bend my head to my knees. I thought of Alice in Wonderland after she ate the cake and grew gigantic in the rabbit hole. This was nothing like my memories of the hours I used to spend here, comfortable and eager. Now I was cramped and depressed.

Yesterday Mom had told me something profoundly disorienting. I felt the blood pound in my ears as her words entered my consciousness. She said that a few days ago Thayer Greene had performed an exorcism on Dad. Mom told me this when I asked her why Dad seemed to be getting worse all summer even though he had a job at the university and we had sold the house. She said she was baffled but, as always, was sure things would get better. Our minister, she said, thought Dad felt haunted by evil, so in desperation Mr. Greene tried something he had never done before. Dad sat in the empty church with the Reverend. They faced the cross. Mr. Greene put his hand on Dad's forehead while Dad held a small cross. Dad wept as the towering minister with his quavering bass voice called on God to expunge the Devil from this good man. He didn't follow an exorcism mass, but he was a reader of Carl Jung and had an abiding belief in the power of myth and ritual. Using religious language, he created his own ceremony. I wished I could have heard Mr. Greene's words. I knew they would have been uttered slowly, chosen carefully, and they would be—as I had heard from the pulpit—unabashedly fervent, steeped in the mysticism of Mr. Greene's New England ancestors. What did he say? I imagined "O Lord cast out the demon!" And "Deliver this man . . ." I'd heard him speak stirringly about deliverance. I'm sure he'd use the phrase "Hear my prayer, O God." And wouldn't he have intoned the Lord's Prayer? "Our Father, who art in heaven . . ." I said the whole prayer to myself in the dumbwaiter. It always had a stabilizing effect on me. If only it were true that Dad was possessed and Thayer Greene had chased the evil spirit away. How blazingly simple. I wanted to believe, but with all that I'd seen in the last few years, I couldn't credit an outside force. Dad, in some inexplicable way, was ill with his own life. And yet, amazingly, I think the exorcism must have done some good, because Dad had seemed calmer in the last few days. Last night, for no reason, he gave me a hug and smiled mysteriously.

Years ago I thought goodness and happiness went hand in hand. How could I not take that lesson from my family's books? The one verity in our family's writing was that tenderness of heart triumphed over baseness. Now, against everything I'd learned about narrative, I saw my kind, gentle father battling an unhappiness so malicious that it threatened to obliterate him. I didn't believe the dark force would win in the end. How could I? Especially if Thayer Greene enlisted God for our side.

In the symmetry of all the Garis tales, the ending should fit the beginning. I situated our beginning in our move to The Dell, a time overflowing with hope. How would our story turn out? Perhaps we were just entering the part where everything looks desperate, just before something shifts in the plot and the hero rallies. Of course, I saw it now. The move to Amity Street would be the beginning of our happy ending. We were leaving our ghosts behind.

PART THREE

* * *

CHAPTER TWENTY

Spring Street and Amity Street—their very names contrasted suggestively. One brought to mind primal energy bubbling from the earth, while the other stood for harmony, peace, tranquillity, and friendship. At that point we were interested in the comfortable values of a serene neighborhood, with all the cozy safety implied.

Since I'd lived all but the first four years of my life at The Dell, our new house took some getting used to. For example, there were no secret spaces or indeterminate little rooms in which a child could close a door and imagine a tower or a ship, or, most satisfying of all, a private study. Every room at 279 Amity Street was spoken for. As there were no alternate sitting rooms, the living room was for reading, conversing, or playing the piano—sometimes all at once. There was a dining room for meals, a kitchen with a small table, a ground-floor suite for Grampy consisting of a bedroom, bath, and study, a single staircase ascending from just inside the front door, and four bedrooms upstairs—two at each end of a short, narrow corridor. The exceptions to this simple plan were a porch off the kitchen—what my mother cheerfully called the sunporch, which looked over a backyard in dire need of tidying up—and a paneled passage between the kitchen and Grampy's bedroom, in which he put his oversize collection of Dickens.

Mom had placed most of our furniture in storage, so that now we had a comfortable version of the basics. There was a new clarity in our lives.

One of my mother's first purchases was a large freezer; in her mode of constant-motion thrift, she could put up supplies bought in the fall to last the winter. At some point in every Amherst fall that I could remember, Mom bought wooden crates of apples picked at Atkins's orchards. Grampy was always part of this routine, which, in all its details, took a good long week to complete. At Amity Street he and my mother sat on the sunporch preparing the apples for freezing. He loved to peel and core them; it reminded him of childhood summers in upstate New York on his grandmother's farm. Sleeves rolled up, elbows on knees, he leaned over a pail and, using his favorite whittling knife, peeled the red skin off in one deft spiral that fell into the pail. Then he expertly cored the apple and added it to the pile in a big bowl. Mom sat next to the bowl and sliced the fruit, which she then covered in sugar and, laying the slices side by side in a pan, prepared them for freezing. Pies, applesauce, and other apple confections appeared at our table all winter.

However, early on a mid-September morning, after being in the house less than a month and only partway through the apples, Grampy collapsed in his room. An ambulance was called and raced noisily off to the hospital, but the doctors made light of the incident by calling it a minor heart attack, and in a few days he was home, a little chastened by his brush with ill health. He was inordinately proud of his robust constitution, including his perfect teeth. He liked to boast that in his entire life he had never had a single cavity, even eating on average a box of chocolates a week.

Despite Grampy's short scare, this particular autumn was one of hope for all of us—except, perhaps, Dad. He had done what his wife required of him, but none of it was sitting well. He felt demeaned by his job. His last salaried position had been with *The New York Times Magazine* just before we moved to Amherst, and when he agreed to go back to work, I later learned, he wrote to magazines and publishing houses all over the East Coast trying to get an editorial position. Our mailbox was full of rejections, not only for his job inquiries, but for *Amusement Park,* which he was still trying to get produced. One letter personified this whole time for him: "I'm sorry if you got the impression I meant to be encouraging."

So now he was working for the university's agricultural school in Munson Hall, a curvy and picturesque stone building, one of the oldest at the University of Massachusetts, which had been founded in 1863 as a land-grant institution called Massachusetts Agricultural College.

It was Dad's task to put some grace into the lumpy language of "aggie" writers who were theorizing about such topics as the most cost-efficient way to package corn. Not only did these subjects bore him, they had a positively toxic effect on his fragile self-esteem. How low he had sunk seemed glaringly evident to him every time he entered that building.

The house move was the other element that rocked his equilibrium. I like to think that it wasn't so much that he was a snob and wanted to be the man in the mansion, but that the new space itself challenged his identity at a precarious time in his life. He experienced the move as a change from amplitude to constriction. He told me that he had decided that living, really living, takes much more than is ordinarily asked of a person. Real living, he said, takes dreaming, the freedom to soar with ideas. And for that you need the right space; you need more space than is necessary for existence. If you always know what is expected of you in a house, he said mysteriously, you might as well be . . . I can't remember the exact image, but it was something like a robot. You might as well be a robot.

He said this one afternoon when he returned from "the office" and criticized the strangled little area at the bottom of the stairs that should, in his view, have been a real hall instead of a scant way station between living room and dining room. But the architect had seen no need for a hall. What was the use of a hall? It was merely wasted space. My father liked a certain amount of waste in his life. He told me that one of the greatest pleasures of staying in great hotels was using a big, soft towel once and throwing it on the floor for the maid to pick up and exchange for a clean one. That somewhat shocked me, but our dad was from another time; the luxuries in his past were part of a man the family he started in his forties never knew.

Dad wanted to make this move work. He resumed psychotherapy with the Springfield doctor who had originally recommended Riggs. To get his health back after the previous year's hospitalizations, he swam several times a week at Amherst College's Pratt Pool. Sometimes I went over there after school and watched him complete lap after lap. He was a strong, graceful swimmer.

Brooks liked our new house. At The Dell, he said, we lived between a scary attic and a scary basement in rooms that were too big for us. This was a real house. The rooms were just right. He was having his usual problems at school, but he began to learn the guitar, eventually enlisting the virtuoso Bill Keith as teacher, taking up the twelve-string, and becoming expert surprisingly quickly. It turned out he had real musical talent.

Dad took Bud to Aubuchon Hardware, next to the men's clothing store House of Walsh, to buy him his first bike, a one-speed Rollfast. Soon he was flying off on his red beauty, down the hill of

Amity Street, across farmland, over to Munson Hall, where, before riding home, he would share with his dad a Coke from the office machine. It was a happy time for Bud, although he said more than once, in what must have been Dad's language, that his father "loathed" his job. Mom would answer, "Work is work. We can't be too choosy."

She was at her peak of certainty. Her thinking must have gone something like this: *If we sell the house, if Roger gets a job, if I put up preserves, if the children go to public school, we will be off this teetering Ferris wheel in this crazy amusement park, and we will be moving ahead unobtrusively like a sensible, realistic family.* My mother was a great believer in appearances, insisting that we all dress according to the current code. She set a lot of store by how people reacted to her. Not only did it confirm her sense of reality, but she believed— although she would never admit it—that judgments from the out- side world were probably correct. She also believed—and why not?—that if we asked less of the gods, we would be rewarded with an ordinary—i.e., secure and happy—life. She was essentially an optimist.

Sometime that fall—I remember that it was warm and over- cast—I walked across town to The Dell. It was the first time I'd been back. I didn't know until a few days later that the college had made the decision that keeping up the grounds as they were, with paths and gardens and hedges, was too expensive. The idea was to reseed the property as a large open lawn. They set a controlled fire to clear the land; it was thought that ashes were good for fertilizing soil. Unaware of this scheme, I could hardly believe my eyes when I got to The Dell and saw the missing plantings and the ground deep in ashes. How had the exquisite landscaping been reduced al- most overnight to this desolation? In a dramatic gesture I took off my shoes and walked barefoot through the ashes, sobbing as I went. My feet turned charcoal, and my shirt was soaked with tears.

Anyone looking out from an upstairs window would have thought I was demented. Making ashy footprints, I went up to the terrace and peered through the library windows. The desk and couch were still there, but the shelves were bare.

I stared and stared until the room came to life. Grampy's face looking down at the typewriter, his hands poking at the keys, his white shirt open at the collar, sleeves rolled up, his dark blue eyes focusing softly on a place in the air . . . Then his image dissolved, and I saw Dad sitting on the couch a year before his parents came to live with us. He was about to speak to me. It snowed that day. "I know why I bought this house," he said, as happy as I'd ever seen him. "I bought it so I could start a magazine. I'm calling it *The Pioneer* . . ." All the choices in his life made sense to him that day. I looked out over the terrace wall at a transformed landscape. If only . . . I never told anyone about my walk through the ashes.

By the time we moved to Amity Street, our eighty-five-year-old storyteller had retired from writing new Uncle Wiggily episodes for newspapers, and since Dad no longer had office space at home or in Jones Library (they were renovating the upper floors), the two men shared the desk and typewriter in Grampy's sitting room. Dad worked on weekends and some late afternoons; Grampy liked the early morning hours. He always had a project, often an adventure story. I didn't question the arrangement. It didn't occur to me, for example, to wonder if Dad minded not having his own desk. In fact it was more his father's desk than his own, so it was almost like a little boy using his daddy's desk when he could. But I didn't think of that then.

In high school, I was having a romance that sweetened my life to a miraculous degree. I could almost forget what was going on at home. I was in love with Earl Shumway. There's little to say: he was the handsomest boy in school; he was from a "town" (as opposed to a "gown") family. I wore his signet ring on a gold chain around my neck, which my father thought was tacky, although he would never have used that word. I secretly agreed with him, but that was part of its appeal. Wasn't I just being a normal American girl? I also sang in the church choir, which rehearsed Wednesday nights, and I had an after-school job in the biology department of Amherst College, feeding newts and performing other menial tasks for Dr. Oscar Schotte, the amputation/regrowth futurist. But mainly my life was tied up with dark, shy Earl of crackly voice and dewy skin. His older cousin owned the Amherst equivalent of the soda shop in the television show *Happy Days*, where all the high school kids go. It was called Shumway's. When Earl and I walked side by side down the school halls, carrying our books sideways on our hips, I was in a state of ecstasy.

ROBERT FROST CAME TO CALL. The two elderly men sat together in Grampy's sitting room in the late afternoon, drinking something besides tea. They sat in high-backed chairs in front of the fireplace, leaning forward toward each other. After a while they left the house and walked up the hill into town. Grampy came back on his own in time for dinner.

A good feature of our new life was that now the Hewletts lived across the street, in a long house that seemed on hinges, as the rooms were set at angles to one another. The Hewlett children, Betsy and Tut, were in a group of friends of which Brooks and I were a part. Buddy was often there, too. I spent many happy hours in that house, which smelled of whiskey, cocktail onions, and salted peanuts. My parents often went over there for cocktail hour, as everyone called it, although Dad rarely imbibed. Mary Hewlett, exotically beautiful in large pieces of Navaho jewelry, and Bud Hewlett, handsome like Henry Fonda, were devoted to each other and to their friends. The children banged on the piano in the den, played cards, ran around, and generally had a convivial time of it. All the Hewletts were so polite and soft-spoken that when Mrs. Hewlett ruined a new dress by sitting on a lawn chair Mom had just painted, she laughed as if nothing more amusing could have happened to her and complimented Mom on her tireless pursuit of house projects.

As fall turned cold, and then as Christmas passed into a typical bleak New England January, my father's depression gripped him again. I have often wondered if his boyhood memory of being taken by his father to a psychiatrist who gave him a jolt of electricity had something to do with Dad's desire for a more sophisticated version of the same treatment. Even though that long-ago day must have been traumatic for the little boy, he would have known at the time that his father's motives were loving: he wished only to help his distressed son. Perhaps in an obscure way the love and the electricity had melded in Dad's mind. In any case, on that January morning in 1959, his thoughts blurred by his immediate despair, Dad underwent electroshock treatment at a hospital in Hartford, Connecticut, on a street named Asylum Road.

His homecoming was traumatic. His arm was bandaged so tightly to his chest that it looked as if the limb had been sheared right off at the shoulder. Shock treatments were primitive in those years. Electrodes were placed on head and body, and the doctors gave the patient a tremendous jolt of electricity. Unfortunately, the literal shock to Dad's system caused the convulsions of a grand mal seizure, in the course of which he dislocated his shoulder. The doctors put it in place and bandaged him up, but it was never right again. Among other consequences, his beautiful swimming stroke was finished. As for his mood, the treatment only seemed to have made him worse. His memory was temporarily impaired, his shoulder was in pain, and the seizure had terrified him. He had found himself on the floor, hearing alarmed voices, not knowing where he was, with his shoulder on fire, wires pulling his skin, orderlies holding his arms. At home he got into bed and stayed there for a week. The swelling in his jaw from the mouthpiece took almost that long to go down.

Physical therapy was required for his shoulder, with the unnerving result that in the basement room a contraption was set up that made a loud noise, like gears grinding in a torture chamber. A pulley was suspended from the ceiling through which a rope was threaded. Dad would grab onto each end of the rope with his arms straight out from his sides. As he pulled one arm down, the other was forced up. Squeak! From upstairs we heard the sound and knew Dad was working on his bad shoulder—and that it hurt. Sometimes we would look at one another and dare tiny smiles. As if it were a ghoulish joke.

On February 22, Dad's play *The Pony Cart* opened in London to good reviews. The director and producer, Glen Farmer, was also negotiating with an English company, Hammer Films, for a movie sale. Dad's mood was so low that this good news seemed to have no impact on him. The play was on a small budget, so Dad wasn't invited to fly over—nor would he have paid for such an expensive trip—but still, I could hardly believe that he remained untouched by this professional upturn. Mom told me of a remark a psychiatrist made to her after *The Pony Cart* failed in New York. When she said that Dad's breakdown was the result of his bad reviews, the doctor disagreed: "The reviews had nothing to do with it. I would have been more worried if he'd had a success." Suggesting that his illness was independent of his professional life and would rage on, following its own course. Watching Dad stumble around the house in the evenings, his voice clotted by drugs, I reluctantly agreed. It was a watershed in my understanding of the intractability of his illness.

He wanted to be a full-time writer again. He had never wanted to be anything else. So, over Mom's objections, he quit his job. His employers must have expected it, since he had missed so much work that winter. He still had hopes for *Amusement Park* (a new agent, more rejections, but always someone else interested), he thought his air force TV series had real possibilities, and he was still working on his comedy, *The Blue Balloon*. Since the recent *Pony Cart* production, I had had the sinking sensation that nothing would matter, but he had his dreams and they kept him getting up each day. Things were definitely getting strange at home. I began to notice that Grampy was slurring his speech at dinner, although I never saw him with a drink in his hand. He was obviously tippling sherry in his room. Was it still sherry? I wondered. I tried to figure out when his drinking became obvious every day, but I couldn't pin it down. I thought it was probably since we'd lived on Amity Street.

Dad, also, was in a new stage of addiction. One night I went to his bedroom to tell him that dinner was ready. He'd told us he was going to stretch out before dinner, but when I got to his room, he said from his bed that he wouldn't be down tonight. I offered to bring his food up. We made him a tray: hamburger with elbow macaroni and string beans. I put ketchup on the plate, gave him a cloth napkin, a glass of water, salt and pepper. In the bedroom, I found him sitting in a chair that was pulled up to a small table. In an extremely subdued, barely audible voice, he thanked me. After dinner I went upstairs to collect the tray, and there he was, pitched forward with his head in his food, his face in the ketchup. He appeared unconscious.

Afraid, appalled, reluctant to touch him, I ran downstairs to the others. Brooks said to Mom, "I'll go. You call an ambulance." Just like that. He was fourteen. I was shaking, and ashamed that I didn't offer to help Brooks. But I went upstairs a few minutes later and stood away from Dad's door, close enough to hear that he was moaning and Brooks was talking to him.

"Brooks?" I ventured timidly, speaking from the hall.

"It's okay. I'm putting on his shoes. I think he can walk downstairs. Tell the ambulance men when they come. I'll get him downstairs."

I don't know where Buddy was during all this, but I do remember Grampy hovering around Mom, who told him gently to go into his room because there was nothing he could do. So he shuffled off, seeming to have aged ten years in the last ten minutes.

Then our front rooms were filled with a moving light from the ambulance, and the doorbell rang. As my mother admitted the two men, my father and brother appeared at the top of the stairs.

Dad, a head taller than Brooks, gazed down fearfully with eyes that looked like smudges, as if they'd been rubbed out. His skeletal face was an unearthly pale hue, his cheekbones jutting out like rocks under his skin. Brooks went down a step and turned up to his father, holding out his hands. At first Dad took his son's hands in his, but when Brooks saw that Dad was having difficulty staying upright, he held Dad by his upper arms, trying to support his weight. Dad leaned forward and put out a tentative foot. Slowly, Brooks going backward, they began to descend. The men, by this time, were standing at the bottom of the stairs. No one spoke except Brooks, who murmured softly, "That's good. Here's another step. Good, Dad. You're doing fine, Dad."

So thin! He was like a rag doll. His wasted body was held at the points of Brooks's hands while the rest of him sagged and weaved around Brooks's grip. Suddenly Dad lurched sideways and fell past his son. Brooks tried to grab him but failed. At that moment the boy let out a dreadful sound—a gasp or a sob, an animal sound of defeat, and I thought in that instant that nothing would ever be the same for Brooks again. Brooks, the sweet, dutiful son, had been the one to help his increasingly drugged father tie his shoes for the past year, always there for him when he couldn't dress himself. But something broke in Brooks that second. I believe he understood in a rush of horror that he was quite literally helpless against his father's downward trajectory.

The men bounded up the steps and caught Dad in midair, almost upside down.

"Got him! Bring the stretcher."

Mom, sounding desperate, asked, "A stretcher? Do you have to take him out in a stretcher?"

"Sorry, ma'am. It's best for the patient."

Chastened because she realized how beside the point it was not to want the neighbors seeing her husband carried out on a stretcher, she put her hands over her face and collapsed into a chair. Watching Mom's reaction, I wondered for the first time how much the neighbors already knew.

No one ever explained to me exactly why Dad had lost consciousness, but I figured out something quite logical, which I don't think was incorrect. The drugs Dad was taking tranquilized him, slowing his anxiety to a crawl. With his inevitable addiction, it took more medicine for him to reach the no-anxiety barrier. It was my conclusion—after watching him for the last year slur his words and move like an old man—that the drugs slowed down everything in his body, including his heart and lungs, which would eventually curtail the oxygen flowing in the blood to his brain and lead to unconsciousness. Retard body functions enough, of course, and a person dies. The chemistry of barbiturates is obviously much more complicated than that, but my explanation, I would later find, was close enough to the truth.

After the critical stage was over and Dad was out of danger, they kept him in the hospital, trying to diagnose his illness. They could find no cause for his emaciated, weakened state. He was desperately sick, they could see that, and they tested for a biological cause. But his illness defied them. How could such a deteriorated body have apparently healthy bone, blood, organs, and tissue?

Mom took over Dad's correspondence, writing letters to Glen Farmer in England, who had finalized the movie sale of *The Pony Cart* just days before Dad's overdose. The film title would be changed to *Never Take Sweets from a Stranger*. So Dad's professional life was showing promise, but whatever was dragging Dad down was more elusive than ever.

While Dad was in the hospital, Mom got her first call from an Amherst bar asking her to come get Grampy. They were very polite, saying something like, We didn't feel right sending the old man off on his own. He's such a nice gentleman, is Mr. Garis. Mom was devastated. She went to get him, brought him home stumbling up the walk, and put him to bed. He was uncharacteristically quiet, although he had apparently been loudly grateful when she came, saying "mighty kind" and "no need." What was unspoken among us was the growing belief that if it wasn't for Dad's state, Grampy would never have been getting drunk in Amherst bars. It was in these days that the guilty sensation of blame began to grow within us.

Along with the blame came my stubborn, unreasoning hope that maybe there was still a way to mend him. I sat with Dad on many afternoons, just the two of us, he with his head in his hands, I looking at that head and wondering how I could penetrate its labyrinths to adjust whatever was going wrong in there. I would recite lists of good news: I'm doing well in school, Mom's singing is better and better and now she's a member of the Amherst Community Opera, Brooks is great on the guitar, isn't Buddy getting big . . . Surely there must be some good news connected to Dad himself. Alas, his writing wasn't going well. But how could it? He took too many pills.

I was sixteen now and had plans for my life. I wanted to go to a good college and have a career in words—writing, reading, editing, journalism. I didn't know the details, but I had ambitions. Even with everything I had seen, I was drawn to the family business, and I thought I had more chance of being good at it than anything else. I knew that Dad's slide threatened to bring us all down, and I was determined not to sink with the ship. These thoughts brought more guilt.

Our piano was in the back of the living room, and I practiced more than ever. I was beginning to master some Bach pieces, and there was something about the Bach under my hands that brought order into my life. The themes separated themselves and intertwined without losing their integrity. Each theme played itself out and came together with the others in a perfect major chord—a happy ending. Even if the piece was brooding and dark as it went along, the themes resolved, sometimes piecemeal, separating again, going off on their own, but coming together at the end in harmonic simplicity. I felt an exhilarating oneness with the world when I played Bach, as if life made sense. Added to that was the physical sensation in my hands, as if my fingers could make magic. I had a very good teacher, so the back of my hands and my lower arms were relaxed and still. My fingers, as I practiced scales, began to move powerfully and fast. In playing Bach, I found one of the most exquisite feelings I had ever known. I played other composers, too, a lot of Schumann, a little Mendelssohn, a little Chopin. I loved listening to Chopin, but not playing him. I didn't like what my left hand had to do. I felt insecure while it was up in the air moving from a bass note to a chord a few octaves above. In the time when my hand was off the keys, I would worry that I might not come down on the chord, and I'd panic. Which may have been the beginning of an acute self-consciousness that I was only then, in the subtlest ways, beginning to feel—maybe first in the left hand of Chopin pieces. But that self-consciousness would take a few more months before it blossomed into something that impeded my life.

Meanwhile, I kept looking at my father and hoping that he was going to reverse his course and find the strength to be well.

I put all my passion into Earl Shumway. I thought that his superb face, his perfect frame, would somehow lift me from the morass that had become my family life. I remembered what Dad had told me about Santayana's *The Sense of Beauty*, in which was formulated a sort of philosophy of beauty, as if beauty were a moral necessity. Dad responded deeply to these ideas, and I, with youthful passion, was captivated by a similar impulse. Earl became my obsession. After dates we parked outside my house, and he would say, "Shouldn't you go in?" and I would want more kisses (we were both still virgins; having actual sex was unthinkable). But I drove him away with my worshipful fervor. It scared him to death; it was out-of-bounds. So in the spring he broke up with me. I thought I might never recover.

By summer I had no boyfriend and my father was showing every sign of going straight down. It was at this time that somehow or other my parents put a little money together and took a month's rental of a house in Wellfleet, at the end of Cape Cod.

I had just gotten my license and wanted to drive, so Dad went with me in a little secondhand car while Mom drove the station wagon. Grampy and the boys went with her. My car was in the lead.

We made it to Route 6 on the Cape with no mishaps. The road narrowed to two lanes. Suddenly I got very restless. I could feel something foreign growing in me, taking hold. I had to pass the car in front. I couldn't contain myself. I put my foot down on the accelerator. It was an underpowered car, so it didn't immediately burst forward but slowly gathered speed. I kept my foot pressed to the floor, and we began to go faster. I had my mind on getting past the car in front. I started to pass, and as I did, I felt a certainty and determination, and I seemed to leave my body as I pressed and pressed on the accelerator. I must have been in a trance. There was a car coming right at me, coming closer and closer. I either didn't see it (which is impossible) or I decided it didn't matter. It wasn't in my realm of reality. I just kept on going forward. And part of me thought—I didn't think, but part of me felt—that dying, especially Dad's dying, was not a bad thing. Suddenly Dad yelled, "Jesus, Les!" and I snapped out of it, and here was this car almost upon me. It swerved off the road and went into scrub grass. I veered back into the right lane. The other car pulled off the grass, got back on the road, and we drove on. I don't remember Dad saying anything at all. I shook the whole rest of the trip. I didn't know where I'd been, what had happened, why I had done that. We continued in silence. When we arrived at the house in Wellfleet, my mother and brothers ran up to me, asking what had happened. What was I thinking? I had no answers.

CHAPTER TWENTY-ONE

The fall of 1959 was one of the most beautiful in memory. The crisp air smelled of new-mown hay and pinecones sticky with sap, and here and there, as you walked across a meadow or down a sidewalk, downy white milkweed floating on the wind might brush your face. Grass, not as often mowed now as the nights grew colder, bent in the wind under watery sunlight. The town was abuzz. From Friday, October 16, to Sunday the eighteenth Amherst would celebrate its bicentennial, and a program was in preparation, under the chairmanship of Horace W. Hewlett, our friend. The commemoration of Lord Jeffery Amherst, a military hero remembered for slaughtering Indians, would be presented by the eminent historian and loquacious Amherst College professor Henry Steele Commager. Emily Dickinson was to be honored by a panel of the poets Louise Bogan, Richard Wilbur, and Archibald MacLeish. Elderly Millicent Todd Bingham, daughter of the still controversial Mabel Loomis Todd, who edited Emily Dickinson's poems for their first published edition, would be given a reception at the Alumni House, which had an exhibit of the Emily Dickinson Papers given to Amherst College by Mrs. Bingham.

My mother and I had both auditioned for—and been accepted by—the Bicentennial Chorus. The town of Amherst had commissioned Randall Thompson, the American composer and professor of music at Harvard, to set Robert Frost poems to music. Professor Thompson chose seven poems: "The Road Not Taken," "The Pasture," "Come In," "The Telephone," "A Girl's Garden," "Stopping by Woods on a Snowy Evening," and "Choose Something Like a Star," for which he created choral pieces for men's, women's, and mixed chorus accompanied by piano. He called his composition *Frostiana*.

Rehearsals, led alternately by Mr. Thompson and the pianist Henry Mishkin, professor of music at Amherst, were my first experience of the solace of making collaborative art. My father's unhappiness lived inside me like a stowaway in a moving vessel and fed on my youthful supplies of energy and optimism, undermining me in ways I barely recognized. And yet, as if in open defiance of my father's darkness, my mother and I spent six hours every week soaring above life with our voices, part of what seemed at the time a monumental work of art—if Frost's poetry could be called monumental, and I believed it could—since the music perfectly expressed the poems. In those hours I was outside my troubles.

In early October, Dad had another near miss with drugs. After his last hospitalization, he had immediately gone back to his pills. So, after much coaxing, he voluntarily checked himself into a rehabilitation hospital in Ashfield, Massachusetts. He was therefore absent from our performance.

As the audience shuffled into the auditorium on that Sunday afternoon, my mother and I exchanged anticipatory glances. We were both profoundly stirred.

" *I'm going out to clean the pasture spring . . . ,* '" the chorus sang. I could see Robert Frost in a center seat near the front. His blunted face expressed its usual worn gravity. But I thought he looked hesitant, as if something were about to be asked of him that he might be unable to fulfill. Randall Thompson, a trim white-haired man, conducted us with what I had come to understand was passionate warmth beneath his dignified reserve.

"I'll only stop to rake the leaves away . . ."

The voices floated the words in the air with unadorned melody and Frost's own rhythm.

"(And wait to watch the water clear, I may)
I shan't be gone long.—You come too."

Something new came over Frost's demeanor: a gentle surprise, a softening of the muscles around his eyes.

"Stopping by Woods on a Snowy Evening" was scored for men's voices. The piano rolled large chords around the words, and the pace was largo in continuous forward motion. "A Girl's Garden," for women, naturally, was sprightly and amusing in a countrified way.

All too soon we came to the last poem, in which the fullness, layered harmonies, and startling silences of the full chorus seemed, to my young sensibility, of nearly unearthly quality.

"O Star (the fairest one in sight),
We grant your loftiness the right
To some obscurity of cloud—
It will not do to say of night,
Since dark is what brings out your light.
Some mystery becomes the proud.
But to be wholly taciturn

In your reserve is not allowed.
Say something to us we can learn
By heart and when alone repeat.
Say something! And it says, 'I burn.'
But say with what degree of heat.
Talk Fahrenheit, talk Centigrade.
Use language we can comprehend.
Tell us what elements you blend.
It gives us strangely little aid,
But does tell something in the end.
And steadfast as Keats' Eremite,
Not even stooping from its sphere,
It asks a little of us here.
It asks of us a certain height,
So when at times the mob is swayed
To carry praise or blame too far,
We may choose something like a star
To stay our minds on and be staid."

In the hubbub of applause I could see Frost getting to his feet with difficulty. Eventually the sounds fell away, and all eyes were turned to the tall, round-shouldered old man. He was crying. He couldn't speak; he was overcome. But then he found what he wanted to say: "Sing that again!" And we sang his star poem one more time.

THE HOUSE THAT GREETED US, as Mom helped Grampy up the walk and the boys walked on ahead, was cold and dark. Buddy switched on all the lights; Grampy turned up the heat. I went to the piano with the printed handwritten score each of us had been given by Randall Thompson. I'd been practicing the piano part. I kept my hands close to the keys, palms almost touching the ivory, as I played Thompson's chords. I didn't want to break the spell. I would fix my life on the star that would stay my mind.

Ten days later Mom received one of those telephone calls that pushed her down into the nearest seat. It was the hospital in Ashfield, and the woman was irate. A nurse had found Dad standing on a chair, his hands reaching up high into a crevice behind a pipe. The nurse knew instantly that Dad was groping for drugs he had hidden up there. With Mom's desperate permission they packed him into an ambulance and sent him to the Northampton State Hospital—what the locals called the loony bin, the last refuge for the mentally ill.

Drained, angry, Mom wouldn't go see Dad at first. It was almost as if he were a criminal who had ended up in jail after ample chances had been given. She was being called regularly now to pick up Grampy in town bars. It took her several weeks before she could face seeing her husband in the state institution. So I called our minister, Mr. Greene, who immediately agreed to take me to see Dad. I didn't tell Mom.

We sat together in a room with worn chairs and grim walls that had been painted with the notion that yellow was cheerful. But the color was faded and anemic; the windows were grimy with dust. Dad was led out to us. His legs looked like pipe cleaners inside his tweed pants. His eyes were glazed, his spirit all but broken. There seemed to be nothing left in him. He could barely look at us. His voice was soft. Did he say, "It's okay, Les, don't worry"? I think he did. What he did not say was "I'm miserable, get me out of here." He was like a man who had lost all hope of reprieve. The three of us were gripped with numbness.

In the car going home with Mr. Greene, I cried lightly as I looked out the window. The gentle reverend tried to comfort me with hopeful scenarios. He said all was not lost. It was a dark, misty afternoon. The trees had no leaves. The world was desolate.

CHAPTER TWENTY-TWO

It was time to concentrate on colleges. I thought perhaps Bennington, or—and this seemed a leap because it was associated in my mind more with urban sophistication than New England stodginess—Vassar. In those years, what were called the Seven Sisters—Bryn Mawr, Radcliffe, Smith, Mount Holyoke, Pembroke (now merged with Brown), Wellesley, and Vassar—were the most competitive women's colleges. I had my job at the biology department, still sang in the choir, and I took two extra honors courses, one in French, one in music. I thought I was a good candidate. But something began to go wrong.

I would be in a social gathering and find myself with someone I hadn't met. We would put our hands out to shake, the other person would say his or her name, I would open my mouth, and before me was a blankness, a fathomless blankness in which my name was nowhere to be found. I would understand from the power of the engulfing void that all personal information was irretrievable. This included where I lived, the names of others in my family, where my town and state were situated in relation to other towns and states, how long I had been upon this earth, where I went to school. It was all gone. I would stutter and blush, and the other person would either rush in to fill the breach or, more often than not, smile in confusion and superiority and move away. This blankness was preceded by a flash of extreme self-consciousness. What if I can't remember my name? I would ask myself in the time it takes to flip a light switch. In less dramatic circumstances I would be in the midst of a conversation and reach for the word—say, "thrifty" (I could never get that one) or "precious" or "environment"—and like a person who has had a stroke, I would find ways to come around the concept, although I couldn't get astride the precise word. It was the opposite of language carrying thought. My thoughts were slipping, raftless, down a stream of inarticulateness while I reached for anything on the shore to pull me to solid ground.

My Bennington interview was a case in point.

"What courses are you taking?"

"Well, English, and . . . umm . . ."

Long silence.

"I imagine you must be taking history."

"Yes, history, and . . ."

I perspired through a cotton blouse and the gray wool jacket of a suit. A dark stain seeped from my armpit down to my waist.

"I know there are other courses. I don't know why I can't remember them. I'm sorry."

I didn't get into Bennington. The interviewer must have found something to recommend this preposterously tongue-tied girl, however, because I wasn't turned down altogether. I was wait-listed.

Dad stayed in the state hospital for only a little over a month. He came home at the beginning of December. Ordinarily, I would have told him about my Bennington interview. He would buck me up, make me laugh, tell me that the world was full of random indignities that meant nothing. But I didn't tell him. He was too broken.

To Mom's dismay, he was now unable to sleep without a lamp on. He was afraid of the dark. One doctor thought he was afraid of something *in* the dark.

A reporter from Grampy's old paper, the *Newark Evening News*, arrived on our doorstep for an interview. Grampy had put on his red corduroy vest and wild tie in preparation. The two men sat by the fire in Grampy's study. I could hear Grampy talking loudly and the reporter laughing. Dad didn't make an appearance, although his first job was on that same paper.

I overheard what he was saying: "My goodness, yes indeed, I did write a few adventures for boys before I worked for Mr. Stratemeyer. And they weren't half bad, if I do say so myself. One about salt was my particular favorite."

I hadn't read any of those books, although we had them on our shelves. I should read them, I told myself, if only to understand him better.

Dad came down for dinner and managed well. Grampy was florid-faced and high-spirited, buoyed by the interview. I had noticed during a visit to his room that he had a stash of Four Roses whiskey. His closet door was open and I spied the bottles inside, on the floor by his shoes. So he had progressed from sherry, as I'd suspected.

"I told that young man Uncle Wiggily would have managed that spaceflight just as well as Sam."

A week or so earlier, a chimpanzee named Sam, wearing a space suit, had been propelled out of the earth's atmosphere in a spaceship and returned the same day by parachute-guided capsule. Sam, who had undergone training for his mission, was the first being sent into space from the earth, proving that it might someday be safe to send humans. Pictures of Sam in his space suit, his narrow, frightened eyes peering out of his headgear, had captivated all of us. Buddy, who had cut out a photo and put it up in his room, said logically that Sam was actually a real hero, whereas Uncle Wiggily was make-believe.

"You're right, Bud," Grampy said doubtfully. The man is deluded, I thought. We've had enough pretending in this family. I gave Buddy a wide smile to show I agreed with him.

Dad said he wanted to get to New York to see a play called *Five Finger Exercise*, the first stage play of a young Englishman named Peter Shaffer.

"It got stupendous reviews."

"Not that that means anything, Roger," Mom said quickly.

"No."

"You can't trust reviewers."

"What's the play about, Dad?" I asked.

"It takes place over a weekend in the English countryside. A young German tutor arrives to teach the schoolgirl daughter. There's a mother and father and a university-age son. They're all at each other's throats, as far as I can gather, but they put up a good front, so the German tutor doesn't know what's really going on. They appear to him the perfect English family. Anyway, with him as catalyst, they pretty much fall on each other. The tutor is shattered; a lot of points are made about class and art and money. The university son is undermined by a selfish and suffocating mother." He took a small bite of food, which made him shiver. "It's apparently a stunning piece of ensemble acting."

"Jessica Tandy, isn't it?" Mom asked.

"Jessica Tandy, Brian Bedford, Juliet Mills as the young girl, Michael somebody—Michael Bryant, I think, as the German tutor, John Gielgud directing . . . I want to see it. I may go next week," he added with a note of defiance.

"But next week is Christmas."

"Oh yes, well, soon after." The long speech seemed to have exhausted him. He was visibly shrinking.

"What time is Ed Sullivan?" he asked.

"Eight o'clock," I said. "And Alfred Hitchcock is on tonight, too."

"Good. I'll be down in time for Sullivan."

"We'll take care of the dishes," said Mom, signaling that it was all right for him to go upstairs. She didn't seem to miss having our former cook, Jean. Mom's life had become much more isolated because of Dad's illness and she never liked being idle, so she put all her energy into maintaining the household.

I went to sleep that night happier than I'd been in months. Perhaps I'd been wrong about an inexorable downward slide. He was great tonight! Almost his old self. I decided to tell him tomorrow about my Bennington interview and that I had another coming up at Vassar. He could give me tips. I just had to keep my wits about me. Perhaps I really had my father back. It had been a long road . . . I nestled down in the covers. I said the Lord's Prayer silently. It always sent me immediately to sleep.

I was startled awake by a loud bang. After the bang came moaning. I arrived at the bathroom at the same moment as Mom. Dad was crumpled on the floor, his face sideways on the tile, with the medicine cabinet—formerly attached to the wall above the sink—half on top of him, pill bottles rolling on the floor, Q-tips, toothpaste, and other supplies scattered around.

"Help me up!"

"Go, Les," Mom said.

"I can help you, Mom."

"Goddamn it, help me up!"

Mom and I lifted the metal cabinet off him, then reached under his arms and pulled him up. His legs were rubber; he couldn't stand.

"Come on, Dad."

"Here you go, Roger."

We practically dragged him the short distance into his bed. Mom pulled the covers up under his chin.

"I'm sorry," came a muffled voice. "Forgive me."

"Pills," my mother practically spat at him with bitter disgust. "Pills."

THE NEXT DAY, Mom was in a frenzy. She vacuumed downstairs while she practiced the aria she was currently studying. Her voice had some extra breath in it but was otherwise clear. In the afternoon she took apples out of the freezer and banged them with a hammer to separate the slices. Grampy peeked into the kitchen.

"What's the row, Mabs?"

"Just cooking."

"They'll thaw after a spell."

"Don't have time."

Grampy came back with his coat on, at which point Mom burst into tears.

"Please don't go into town, Grampy."

He looked deflated. "I'll be back lickity-split. Just a few errands, you know."

"No. Not today. Not today."

Slowly he removed his coat and shuffled off. He got his whittling stick and knife and sat in his big chair.

I went to the piano and began to play a Bach fugue. I pushed my fingers into the keys so hard that it felt as if I were making depressions in the ivory. Even though I played the notes as written, for the first time I had the impression that I was forcing the themes to crash into each other as my playing got louder and harsher. I'd never known how percussive the piece could sound. I had a glimmer of the feeling I'd had when I drove the car blindly that day on the Cape. I drove the themes on. I saw cliffs before me that I had to ram through.

The next thing I knew, Dad was standing there with tears in his eyes.

"Please stop, Les. Please stop."

"My teacher says I should practice." I didn't stop.

"But please don't play that way."

Then I knew that I was playing the piece against him, to vanquish him.

"I have to practice."

He turned and walked down the living room and away.

I played on. I had to. I couldn't stop.

CHAPTER TWENTY-THREE

I'll tell you a story," my mother began.

There was a man upstairs, fixing the cabinet. We were in the living room, decorating the smallest tree we'd ever had for Christmas. Lately I had been asking her a lot of questions about my grandparents. I was trying to untangle the threads that ran through their lives and still, in some ineffable way, entwined us. I asked her how Grampy had been such a devoted husband to Granny. How could he continue to love her?

"Well . . . ," she began in all seriousness, but then she started to laugh. "I think you're old enough to hear this."

"Of course I am!" Whatever it was, I wanted to hear.

"One day, when your father was a young man still living at home, he heard his mother shriek 'Howard? Howard? What *is* this?' She was waving a telegram addressed to Grampy. And do you know what it said?" At this, she broke up laughing. "It said, 'Don't come Thursdays anymore.' "

And from that moment, when I realized that Grampy had a life apart, besides the imagined universe in his head, and that he knew how to keep himself happy, I felt much better about him. He wasn't a beaten-down husband after all. He was a man who knew how to manage his life with the least stress and the most joy.

After a while, I asked her if she would tell me something about Granny and Dad—anything that would shed light on her attitude toward him. And so she obliged.

"When your father and I were engaged, we went to a house on the shore in Connecticut with my family. It was the end of the month, and we were closing up the house—Doris, Joe, Nana, Grandad [Mom's sister, brother-in-law, and parents]. Your father and I were going to go to Martha's Vineyard with Nana as chaperone. The morning we were leaving, there was a knock on the door. It was a bellboy from a nearby hotel. He had brought a telegram for Roger. Roger said, 'I'm not going to open it. It's from my mother.' I didn't believe him. Even if it was from his mother, why would she send a telegram unless it was important? Telegrams were serious messages. I said, 'You must open it! It's a telegram!' He refused. He said, 'I'm not going to open it. I know what it says. It's raining. She's going to tell me to take an umbrella.' Of course I didn't believe him. I told him, 'No one would say that in a telegram!' I tore it open. And that's what it was. IT'S RAINING. DON'T FORGET TO WEAR YOUR RUBBERS AND TAKE AN UM-BRELLA. Signed, YOUR MOTHER. This was 1940. He was thirty-nine."

We worked on in silence. There was nothing to say about this stupefying story.

"She would call me up and ask me what socks Roger was wearing. I would say I didn't know. 'Are they the lisle ones?' 'Yes,' I would say, just to please her. 'He's wearing the lisle ones today.' 'He mustn't wear the lisle! It's too cold for the lisle!' she'd say."

"What do you think it was all about?"

She shook her head. Then she picked up the blue glass swan that she'd had since she was a child. She hung it on a branch, but the tree was so skimpy and limp that the weight of the glass bent the branch precipitously. With a sigh she removed the swan and held it in her hand.

"I'll tell you what I think," she said almost in a whisper. "I think when she was alive, Roger could fight her. He could defy her low expectations of him. He could be a man, he could write successfully, he could be a husband and father. She never thought he could do or be anything. But when she died and he didn't have her to fight anymore, she became a ghost inside him, she inhabited him, she took him over. She won."

"Do you really think that, Mom?"

"Yes, I do."

"But it can't be as simple as that."

"You think that's simple?"

"Well, I mean . . . there's got to be more to it."

"I've just told you what I think. There it is."

"But surely there's—you make it sound irreversible."

"No, no, I don't mean that, Les. He could get better. I have to believe that. But life's not all beer and skittles."

As she said that, her voice cracked. It was an English saying her parents used when they were trying to tell her that life was hard.

THE LONG WINTER gradually turned into a wet spring, but we hardly noticed, so disoriented were we by the ceaseless atmosphere of emergency in our house. One of the most painful changes taking place was my mother's increasing loneliness. It was no longer possible to have anyone come to the house. In The Dell they used to entertain, but now, at Amity Street, with my father so ill and my grandfather's drinking becoming more and more of a problem, with my mother drained and frightened and our finances stretched to the limit, no one ever came over. Eventually, no one even called.

Robert Frost stopped Mom one day in town and asked when we were going to invite him over again. Mom made a graceful excuse, went home, and asked the two men, but both of them said they didn't feel up to receiving him. The only friends my mother saw now were the Hewletts, and they never ceased to be a solace to her.

Dad's addiction was in full flower. Ambulances at our house were no longer rare occurrences. I hardly dared think what the neighbors said about us. On one fantastic occasion we had two ambulances on the same day. In the morning Dad was taken away in another near coma, and in the late afternoon Grampy, inebriated, fell in the bathroom. By that evening, both Dad and Grampy were in Cooley Dickinson Hospital. Late at night, when my mother returned from the hospital, she broke down sobbing, saying that was the worst day of her life.

The question of where Dad got his drugs was always in the air. Local doctors, finally aware of his dependency, had stopped prescribing them. There was a man, however, who worked at College Drug, a very fat man, the one who was rude to my brothers and me, and it might have been he, I believe, who supplied my father. I remember this man in his huge white coat, saying to me crossly, "Your father is a very sensitive, special man. See you are kind to him and don't cause him any trouble." I had no idea what he was talking about—just as Brooks had been mystified as a little boy when Granny had said something similar. Years later, I realized that this man must have been at least a little in awe of my father, and might have counted it his privilege to give Dad whatever he needed to keep him going, even if it meant breaking the law. I think also that Dad had doctors in other places—including New York City—who wrote him prescriptions. There were so few medications available to fight depression, and it was still an era when doctors were sensitive to issues of privacy, so they were less likely to probe patients about addiction.

Brooks and Bud, under unmanageable stress, were now nearly failing in school, although Brooks had his music, which steadied him. Very early one Saturday morning Brooks took his guitar, his bullwhip (I don't know where this hobby came from, but he'd gotten proficient at cracking it), and a little money, and he set off for New York. He was running away. Standing outside, watching his breath in the freezing air, he had second thoughts. Not only about the idea, at fifteen, of handling life on his own, but also about the pain his abandonment would cause his wounded father. He decided he couldn't live with that guilt. So he went back home, walked into Dad's room, and said they needed to talk. Years later, Brooks told me that Dad could barely rouse himself from his torpor to pay attention to his son. "I realized," Brooks said, "that Dad just didn't have his heart in what was going on around him and had no creative resources to expend on me. Those hours that morning gave me some distance. They also deadened me some, too."

As for me, I was accepted at Vassar. When the letter came, Dad was in the study, working on his comedy. How could he be working on a comedy in his state? Why did he turn away from writing about what he knew—the despair, the loneliness? I interrupted him with my news. He rose from his chair and engulfed me in a hug.

"I've always believed in you, Les."

His cheek was rough against my own; I gulped hard to hold back tears. We both knew I was beginning my journey away from the family.

SOON AFTER THIS CONVERSATION, perhaps because I would be going away and was guiltily counting the days, I picked up one of those Howard Garis books I'd always meant to read. It was called *The White Crystals*, published in 1904 by Little, Brown. I'd never even opened its cover before. Settling into a chair on the porch, warm spring air wafting pleasantly over me, I began to read:

To My Son Roger this book is affectionately dedicated.

Dad would have been three years old in 1904, and two years old during the time his father was writing it.

I read on:

Dr. Glasby looked over the rims of his spectacles at the boy before him. Then he glanced at Mr. Anderson, cleared his throat with a loud "ahem" that made Roger start, and said, very ponderously:

"Um!"

"Well?" asked Mr. Anderson, a little anxious tone coming into his voice, "what's the verdict, doctor?"

"Um!" said the physician again. "Nothing very serious, Mr. Anderson. Roger, here, is a little run down, that's all. He's been studying too hard, his eyes are a trifle weak, muscles flabby, and his blood hasn't enough of the good red stuff in it. In short, he must live out of doors for a year or so, and then I'll guarantee he will come back with red cheeks and a pair of arms that will make you proud of him. Eh, Roger?" and Dr. Glasby pinched the rather small and soft biceps of the boy, smiling the while, good naturedly.

Strange! He's named the character after his real son, who was a healthy toddler, and given him what was called in those years "a nervous ailment." Astounded, I continued:

"No disease, then, doctor?" from Mr. Anderson.

"Nothing, my dear sir, except a general poor condition of the system."

*"Don't he need medicine, a tonic, or something? His mother
and I are quite worried about him."*

*"Not a drop of medicine for this patient," exclaimed Dr.
Glasby. "Fresh air, fresh country air, and more air. That's all."*

*The physician turned aside to replace the apparatus he had
used; the stethoscope, with which he had listened to the beating of
Roger's heart, the eye-testing mirrors and lights, and the lung-
cylinder, into which the boy had blown more feebly than Dr.
Glasby had liked to see.*

I couldn't help thinking about Dad's stay in the hospital a few
months ago, when the doctors tested him for every ailment known
to them and came up empty.

*Roger Anderson was just past his fifteenth year, rather small for
his age, and not nearly as strong and sturdy as his parents
wished he was. Lately his eyes had been troubling him, and he
had complained of frequent headaches. He was in his first season
at high school, and, what with taking up Latin and algebra, two
new worlds of study for the boy, he had been rather closely applied to his books at night. As he was ambitious he threw himself
into the vim of learning with an energy that was pleasing to his
parents and teachers, though it had a bad effect on his health.
For, after a few weeks of school, it was noticed that he was failing in energy. There were many days when, in spite of his desire,
he felt disinclined to go to his classes, and he was troubled with
dizziness. In short he seemed in such poor shape that Mr. Anderson determined on a visit to Dr. Glasby, the old family
physician.*

Headaches, dizziness, failing energy—all this visited upon
Roger, the fifteen-year-old protagonist with the same name as

Howard's two-year-old son, his son who would one day suffer all these symptoms to a crippling degree. I hardly knew where to start thinking about this puzzle. Perhaps Howard had been inspired by the symptoms of his neurotic wife, the mother who would be both the genetic forerunner and emotional catalyst for her son's lifelong illness.

Mr. and Mrs. Anderson decide to send their son Roger to "Uncle Bert," who had a farm in Cardiff, New York. Incredibly, when Dad had his first nervous breakdown at age thirty, his father insisted on Dr. Glasby's cure: " 'Not a drop of medicine for this patient,' exclaimed Dr. Glasby. 'Fresh air, fresh country air, and more air. That's all.' " Prevailing over his son's plan to enter a White Plains psychiatric hospital, Grampy sent him to the same area of upstate New York as where his real-life uncle Bert had a farm. Dad must have been too drained by his illness to go against his father's wishes. I'd heard about this "fresh-air cure" from my mother, and apparently it did some good in the short run, although it didn't come close to addressing his underlying difficulties. Grampy . . . Glasby . . . the words looked almost the same, as if one were the code version of the other. I had to put the book down because I began to tremble violently. I didn't understand. I couldn't understand. I resisted devolving into magical thinking. Of course Grampy hadn't *caused* his son's condition by writing about it before it happened. But somehow, when he was a thirty-year-old father with a toddler son, he wrote himself into a future when his son would have a nervous breakdown at the same age the father was now and be sent to the country instead of a hospital. And then, when Dad really did go to mental hospitals, when he went to McLean and Riggs, Mom told Grampy that Dad had gone for a "health cure." I remember hearing Mom say that to Grampy in the downstairs hall and wondering why she couldn't tell him the truth.

All those years ago, had Grampy seen something in his baby

son? Almost nothing is created out of whole cloth. Was there something about the child that suggested to his father a hypersensitive disposition? How does a man discern a malady coiled and hidden inside a beloved child, prepared to spring decades hence?

He also had the example of Lilian's headaches, naps, and medicines. But even she wasn't so visibly depressed in those years. She was writing full-time and had a vibrant life outside her home, fighting for women's and children's rights. Perhaps Howard had an unconscious intuition that Lilian's nascent depressive hysteria would undermine their son's health.

I was losing my place in time. I saw Grampy as if before me, a young man with a baby, his life sweet with promise, his conviction stout, conceiving an idea constructed from information provided from thirty years on, and I pictured the old man in our house now, confused by his son's bizarre symptoms, which he wrote in rough form fifty-six years ago.

I picked up the book again. Hours later I had lived through Roger's adventures on Uncle Bert's farm. Of course he became a hero and saved the farm from being lost to the bank. He discovered a salt mine—the white crystals of the title—on Uncle Bert's property. It was a ripping adventure story, full of local incident—a mountain lion in the woods, a race on homemade toboggans, Onondaga Indians nearby, buggies hitched to faithful horses—but most important, Roger came home strong and rugged, ready for anything life could throw at him. Here was the dream Grampy had for all boys, a dream he would apply to his own son in a situation where neither the method nor the hoped-for result was realistic. Well, I thought, realism has never been this family's strong suit. Only recently Grampy had said that Uncle Wiggily would have done as well in space as Sam the chimp, and when he said it, I had the disquieting impression that he half believed his assertion. Uncle Wiggily was real; mental illness was a chimera.

I had to get out of Amherst to find solid ground. I thought of my bedroom wallpaper at The Dell, with its lines never completing a figure but wandering across space to begin another shape.

Brooks finally failed at school. It was decided he would enter Tabor Academy in Marion, Massachusetts. They would help him pick up his ninth-grade work so he didn't fall further behind. Both of us would be leaving. Buddy would be the only child at home.

In the next weeks there was anxious talk about how to pay for these schools. I had been awarded some financial aid, but there would be a shortfall. Mom said she'd get a job. Dad told her she couldn't, she was needed too much at home. We asked my father's sister, Cleo, for help with my tuition, but although she could easily afford it, she turned us down. However, she offered $300 if I went to the University of Massachusetts. Her message was that I was overreaching. Girls with no money had no business pursuing a Seven Sisters school. I was reminded of Granny's telling Dad that no professional actress would want to work with the likes of him.

However they did it, my parents packed Brooks and me off in the fall. As I stood on the steps of Lathrop House at Vassar and waved goodbye to their departing car, I thought, *I'm free. I'm finally free.*

CHAPTER TWENTY-FOUR

I was seventeen when I began my first year at college, unnaturally weary for my age, and naive about how easy it would be to escape from my family. Along with the voluptuous pleasure of privacy came an almost unbearable guilt at fleeing the field of battle.

Once I started living at school, I viewed my father in glimpses, like dots of light on water that moved to its own current when I could not see it. I spoke to my family on the phone, although weeks would go by when Dad was "unavailable." The first Thanksgiving, I brought home a new friend, Mary Peacock, who lived in Florida. Dad must have kept his drug taking to a minimum, because his walk and speech were fine. Grampy was delighted to have a visitor, and he stayed reasonably sober. We seemed like a normal family, even an enviable one, with our obvious closeness, Dad's worldly courtesies, and Grampy's boisterous humor. Although Dad was still painfully thin, he seemed to have put on a little weight. His hair was almost entirely gray, but his mustache was still blond. I asked him what he was reading currently, and he said Yeats, but since I hadn't read any and I wanted to spend time with Mary, we didn't discuss it further.

After Christmas, the next time I saw Dad was that spring, when he organized a big celebration for his father's eighty-eighth birthday. All the children of Amherst were invited, and an enormous crowd of them showed up. *Look* magazine covered it and ran a full-page photo of Grampy standing in the midst of the children, looking down at them as he told stories. With his beak nose, his furrowed skin, and his eyes encircled with dark rings, he resembled a great bird bending over its nest. How tired he seemed! His voice had lost much of its strength. Dad was charming to those who dropped off their children, some parents staying for the afternoon. I flirted with the dark-haired young *Look* photographer, Sam Caston (who later was one of the first journalists killed in Vietnam). Dad was holding his own in the midst of this party, in fact appearing to take strength from it.

In the summers I found jobs in New York City or on Cape Cod, creating a life where I was at home for barely a few days between school years. I supported myself by temping in offices and waitressing and I tried to be happy, but I couldn't shake a sensation of doom that followed me wherever I went. I talked to both my parents over the phone a great deal. One call from my father, in my sophomore year, stands out in my memory. He was excited in a way I hadn't heard him in years—actually since my childhood. "Les," he said. "There's a play in New York you must see. I don't care how you do it, but you *must* get yourself into New York to see this play. There has never been anything like it. Never. It's the most original play I've ever seen. It's by a young man named Arthur Kopit, and it has the most incredible title: *Oh Dad, Poor Dad, Mamma's Hung You in the Closet and I'm Feelin' So Sad.* Isn't that remarkable? Have you ever heard anything like that? It's brilliant! You *must* see it! It redefines playwriting. I could never write anything like it."

And when he said that last part about not being able to write like that, he didn't sound despairing. On the contrary, he was flying with enthusiasm. He had never told me to go see something in New York before, and I knew I would disappoint him terribly if I didn't make it happen.

So, with my friend Dorothy Tod, I went into New York to see the play. We could only get standing-room tickets. It starred Jo Van Fleet in the role of Madame Rosepettle, a hilariously exaggerated devouring mother, Austin Pendleton as her stuttering, frightened son, and Barbara Harris as the enticing young woman who sets the action into riotous motion. It was the funniest play I'd ever seen. And Dad was right; it was also the most surprising. There *hadn't* been anything like it. Unlike well-made realistic plays, the narrative made sense only in an intuitive, highly comic, absurd universe. The last line, delivered by Madame Rosepettle in high dudgeon, was emblematic of the whole piece: "As a mother to a son, I ask you, what is the meaning of this?"

My conversation with Dad later was different from our last one. "I'm in a foul state," he said, by way of excusing the extreme hoarseness of his voice.

"I went to see the play you told me about."

"Oh, great, Les. What did you think?"

"It's everything you said it was. And more."

"It's very well done from a professional angle," he said as if by rote.

"It's about a nightmarish mother—the worst I could imagine. You didn't tell me that. The mother is mythically destructive."

He didn't say anything.

"Dad?"

"I'm here. I have to get off now, Les."

"I'm glad you told me to see it. Thanks for getting me to go. I'll never forget it."

"I won't either, Les. I'm so pleased you saw it."

"So I wanted to thank you, Dad."

"Okay. Goodbye, dear."

"Bye, Dad."

"THE MOST AMAZING THING happened to Grampy," Mom said over the phone. I was in my room at college. "I've got to tell you about it. You just won't believe it."

Grampy had been taken to the hospital a few days before, suffering from dizzy spells. "Sadly, they discovered that he has leukemia."

"Oh, Mom . . ."

"Don't say anything, Les. Wait until you hear what I have to tell you." She gave me time to settle down, then continued her story. He was given a blood transfusion, but within forty-eight hours he had begun to "fade." A nurse called the house saying he was "going" and they should hurry over. They didn't expect him to last long.

"Oh, Les, you should have seen him when we walked in. He looked as if he had already gone, he was so pale, the dear man. We each took a hand. It was heartbreaking. He barely knew we were there. And then—well, you just won't believe it."

Two nurses came into the room, each carrying a large postal bag. They greeted Grampy cheerfully, telling him that they had something for him. They untied the bags, and hundreds of letters tumbled out. "They're all for you, Mr. Garis," one nurse said. "They're from children." As they began to read the letters—"Please get well soon, Uncle Wiggily, from your biggest fan" was the general message—Grampy opened his eyes and turned toward the nurses. They held up a crayon drawing of a rabbit under a yellow sun, another of a train with animals, another of Uncle Wiggily's airship, all with get-well messages written in the labored scrawl of childhood.

"For me?" Grampy asked incredulously. "Those are all for *me?*"

A little while later he was sitting up, with the letters strewn over his bedclothes, shaking his head, chuckling, exclaiming in his weak voice.

Teachers in the Amherst elementary schools had told their classes that Howard Garis was in the hospital. It must have been a school project to write all those letters, but neither teachers nor children could have imagined what a miraculous effect their warm-hearted wishes would have—they gave him seven more months of life.

CHAPTER TWENTY-FIVE

After assiduously avoiding home for the past two years, I spent a month there in the fall of 1962, during my third year of college. As a matter of fact, I had a mini-breakdown. One Saturday morning in the living room of my dormitory I broke into hysterics. Something just crashed in me, but I had been increasingly unstable. It felt as if I were being eaten alive by self-loathing and guilt. In class I would double over with a burning in my gut, as if I were being destroyed from within. It was painful—like the mythic fires of hell. My concentration and memory were barely functional. I might, if I'd been more aware, have thought that I had caught the family illness, and perhaps I had. But I was spinning into space, propelled into a void that contained no connections to anything that had happened before. Then one bright Saturday, entering my dorm after a walk, the view before me—a long sitting room with couches, chairs, a piano—exploded before my eyes. The furniture flew in all directions, and I began to scream and couldn't stop.

I don't remember anything after that until I was being driven home by my parents. I kept crying, "We're going to crash!" They assured me we were safe, and I thought, Really? I'm really safe? My parents will take away the pain?

At home they put me to bed, where I stayed for weeks. My mother was unfailingly soothing to me. I can't imagine how it must have frightened her to watch yet another family member go under, if only temporarily. Gradually I began to feel strong again; whatever had hold of me loosened its grip and let go.

As I rested and read, I had a good look at the entrenched melancholy that pervaded Dad's life. His days divided themselves into quadrants of pain: bearable, less bearable, unbearable, semiconscious. Early in the night, wide awake, it started all over again. He told me he slept not at all, although that was hardly credible since he spent so much time in bed. He must have dozed now and then. I spent hours by his bedside or in the living room talking with him. Hearing about my life in college distracted him from himself. While at home I was supposed to be reading Aristotle's *Poetics* for school, but when I picked it up after much procrastination, I found that I had already underlined and annotated it before I left school. Dad and I had a sour laugh over that. We talked about music. He was listening to a lot of Brahms, especially the Second Piano Concerto, which he told me had an "unearthly beauty."

As before, when I was a child, I felt that he and I were kindred spirits. I suppose, aside from something ineffable that connects people who have the same DNA, there was a sense of a palpable dream before him that he was still hoping to enter. I, too, had hovering about me a secret presentiment of a glowing future, so that together we were both inside our collective nimbus. Even after all he'd been through, he still had hopes that he would write something that would change his life.

One time when he was particularly bad and still in bed at midday, I sat by him in his darkened room, the shades pulled down because he had a "splitting" headache. He had been crying. In an effort to pull him out of the moment, I asked him how his work was going. I will never forget his answer, spoken with his customary formality, even in that state.

"I have fallen prey to the incubus which attacks me in unguarded moments and holds my whole unworthiness up for me to see."

I offered the appropriate confidence-boosting bromide, but he put up a shaking hand to stop my talking.

"I know the cure, or the weapon, which defeats this monster: it is to deny the unworthiness, especially if one can establish an act which restores self-confidence."

It was then that I understood how he was able to haul himself to his writing desk day after day. He was trying to save his life.

"Just for this little moment I am stumbling," he said. "I'll find the handrail shortly."

I said again, as I had so many times in the past, that he was a good writer and would find his way.

"I'll go on as soon as the Devil releases me. I think that will not be long."

MOM WAS AS DESPERATE as Dad was sad. Her domestic stratagems were failing to bring her husband back to health. In addition, our money troubles were worse than ever. We were managing on the proceeds of the Uncle Wiggily Game and a trickling of royalties. Mom had taken the only job she could find: canvassing houses for the animal census. She was tiny, and the dogs were large. It was a frightening job.

One day she called me very softly from somewhere in the house. Her voice was so quiet that at first I didn't recognize the sound as my name. When I did realize that she was calling me, I heard no alarm in her voice, only an eerie lifelessness.

I found her standing on the stairs, halfway down, one foot on a lower step than the other, her hand on the banister. She was absolutely still in that position.

"Les," she said, her lips barely moving, her face expressionless. "I can't move. Literally. I can't move."

I went to her side and put my hand on her back to ease her forward. She didn't budge.

"I need to go out. I have to get to my job. But I can't unbend my legs," she whispered. "The knees, they won't move."

Here she was, frozen on the middle of the stairs. After a while I was able to help her sit on a step. Slowly she worked on her legs, bending and unbending them. At last I got her down to a chair in the living room.

"I felt so odd when I got up. I didn't know how to get dressed. I didn't think I could do it. Then I told myself to put on my stockings, just put my feet in the toes and pull them up, then my sweater. I talked to myself all the while, telling myself what to do. Then I started to walk downstairs—and then—I couldn't take another step. I was paralyzed."

Her face looked wiped clean of all emotion.

"I can't go back to that job."

"No, you mustn't. I'll call for you."

"Would you?"

"Of course."

I did, and Mom never went back to counting animals.

SINCE I HAD BEGUN COLLEGE three years ago, Buddy had changed. No longer the bright little boy bursting with energy, he was now a withdrawn adolescent. There was something hidden about his expression, and he didn't smile much. Always precocious with language, he had a mature articulateness, as if he were already a man.

He told me that he had tried to convince Dad to write some junk to make living expenses so he could work on his "great opus" without pressure. "I even suggested a name, 'The Right Hand of God.' He was charmed with the suggestion, but he demurred."

We took a walk one day. "I don't know what Normal is," he said. "I visit other families, trying to learn what their lives are really like, looking for a definition or example of this Normal. I think I see it. But I still don't know what it is." I realized with a pang that he had been asking almost the same question five years earlier when he pored through those old magazines. He was on a search.

"I don't know what normal is either. But it's not necessarily something to be desired."

He shook his head, as if saying no to everything. He had inherited his father's slim build and narrow face. I couldn't bear seeing the effects on him of living at home. He seemed to have lost the joy of childhood. There was a new sternness to the set of his mouth and the cast of his eyes.

"You know," he said, "since you and Brooks have gone away and I'm the only child in the house, the balance has gone haywire between Dad and me. I rely less and less on him, and he relies more and more on me. It's too soon for that. I'm only fourteen."

I put my arm around his shoulder as we walked back up Amity Street from the lower fields. It seemed to give him genuine comfort.

GRAMPY, TOO, had entered a new stage. Six months after his near-death experience, he was weakening visibly, day by day. A truly dreadful moment occurred while I was at home that month. Mom came upon him sitting with his head in his hands. She asked him if he was all right. He shook his head. "What is it?" she asked in alarm. He looked up at her and said a terrible thing: "My whole life has been a failure."

Mom was stunned, shattered. Despite everything, he was the rock in her life. His simplicity and kindness still moved her; she loved him deeply. She protested, telling him he was a great man. He didn't answer her. He never alluded to it again. But the wind had gone out of his sails for good.

I returned to school, changed by my month of "rest." College life took on a serene aspect compared with life at home. Studying was a simple task, solitude was a gift.

CHAPTER TWENTY-SIX

Back in Amherst less than a month later, I was in St. Brigid's Catholic church sitting next to my mother. Brooks and Bud were to my left. Dad was on the other side of Mom, his bony fingers holding his mother's onyx rosary. His face was puffy, like a swollen wave about to break. I looked past my mother's heaving chest (she was doing her best not to cry) at my father's trembling hands clutching the black beads. The priest was saying a high mass for Grampy, who had died a few days earlier, on November 5.

Dad's sister and her husband, Cleo and John Clancy, and their daughter, Carroll, were sitting behind us. The church was packed. Amherst had turned out to say goodbye.

The closed coffin lay on a bier in front of the altar. When the priest said the blessing at the end of the mass, he came down and stood next to the coffin. Breaking tradition—because a high funeral mass has a prescribed form—he looked down toward where my grandfather lay, and he said quietly, "Bless this man who has brought so much joy to so many children." I heard my father gasp.

At the cemetery, when the coffin was lowered into the ground, Dad suddenly lurched forward, losing all control. He fell on the ground, sobbing loudly, "Dad! Dad!" The priest gently helped him up, but the friends and relatives who were gathered were embarrassed. Cleo gave a snort of contempt. "A grown man," I heard her whisper to her husband. "He's sixty-one years old. Disgraceful." I burned with fury at her when I heard those words, although I, too, was embarrassed by Dad's outpouring. There was something wrong with it, but not because it was unseemly. Yes, it was so obviously raw, so unguarded for this most dignified of men. He wouldn't have wanted his intimate cry heard in public if he could have helped it. And we were in New England, after all, a place where public feelings were firmly under control. As people no doubt said to each other when they got home, it was very bad form. But beyond that, it showed a shocking parental dependence in a man of late middle age. Surely he was old enough to stand on his own two feet—so the talk would go that evening around Amherst dinner tables.

LATER, AT OUR HOUSE, amidst family and old friends, Dad seemed recovered but exhausted. Thirty-three-year-old Carroll was red-eyed from the funeral. Before our grandparents had left New Jersey for Amherst, Carroll was a constant visitor to their house on Evergreen Place in East Orange. Granny had taken her to see her first color movie; Grampy took her for afternoon walks in state parks; she adored them both. Having this rare opportunity with Carroll, I questioned her about Granny. What had happened to her celebrated energy? I never saw a whit of that.

It was Carroll's theory that it all started with Granny's gallbladder operation in 1930. She had round-the-clock nurses for a year. "And you know how they afforded that?" she asked, beginning to smile. "Grampy won the Irish Sweepstakes! He won five thousand dollars, which paid for all those nurses!"

"But they already had a lot of money," I said. "Why did they need more?"

Her explanation finally cleared up for me how it was that Grampy's money gave out, even though he had made so much through the years. During the 1920s, Granny had fancied herself a brilliant investor, and without Howard's knowledge—he distrusted financial speculating—she put their money into stocks. Then, in 1929, when the market collapsed, they lost all their money. "Their investment base was wiped out," Carroll explained. Investment base. It was the first time I had heard that phrase, and it opened up worlds.

"But didn't they continue to make money from royalties? Grampy wrote so many more books."

Carroll laughed lightly. "Royalties," she said dismissively. "Royalties were fine, but they lost their real money. The crash was a big factor."

So Granny would have felt responsible for ruining them in the market; then she got sick and almost died; then Grampy won the Irish Sweepstakes. Grampy was always lucky, almost mystically so. And Granny was jealous of his magic. It was that magic, that optimistic sweetness and sense of fun and affection for the ridiculous, that made the public buy his books. Even though Granny always thought she was a better writer, she knew he had something ineffable that made his life a triumph. And now here he goes, against colossal odds, and wins the Irish Sweepstakes. Her rotten luck was followed by his golden touch.

Carroll believed that Granny never recovered from her financial loss and her illness. "That must have been it," Carroll mused. "Because I never saw the activist she had been. When I knew her, she was subdued and mostly stayed home." She didn't mention possible drug addiction. My knowledge of that came later.

"Was Granny unpleasant when you knew her?"

Carroll's answer surprised me. It was a firm no.

"It was horrible for her to come to Amherst," she said.

"What? Why?"

"They had just celebrated their fiftieth wedding anniversary when they had to pack up everything, say goodbye to all their friends, and leave the place they had lived in for their entire married lives. How would you feel?"

Shame is what I felt in that moment.

"They were supporting your family and couldn't afford two households. I helped Granny pack. It was like a death."

Like a death? Maybe to Carroll, surely not to them, I protested silently. Grampy had been happy here at first, hadn't he? But Granny . . . she must have been furious at her son for upending her life in her old age. And yet, I remembered talk about Granny's not wanting to go into a nursing home, and I remembered clearly that Cleo wouldn't consider having her parents live with John and her, and that she once called Mom a saint for taking such good care of Granny. It was all so confusing. Carroll didn't seem puzzled in the least, but I wondered if I would ever understand.

Before the Clancys left for New Jersey, Dad asked Cleo and John into the study, where he announced that his father had sold him all the Uncle Wiggily copyrights for one dollar, and that was because . . . He couldn't finish his sentence. Cleo blew up. "It's not the money, Roger, you know that, but how could you deprive the rest of the family . . ." Mom shut the door, where I'd been discreetly listening. But it was glass, and I could see Cleo's severe, still-handsome face blotchy from emotion, her red lips issuing muffled shouts, her bejeweled hands gesturing. Uncle John stood soberly by, watching Cleo's outburst. Dad put his hand over his face and sank into a chair. Mom spoke to Cleo, who listened with a stony expression. I was certain Mom was reciting all Roger had done for the Uncle Wiggily property. After more argument, Cleo started for the door. I moved away fast. As they were leaving, Carroll took me aside and said she had faith in me. It was kind of her. I think she had taken the measure of Dad's emotional state and wondered if I was in difficulty over it. She gave me a long hug, which actually changed the day for me. A gesture of acceptance from one of the Clancys meant that in some way the family was still together.

When everyone had left and the five of us were alone together, we felt our diminishment. Grampy had lived to be eighty-nine, and he was, at the last, ready to go, but the fact of his permanent loss lay heavily on us that night. Bud went into his grandfather's room and sat in the big red chair. It was the same chair I remembered seeing him in when he was a small child at The Dell. He used to stay there for hours, sitting forward so his knees reached the edge of the seat, swinging his legs, listening to Grampy talk to him. Tonight it was hard to find that little boy in him.

Brooks was unnaturally quiet, as if stunned into silence. Mom and Dad moved through the evening talking of practical matters, and there was a palpable tenderness between them. I saw, as I had often seen before, that theirs was a great love.

That night I slept soundly, but awoke at first light thinking about the Salinger story "Uncle Wiggily in Connecticut," remembering its evocation of yearning for lost innocence and thinking about how the best part of my grandfather was embodied in the innocence of his childlike imagination—a state of mind under constant assault in recent years by the realities of his life. And then, in a haze of Salinger and memory, the years of Grampy's drinking and his despair over his son began to fall away in my mind, replaced by the robust fabulist who spread delight among us.

I was also in possession, during that dawn hour, of another, even more comforting thought: Maybe Grampy's death will have a healing effect on Dad. Perhaps what he needed was to be the senior man in his household, and now, at last, he will be all right.

We were in for a change; we just didn't know what form it would take.

The evening of the day Brooks went back to Tabor Academy, after the funeral, they showed a movie in the recreation hall. Brooks sat down with friends, but he began to feel strange. He fainted. They carried him out. When he came to, he insisted that he was all right. Which was true, in the relative way that our family was—for now—all right.

CHAPTER TWENTY-SEVEN

During my last year of college, Brooks did so poorly at Tabor that Mom found a school for him in Switzerland. But at Christmas he told us he wouldn't be allowed back there, because he had spent more time with a family of Scottish musicians in town than on campus. He played his guitar with them and memorized "The Cremation of Sam McGee," a melodramatic poem about the Yukon by Robert Service. But, as in a lucid nightmare, where you know you're in a dream but you can't wake up, his absence from class caught up with him. When ordered by the headmaster to choose between the school and the musicians, he refused and was expelled. Dad was livid. Brooks was in despair. After a brief interim of attending Amherst High School, he went back to Tabor and did much better. Being alone in Europe had given him confidence; an American prep school no longer seemed so daunting.

DAD, NOW THE SENIOR MAN in the house, applied himself with renewed vigor to his work. He started a book called *The Lone Cru-*

sader, based on the life of Florence Nightingale. It wasn't surprising to me that he was fixated on a healer. I don't know why the book didn't work out—it was unlike him to drop anything—but one day that project was over. He was still working on *The Blue Balloon,* but he'd revised it extensively and renamed it *Love and Paula.* I asked Mom to send it to me at college.

Reading Dad's new play was like looking through a camera lens, trying to adjust depth of field, catching it for a moment, only to have the view turn blurry again and again. I became disoriented and from time to time was shocked into the sudden awareness that I must have just lost consciousness for a moment. When I finished reading, I was dazed and shaking. I never mentioned the play to my father—I just couldn't—and he was probably glad I didn't. Perhaps he never even knew that I read it. Years later I found his original notes in pencil. He wrote "Leslie" many times when he meant "Paula."

First we see a slide projection of a little girl (Paula) on the lap of a man with a "ridiculously perfect profile" (Paula's father). He is reading her an Uncle Wiggily story. The play begins years later, when she is at a Vassar-like women's college. She is recruited by "Suicides Anonymous" to work a hotline and, if needed, make home visits. She soon loses her virginity to the cause, sleeping with men to keep them alive. "Is this worth living for?" she asks a desperate man as she drops her clothes. Apparently it is. Later, she saves someone who has taken an overdose of Sodium Amytal (the very drug Dad was taking hourly). She keeps him awake with sex. When a scandal breaks, she leaves school rather than repudiate her methods, but Suicides Anonymous drops her, so she quits her sex therapy anyway. In a confrontation with her parents, she says, "Isn't using sex to help people regain their courage and strength . . . to save their lives . . . isn't that an honorable act? These people need love—the lack of love is what brings them to self-destruction!" In the happy ending, she marries the man she loves, with whom she has so far had a chaste relationship.

Of course this play was a comedy—meant to be broad and satirical. But it made me even more uncomfortable than I had been years earlier when he wrote *The Pony Cart*, about a girl my age at the time who was molested. In *Amusement Park*, which I read at fourteen, a thirteen-year-old girl sacrifices her life for her father's happiness. Now I was the age of this new heroine—a girl who had been read Uncle Wiggily stories!—and her sacrifice was too creepy to contemplate. Did he believe that some unconventional love could save him? I couldn't and wouldn't think about it. I had to believe that all the drugs he was taking had confused his mind and, in a mix of real life and fantasy, he had unconsciously concocted an amalgam of unformed desires.

There was never anything sexually suspect in my father's behavior toward me, but I see now that his love for me wasn't wholly within the boundaries of an ordinary father-daughter relationship. I did recognize early on that I was a lifeline for him, and as a young child I was flattered by his regard. As I grew older and he continued to need my assurance, his formality and my determined independence kept us on a manageable footing. Nevertheless, reading *Love and Paula* was a shock I have never gotten over.

BY 1964 his accumulated rejections had grown into an enormous burden that went everywhere with him. One day when Mom wasn't looking, Dad committed a peculiar folly, as if he might hoodwink the gods of rejection letters by taking on the disguise of success. He bought a secondhand Lincoln Continental Mark IV convertible. It had red leather seats and was a ridiculous car for him to own. He looked eerily natural driving it, but where had the money come from? He bought it just before I graduated from college, so that when he drove up for the great day, he came in style. I thought it was a lark, but my mother and brothers were smoldering with anger. I'd had to borrow the money for my senior year from a wealthy friend, and Mom was frantic about our lack of money.

Meanwhile, Buddy (who was christened Howard John), in an effort to distance himself as much as possible from the life he'd been born into, took on a new, stalwart-sounding first name: Dalton. We were to call him Dalton from now on. But we couldn't do it. Coping with another discontinuity was too hard, so, much to his annoyance, we dropped his new name for the time being.

And there was another change. Within a year of Grampy's death, Mom sold the house on Amity Street and bought a less expensive, smaller, but more beautiful one. A modest but graceful structure, it had been built in the early nineteenth century in Leverett, a tiny rural village about four miles from Amherst center. It sat on January Hill, at Still Corner. There was a little stable on the front lawn, which Dad roughly converted into his work space.

Once we moved into real country, Buddy took to disappearing for days into the woods, telling us he had friends who lived out there. He affected a broad country accent, and under his blue jeans and plain flannel shirt he wore BVDs—the one-piece long underwear of New England farmers. He told us that with a little bacon fat, a pot, and matches he could survive in the wild indefinitely. I think he was trapping.

In my own attempt to establish myself as independent from the family, I moved to France less than a month after my college graduation. With my father's help in the form of a letter to his old *New York Times Magazine* boss Lester Markel, I got a job with the Paris-based *New York Times International Edition*, a short-lived experiment meant to rival the *International Herald Tribune*. I flew to

Paris on Icelandic Air, in a prop plane that took eighteen hours (with a stop in Reykjavik) to make the journey.

I found an apartment over a butcher shop in Montmartre and began my European adventure. I worked in the office where the paper was edited; I was the only woman in the newsroom. I started with a few small jobs—writing the shipping and movie calendars, doing secretarial work for the managing editor—but then the copyboy quit, so I took over his job, and the editor of the letters-to-the-editor column needed help . . . and so it went. During the winter I got my first byline. Paris was numbingly cold and gray. I came to understand why the French use the word *triste* so much; it goes perfectly with the lonely winter atmosphere of those freezing streets. During my senior year at college and the fall in Paris, I had felt more competent than at any other time in my life. I was practical, rational, organized, and able to compartmentalize the problems of my family. But as winter settled into Paris, it was as if my mind had caught a fever that was sapping its ability to cope. I couldn't shake a numbing sense of isolation, as if there would never be a place where I would be happy and safe.

Then, in February, with no physical symptoms whatsoever, my consciousness mysteriously shut down. I was on a short vacation and slept through two nights and two days. I awoke in the dark, completely disoriented. I knocked on a door across the hall to find out what day and what time it was, and when I discovered that I had been out cold for so long, I was profoundly frightened. I went to the one place I knew would be light and cheerful—the Ritz bar—with money enough only for a drink, no dinner. There I met an elegant Russian woman and her middle-aged son, who invited me to join them. During that evening, I could actually feel health moving back into me, establishing occupancy, and I thought, I'm handling it. Life is strange, but I'm handling it.

By the following summer I was convinced that I would never

feel at home in France, and I was becoming anxious about my family. It was time to go home. I returned in the fall of 1965 to a scene just as fraught as the one I left, but one that had taken on new colors.

Every difficulty was more entrenched, and my mother was, at last, coming unhinged. She suffered from intense migraine headaches and diverticulitis, a painful intestinal disorder often brought on by stress. Dad had forbidden her to sing in the house—said he couldn't stand to hear it—so she, who had always depended on song to pull her out of a mood, had nothing to alleviate her anxiety. Almost but not quite dead were her hopes that her husband would cheer up, stop taking pills, and find a way to make a living. He seemed to block her at every turn. He said things like "You have no idea what you're talking about" and "You know nothing of the world" and "You behave like a child," and he said them with bitter antagonism.

I stayed home for a month, settling back into our tortured version of American life after my time in Paris. Buddy was away at school for the first time. He had asked to leave Amherst High School—which he hated—and transfer to Tabor Academy, even though Brooks had graduated the previous spring. At the beginning of October, I went to New York to find work in publishing. My old friend Mary Peacock let me stay with her in her small apartment on Horatio Street in Greenwich Village.

At that stage our family had become so used to Dad's state that one night when he fell out of bed and moaned for hours asking for help, Brooks and Mom, who were there at the time (my mother was sleeping in my room), tried to ignore the sounds they heard, thinking them his usual expression of despair. But it turned out that he had fallen and broken several ribs, and when they finally went to him, he had to be brought to the hospital once more. "Can you imagine?" Brooks told me later. "We were so used to hearing him make horrible noises in the night that we let him lie there? That this was a *normal* sound? It's beyond believing."

In New York I had many interviews, then came home again to await news.

One afternoon in November I was reading in the living room. Brooks was sharing an apartment with friends and working at a local bookstore. Buddy was living with another family, named Williams. Both my brothers had friends who took them in from time to time. The Vietnam War was escalating, and legions of disenchanted young people set out hitchhiking around America to "find themselves." In the case of my brothers, they were in flight from the craziness at home. They wanted to take a breather for a while in calm households. Mom didn't object, because she didn't want the boys exposed to the inevitable scenes my father would cause. On this day, Dad had left the house in a stupor of gloom and gone somewhere in the car. Mom was in another room. A few minutes before, she and I had been talking about her future. She was fifteen years younger than Dad, only forty-eight, and still looking miraculously young. I wanted her to find a viable life for herself, something free from the stress that was dragging her down.

"I can't leave your father. He needs me."

I didn't have an answer for that, nor did I have any real ideas for her. I knew that Dad needed her, but I couldn't see at that point how he was in any way helping her. I was young, and my life so far had taught me to be selfish about my own welfare. I remember a moment in my life—I was sixteen—when I said out loud to myself, "I'm not going down with this sinking ship." The guilt that resolution engendered is with me still, but starting then, I singlemindedly stayed away from home as much as I could. Naively, I had the idea that Mom could do the same thing. She could save herself if she left. She listened to me. The idea of independence

began to enter her consciousness, but she had neither the means
nor the will to take such a drastic step.

"Dad's illness will go its own course," I said. "I honestly don't
think you can have any effect on him anymore."

"I don't believe that, Les," she declared, and left the room. I had
upset her.

The phone rang. It was the publishing house Viking Press,
where I was up for a position as assistant publicity director. I got
the job! I was absolutely elated. I ran to tell Mom. She hugged me.
I felt her despair at being left behind from what would now be my
new life in New York, but she was also genuinely thrilled for me.
"Where's Dad?" I asked. After all these years of seeking independence, I felt like a child wanting to boast of a triumph to her father,
who would inevitably share her happiness. Mom thought he might
have gone to visit Doris Abramson. He'd been seeing her a lot of
late.

I took Mom's little car. I wanted to tell him in person.

Sure enough, Dad's Lincoln was parked in the drive. Dorothy,
Doris's lover, let me in. He's upstairs in Doris's study, she told me,
but be quiet when you go up there. I think she's reading to him.

Reading to him? I tiptoed upstairs as, indeed, I could hear her
beautiful low voice intoning language that I soon realized was poetry.

" 'You do not know how much they mean to me, my friends,
And how, how rare and strange it is, to find
In a life composed so much, so much of odds and ends,
(For indeed I do not love it . . . you knew? you are not blind!
How keen you are!)
To find a friend who has these qualities,
Who has, and gives

Those qualities upon which friendship lives.
How much it means that I say this to you—
Without these friendships—life, what cauchemar!' "

Not sure whether to sit on the stairs and listen or creep in, I hesitated. She read another verse, and another. I didn't know the poem, but all thoughts ceased within me except the layered gist of these words and the knowledge that my father was there in that room listening to them as his friend fairly sang them with her incredible voice.

"*Now that lilacs are in bloom*
She has a bowl of lilacs in her room
And twists one in her fingers while she talks.
'*Ah my friend, you do not know, you do not know*
What life is, you who hold it in your hands';
(Slowly twisting the lilac stalks)
'*You let it flow from you, you let it flow,*
And youth is cruel, and has no remorse
And smiles at situations which it cannot see.'
I smile, of course,
And go on drinking tea.
'*Yet with these April sunsets, that somehow recall*
My buried life, and Paris in the Spring,
I feel immeasurably at peace, and find the world
To be wonderful and youthful, after all.' "

"*Youth is cruel, and has no remorse.*" I'd just told Mom she should consider leaving Dad. But it's not true there's no remorse. Friends . . . his friend is with him . . . Paris in the spring . . . a buried life . . . I felt as if I were crumbling from within, as if everything and nothing had meaning and the future could only dissolve. How was he sitting up there? In a chair facing Doris? Looking away? Did he choose this poem or did Doris?

Silence. I waited. More silence. I dared the last few steps and entered the room. I was not expecting what I saw. At first I took in only Doris, sitting in a chair, holding a book. She looked up at me, startled. Then she looked elsewhere, and I followed the direction of her gaze.

She had a small couch in her room. Well, barely a couch, it was an antique American wooden bench with spoked back and arms. She'd had a seat cushion made for it, but it was still a piece of scant comfort. Dad was curled up on it in a fetal position, a blanket covering him up to the chest, his hands, palms together, under his head. His eyes were closed. Incongruously, I noted that he needed a shave and how unlike him that was.

He opened his eyes. "Les—"

I hardly knew what I had come upon. It was as if I had violated an intimacy.

Doris took hold. "He likes me to read this poem to him. He finds it comforting."

I didn't say anything.

"It's one of his favorites," she added.

Dad neither moved nor spoke. Doris put the book down on a table next to her. I saw it was T. S. Eliot. I understood why Dad would come here. There was about Doris an almost supernatural calm. I sensed that whatever their habit of communion, it had not yet finished when I entered the room. And so I left, stuttering something about seeing Dad at home. Walking down the stairs and out the door, I had the aural hallucination of wind thundering in my ears. It didn't stop thundering until I was out on the road, but by then I was crying.

PART
FOUR

* * *

CHAPTER TWENTY-EIGHT

In the summer of 2005, far along in my writing of this book, something remarkable happened. As if in a Victorian melodrama, I discovered a trunk that hadn't been opened since it was packed up by my mother thirty-seven years before. The trunk had sat in a succession of storage spaces since my husband and I helped my mother clean out her garage in the 1970s. It moved, unopened, with us from Vermont to Connecticut to New York. I had no desire to root through family papers, so it took on the sealed impermeability of a relic in the dark. Eventually I forgot about it. And then, with nothing more in mind than tackling my family's storage problem, I pulled aside a few moldy boxes and uncovered the trunk—a footlocker I had used for camp in the 1950s. I brought it to our Manhattan apartment with the intention of disposing of its contents after going through it. When I lifted the lid, I couldn't believe my eyes.

In it were not only my father's old manuscripts, but hundreds of letters, in folders labeled by year or subject in his handwriting. Some letters were to him, but most were from him. He kept car-

bons of almost every word he wrote, and he was a copious corre-
spondent. Here was the history, in his own words, of the last years
of his life.

I also found a battered six-by-ten-inch red leather portfolio
with FRENCH LINE written across the front in faded gold letters. It
bulged with receipts from a 1932 trip to Europe, yellowed, crumbling, but still intact. I unfolded page after page of meticulous accounts, written with the flowering penmanship of that distant
time. Here was a bill from Pensione Mondello, on the Venetian
Lido, and a *carte d'entrée* at the Casino Municipale in Rome; bills
from the Carlton Hotel in Cannes; Hotel Formentor, Pollensa,
Mallorca; Hotel Lutétia, Paris; Sinai Hotel; Hotel Bel-Air, Suez;
Shepheard's Hotel, Cairo; Luxor Hotel; Hotel Cecil, Alexandria. I
found a bill entirely in Arabic and a receipt from Ahmed Soliman,
"Cairo's Perfume King" in the Khan el Khalili Bazaar. Handling
these papers was like rubbing a magic urn and releasing visions of
my father, tall, handsome, gorgeously dressed, his manners polished to a sheen, traveling through Europe and North Africa, buy-
ing perfume, playing baccarat, laughing, flirting, reading in his
room . . . The reality of the papers brought with it the unreality of
looking into the past. Somewhere that traveling man continued to
exist in my father.

FROM LATE FALL 1965 I lived in New York City. I kept in constant
touch with my family by phone call, letter, and occasional visits,
but in fact my eyewitness knowledge of what went on at home was
limited. I last saw my father about six weeks before he died. I was
out of the country at the very end. With the help of the letters
from the trunk and the detailed accounts of family members who
were there, along with my own memories of those days, here is the
rest of my father's story.

*   *   *

THE FIRST THING THAT STRUCK ME as I read through Dad's letters was how much work he accomplished and with what grace he conducted himself professionally. His business letters were full of personal good wishes and gallant courtesies. He managed to pry the Uncle Wiggily Game away from Milton Bradley and make a more profitable contract with Parker Brothers, who created a stunning new board for the game. He also, after several years' negotiation, made a deal with United Artists to produce a pilot for an Uncle Wiggily animated television series. There was a small but honorable rights payment, the major money to come if and when Uncle Wiggily ran on TV. He had reason to be proud of these deals. I was astonished—breathtakingly so—to discover that throughout his illness he'd kept flowing a steady stream of business correspondence.

At the same time, he was continuing his own writing—his comedy *Love and Paula*, which was met among producers with respect but not enough interest to actually mount, and his continuing struggle to get *Amusement Park* on. How he worked so much when he was so impaired by depression and addiction, I cannot imagine.

In 1965 he had a stroke of good luck. He'd written an article about his family for *The Saturday Evening Post*, which a McGraw-Hill editor named Rose Marie Grgich read. She commissioned Dad to write a memoir of his early life. It was to be a fond remembrance.

Dad went right to work, and the book came out in the fall of 1966. To quote from the jacket copy:

> *Any afternoon, at the big old house in East Orange, New Jersey, the doorbell might ring, and a young visitor might timidly inquire whether Uncle Wiggily lived there. As a matter of fact he*

did, and so did much of the spirit of Tom Swift, the Bobbsey
Twins, Baseball Joe, the Motor Boys and countless other fictional
heroes and heroines that delighted young readers, and delight
them still.

For this was the house—aptly called the fiction factory—of
Howard R. Garis, his wife Lilian (alias Laura Lee Hope), and
their children Cleo and Roger, all of whom were enthusiastic
writers of immensely popular, immensely successful juvenile
books. In this enchanting biography of a "writing family," Roger
Garis tells what life was like in a hard-working, wildly imagi-
native family in small-town America.

The sentence that especially interested me was this:

They led the kind of warm and joyous family life for which we
are all nostalgic . . . Roger Garis turns back the clock to take us
right into the "house of magic" in which he grew up, to show us
just how delightful and unpredictable life once was at the side of
a forever jovial, confident, inventive father and a charming, tal-
ented, endearingly temperamental mother.

An endearingly temperamental mother, that was how he presented her in the rosy glow he conjured up to describe his early life.
In the trunk I found a letter she wrote Dad while he was in Mallorca on his 1932 European adventure. It was handwritten in
cramped letters, with a small *x* between sentences to avoid the
usual space after a period. Here it is (without the *x*'s):

Garis Stories
103 Evergreen Place
East Orange, N.J.
Phone: Orange 8416

February 19, 1932

Darling Son: note how I am economizing on space. Your cables are fine, but the cost! Where you are winding up those dollars will be twice as large as they seem to you now. Frankly we worry about the cables; letters are <u>much</u> better. Besides, you do not cut words, we can understand in half that wording. So much for advice, dear. We know you are going to improve. Send us a record in <u>pounds</u>. Now for writing. Here is the G—[I can't read her writing here] Story. It is <u>sharp</u>. Yours are not <u>sharp</u> enough. You see too many little things. That is the curse of the poetic mind. Now, to get something out of all this, just make up your mind to think violently, and write that way. The result should be <u>gentle</u> according to the ideas of others. I hope you get what I mean . . . Now please take the trouble to write, make letters short and send them often . . .

Tell us about the climate, and avoid too much sun. Neighbors are telling us now that you lay out on our damp grass last summer! No wonder you had a <u>bad</u> sore throat.

How is your throat?

I must cease, though I have only just begun. Be wise, be sincere, don't put on the dog, or you will make the wrong sort of friends. The best are not so easily deceived.

With all my love,
Your Mother

What was the message of that letter? That he was heedless of cost, that his writing was too diffuse and soft, that his health was too precarious for him to relax precautions, and that he must stop pretending he's equal to the worldly people he mixes with, since they will see right through him. And, although she sends her love, she closes with the formality of an abbess.

But my father put all that and much more aside when he wrote his memoir. His parents are lovingly and amusingly rendered, along with his sister, Cleo, who also wrote a few books for Stratemeyer, rounding out the complete "writing family." It's hard for me to imagine what it was like for my father to tell such an emotionally whitewashed version of his parents, although he managed to transmit some truths about himself. For example:

> *As a boy I was subject to rather violent and interesting—at least to me—swings of mood . . . [but a] thread constantly emerged: writing. In between moods I always reverted to that. So my father may have known that, despite all the other horizons, I would one day be a writer—or die trying.*

BEFORE PUBLICATION he had a major disagreement with McGraw-Hill over the title and the jacket. They wanted to call it *My Father Was Uncle Wiggily* and use a jacket with pictures of the rabbit. Dad was violently opposed to both those ideas. I don't know what he wanted to call the book, but it would have been something more sophisticated.

They did an end run around him. Proceeding just as they wished, they sent him a finished jacket. The top half of the design was taken up with these words:

My Father Was UNCLE WIGGILY
The Story of the Remarkable Garis Family who created Uncle Wiggily and wrote countless adventures of the Motor Boys, the Motor Girls, Baseball Joe, the Bobbsey Twins, Tom Swift and the Outdoor Girls

by Roger Garis

"UNCLE WIGGILY" was printed in oversize red letters, swamping the rest of the title. Below the type was a picture of Uncle Wiggily carrying a basket of apples to his bungalow, talking to Peetie Bow Wow on his front walk while Nurse Jane stood in the door, hands on her hips, impatient to start baking a pie—a perfect domestic scene in fantastical Woodland. Dad was devastated, and so was my mother. It was too late, though. The books were already on press.

To cover his disappointment, he told himself it wouldn't make any difference, that the book was good enough to attract the adult audience he had always been courting.

ON A COOL NOVEMBER DAY he went into Amherst to do some errands and visit Hastings' store, where he knew his book was on sale. He had a spring in his step. Approaching Hastings, he saw with a thrill of pleasure that his book was on display in the window. Don Hastings, the wiry, plainspoken owner, was behind the counter and called to Dad as he entered the shop.

"Roger! Great to see you! So glad to have the new book. We've needed another Uncle Wiggily story for a long time!"

My father stood where he was, unable to say a word. Don beamed at him. It occurred to Dad in that moment that his entire life was part of a joke concocted by the great storyteller in the sky. And he would never escape his role in the demented narrative.

That very day, someone stopped him on the street, saying essentially the same thing as Don Hastings. "I see your father has another Uncle Wiggily book out." The fact that Howard Garis died in 1962 and it was now 1966 didn't seem to matter, since people assumed it was a posthumous publication. Dad was amazed and appalled that a person could look no further than the bold letters of

"UNCLE WIGGILY" in the title, then stop him in the street for congratulations. He felt he was moving through a bad dream.

As if he hadn't quite gotten the cosmic message, a cousin called him from Rhode Island asking him to send her "the new Uncle Wiggily book" for her four-year-old nephew. His humiliation was complete.

A FEW WEEKS LATER, in a state of extreme agitation, he went into New York with my mother for his appearance on the *Today* show. Barbara Walters would be interviewing him about the book. As usual, they checked into the Royalton Hotel.

In the room, Dad hurriedly gave the porter a tip and closed the door behind him. Avoiding my mother's eye, before he had even removed his coat and hat, he took a piece of paper out of his pocket, picked up the phone receiver, and dialed a number he read off the paper.

"Hello, my name is Roger Garis. I believe the doctor is expecting my call." After a moment he asked for a Sodium Amytal prescription to be phoned in to a nearby drugstore. He would pick it up within the hour.

When he put back the receiver, my mother lit into him. How could he do that? He had important engagements ahead, etc., etc. She delivered a steady torrent of words until she saw the look on his face and caught her breath. He was staring steadily, malevolently at her.

"Don't ever ask me," he said with deadly coldness, "to choose between the medicine I need and you. I will always choose the pills."

He tore out of the room. She threw herself onto the bed and sobbed.

CHAPTER TWENTY-NINE

At home my parents were alone with each other and arguing a great deal. Brooks, having started college at the University of Massachusetts the previous year, had quit that school and enrolled at St. John's University in Santa Fe. It had a curriculum based on the "great books," and it seemed like a good school for him. What better way for a dyslexic student to learn math than by starting with Euclid? Buddy, having run away from Tabor, was attending the high school and living with the Williams family, who were tender and kind to him. Dad's behavior toward the boys was irrational and often outright hurtful. He criticized them ruthlessly when he was drugged, saying that Brooks had "the guts of a monkey" and that Buddy's school performance was a disgrace. As Brooks described his life then, "I was embarrassed by his addiction. I was sad, too. I didn't want to have that life. I would have liked not to have to take him off the floor. I didn't want my child energy going into him. It was the wrong direction of energy flow." After Dad's scenes with his sons he would sober up the next day and apologize, but homelife was destroying the boys' confidence and undermining their strength. Out of self-preservation, they informally moved out.

After my parents' New York experience, something essential deteriorated at home. Dad's mood plummeted, his terrors attacked with a vengeance, and he lapsed into even heavier drug use. The two of them were barely speaking. Then, suddenly, my mother began to suffer from alarming symptoms. At first she thought her dizzy spells were momentary, but the dizziness increased so much that she couldn't walk. And it didn't go away. She also was nauseated. As she described it to me weeks later from the hospital, her field of vision was in constant motion from upper right to bottom left. The world was on a diagonal and never still, even when she closed her eyes, and when she tried to stand, the commotion in her head was like overpowering vertigo. Lying on her bed, she felt as if she were spinning on a violent carnival ride. The sensation was an intense torture.

My bewildered father saw, as she got worse each day, that this was no passing migraine or weak spell. With much difficulty, since she couldn't walk, he got her to the car and drove her to the hospital. Her eventual diagnosis was astoundingly theme-related: she had viral labyrinthitis, an inflammation of the inner-ear canal. Sick to her stomach, weak, sad, too dizzy to be upright, she was lost in the labyrinth of her own head.

And then, in a replay of previous times, Buddy came to the house for something and found his father on the floor in a near coma. Once more an ambulance came to our house. Both my parents spent the last month of 1966 in Cooley Dickinson Hospital. On December 19 my mother turned fifty, but she was too sick for visitors.

The local paper ran a picture of Dad autographing his book for a group of smiling nurses gathered around his hospital bed. He smiled for them, but to me, the rest of his face was too forlorn for the smile to register.

CHAPTER THIRTY

*He knew that soon the . . . accustomed desolation would fasten itself
upon him with such viciousness and tenacity that movement might be
too difficult . . . But then, as often, came the counter resolution, and he
was aware of the rising rebellion against surrender. If he were not to
surrender he must do something.*

—THE STEPPING STONE
A novel, the last work of Roger Garis

He left the hospital weeks before his wife was discharged. At
home alone, he faced absolute bleakness. The children were
gone—Buddy living with the Williams family, Brooks at school in
New Mexico—and his wife was prostrate. It wasn't just a matter of
waiting a few weeks until she came home. She wasn't planning to
come home. Her sister, Doris, now a widow still living in the simple Naugatuck, Connecticut, house where she had brought up her
three children, had invited Mom to recuperate with her, and Mom
had gratefully agreed. Their mother, also a widow now, lived with
Doris. It would be the remnants of the little Burns family gather-

ing around their ill Mabel just a few miles from Waterbury, where the two daughters had been born. So Dad was looking at a life alone in Leverett, and the prospect sent him into a panic. He knew he wouldn't make it on his own; he had to do something.

It was then that he discovered Gould Farm. Founded by the social reformer William J. Gould in 1913 on 650 acres in the Berkshire Mountains (not far from Austen Riggs), it was a new model for the rehabilitation of the mentally ill. Still in existence today (although now it costs $205 a day and then it was $80 a week), it is the oldest therapeutic community for mental illness in the United States.

The patients there, called guests, were in that stage of illness where hospitals could only maintain them, but they were still unable to function in the world, destined to become more and more isolated. Gould Farm provided a bucolic community, and the work the "guests" were required to do gave them self-esteem from the real sense—often for the first time in their lives—that their contributions made a crucial difference. The population of less than a hundred was divided into one-third guests, one-third staff, and one-third staff family. Everyone ate and worked together. The most prevalent illnesses were bipolar disease, schizophrenia, and severe depression, and the ages spanned early twenties to middle age. Those who were strong enough worked on the farm, feeding animals, milking cows, and tending crops, while those who were too frail for outdoor work helped out in the houses and kitchens. There was a full-time psychologist on staff, but the focus was, in their words, "on the principles of respectful discipline, wholesome work and unstinting kindness." William Gould had had the genius to adopt the tradition of the earlier American Utopia movement for some of the most stricken and marginalized in society.

Dr. Virgil Brollier was the resident therapist at that time, and the executive director was a Congregational minister, the Reverend Hampton Price, although the religious aspects of the program were

voluntary and ecumenical, accommodating Jews, Quakers, and
Catholics. Dad, whose faith was strong, was comforted by the spiritual atmosphere.

On December 29 Dad wrote from Gould Farm to Mom at
Cooley Dickinson,

*This is a lovely place, farm houses, farm, kitchens, and the work
is divided among us. I will not do strenuous work for a time, but
I help with the housework and dishes—things like that. I have a
sweet little room, alone, in a cottage with perhaps 7 others. We
arise at 7, breakfast at 7:30, we sing hymns and pray and work.*

But eleven days later he wrote to his still-hospitalized wife,

*I am so desperately lonely for you that at times I feel physically
ill . . . It is, I suppose, unsophisticated to pour out love like this,
but I have refrained from doing it so long, and finally I thought,
it can't hurt a person to know that she is loved . . . This is a
lovely place, and all the people are kind, and no other place could
be better for me, but I so want to see you, and hold your hand,
and put my arms around you, and protect you from everything. I
work hard here but all days seem to go so slowly. I do not have
the frightful depressions, except at times in the mornings, and
then I work them off. The evenings are better . . . I cannot look
back too intently on all that has happened, because I know this
will retard my own cure, but I feel I have been as good a husband
and father as I could be with the handicaps I had. I tried. I tried
very hard. There were many times I failed, I made you unhappy.
Nor can I look too closely at the future, except to feel that the
change that is taking place in me will, I hope, make our lives
happier. I believe you love me—I cannot believe otherwise and
go on.*

In mid-January 1967, Mom, still bedridden, moved to her sister's house. At this time there was so little money in their bank account that the first letter my mother was able to write to her husband was a sad affair:

Writing is a great effort so I've been unable to do any. I'm sorry my first letter is one of concern. But I can't rest or relax because of two financial commitments. One is Buddy's last tuition payment of $282.15. They should also be notified that he has dropped out of school . . . The second and larger sum is that due St. John's. It is a small sum in contrast to what it would be but for Brooks' grant and job . . . I know you are struggling too so this has been an extremely difficult letter to write. If these two items could be handled (without making Brooks leave school) I feel my recuperation would be more rapid. As it is I can't get them out of my mind night or day. Please help me.

At the same time, her mother was upstairs writing another letter:

Dear Roger:
    Mabel is writing to you downstairs about Brooksie's tuition. Do not tell her that he is not in school because of her weak condition. Just tell her that you will take care of it.

Not only had Bud left Tabor in a flurry of arguments with the school, but Brooks had dropped out of St. John's because New Mexico was too far away from his ailing family. He told his dean that he had to go home "to save my father." The dean tried to talk sense into him, but he wouldn't listen.

It must have been surreal for my father at Gould Farm at that time. He was receiving letters almost every day about the Uncle Wiggily television program. All was going well; everyone was sure it would go to pilot and then to syndication. Parker Brothers sent him the new game, which he showed around at the farm to much enthusiasm. He thought he was getting better at last and that his financial future might just be assured, even though he was broke at the moment. He had weaned his way down to fewer pills than he'd taken in years, and he had plans for his writing. He was working a few hours a day on his novel, *The Actress,* and he felt positive about it. Meanwhile, he was still alarmingly thin. It was like being barely corporeal, as if he were floating in the air over health. He could see safety below him at a distance. He thought he was approaching it. He needed a few more pounds on his bones and a little more confidence, and he'd make a steady landing at last on solid earth.

Dad answered Mom's letter with this one: "I have just come from church, and it was almost exactly like our church in Leverett. I am leaving early tomorrow morning for New York, to try to obtain money for Brooks's tuition and the remainder of Buddy's and to do anything else I can that will help." He said he asked the bank for a loan, but they wouldn't give him any more credit. "I did not know where to turn. Now I have some ideas which I think will work out. I'll send you all the money I can." He ends with a plea: "I would like to ask you this: I would like you to forgive me all the harm I have done you, and all the suffering I have caused you. There is nothing else I want."

Then a bombshell. To a stronger person, the letter he opened at Gould Farm on a wintry day wouldn't have been the blow that it was to my father's fragile ego. Apparently Dad had telephoned Mom and had an argument with her. He was beginning to be obsessed with the fear that she was planning to leave him, and his paranoia, which took very little to kindle, burst into an uncontrollable ball of fire. Whenever he felt threatened, he lashed out, and he said something harsh over the phone. Watching her sister weep after the conversation inspired Doris to write him a letter. When I read it now, it seems mild, but he received it like a hail of bullets.

Dear Roger,

I think I owe you an explanation. I didn't say you were not to call Mabel. I said she wasn't to be upset.

I have an affectionate regard for you as my brother-in-law, but Mabel is my sister and my first concern. I also think you are under the delusion that Mabel has left you. This is not so.

Mabel for the first time in her life needs attention and care. There is no one except Mom and I, right now, able to do this.

Since she is here and I know her condition, I try to lessen her anxiety. Buddy's leaving Tabor certainly did nothing to alleviate her condition, and last week she was progressing beautifully then, "bang" she heard Brooks withdrew from school, which caused a set back.

Mom and I hope she is now responding but it is going to take time. One person can't take the constant pressures and tensions that she has had forever. There is a breaking point for everyone, only to everyone in Amherst Mabel seemed indestructible, and she wasn't.

How many other women do you know who did all Mabel did for her family? Not many.

Who else painted and wallpapered, cleaned the yard and did other manual labor without neglecting her family, or getting any help or recognition for all she did?

Roger, you may think I was a good wife and mother, but I would never, never put up with the life Mabel has.

I hope you will get on your feet soon so you can take care of Mabel, instead of her having to carry the load.

We are a small family and here to stick together.

> *With best personal regards,*
> *Sincerely,*
> *Doris*

He answered her letter, sent it off special delivery, then phoned, begging Doris to rip it up before she read it. Ten days later he wrote her again. In his first response he said, "It seems to me that through this letter you have cast me in the role of a villain and Mabs as my victim." He quoted phrases from her letter, then wrote,

I am sure your mother believes as you do. Perhaps, in fact probably, Mabs feels this way too . . . It is most difficult for a man to live under this load of blame. Whatever good he did, however much he loved his wife, whatever he did for her, is lost. All he has left is guilt . . . She underwent great strain during my illnesses. But putting the entire blame on one person . . . is no way to help that marriage . . . I am not a villain, and I cannot accept being cast as one.

In the next letter he wrote that Doris made

accusations which I feel were completely unjust. Furthermore, it was sent to me when I was ill, in a hospital for persons with emotional difficulties. I was also trying to bring Mabel and me together again, by letters and telegrams. I was also trying to write a book, which would bring in some money . . . Perhaps it is difficult for you to understand a person who could be made ill by receiving a letter like that. But that is what it did to me. The accusations . . . had the effect not only of making me sicker than I was, but of making me despair of ever getting together again with Mabel, as we once were. If those thoughts were in her mind also, certainly she could not bring herself to live with me again . . . a letter such as you wrote tears down everything I have been trying to build. It saddles me with a load of guilt. I will not accept the role of villain . . . I don't know what the end of this will

*be, but I do know the injury I—and perhaps Mabel—has suf-
fered from your letter.*

Although Dad's reaction was somewhat hysterical and self-
pitying, I reproduce it here because it was his truth as he understood and felt it. The day before he sent that letter to Doris, he
wrote to Mom:

*I just want to talk with you. I'm lonely as hell. I think about you
all the time and wonder if I ever really will see you again. It's
been so long. Are all the good things we had together gone?
Where did they go to?*

*And I don't have anything to say. Rose Marie Grgich didn't
like the first draft of the novel, and I have to do it all over again.
But that isn't bad. I can do it.*

*. . . Some new people come to the Farm, and some leave.
Many of them have no homes. I'm not sure I have a home. It's so
long ago. And the children—I haven't seen them, except that I
saw Leslie in New York, and she was most, most kind, apparently sensing my loneliness. I don't think women get lonely the
same way men do . . .*

In another letter to her he wrote,

*Something has gone out of me . . . I don't know what replaces it.
I don't even know what it is . . . If I am the sort of person who
has . . . made you lead the kind of life which Doris mentioned, I
must be either psychotic or a monster. Was I, truly, either of
those? . . . I feel like Mr. K, the condemned man of Kafka, who
never knew what his offense was, and yet suffered for it . . . I feel
as though I have no family and no home . . . through everything
I do creeps this vision of hopelessness.*

When I spoke or wrote to him, I continually bucked him up, telling him that Mom was certainly not planning to leave him and he had a good future ahead. I believe my words helped him for no more than a few hours and then he reverted back to his obsessional fear of abandonment and rejection. I was also still encouraging my mother to strike out on her own. I wanted to give them both the best help I could, and I believed what I was saying at the time. Confusion, guilt, self-accusations of dishonesty, were rampant within me.

As Mom got gradually better and began to plan her return to Leverett, Dad improved enough to go home at the end of February. Brooks and Bud were both in Amherst living with friends, but they occasionally visited with their father, and now he could look forward to being with his wife. The immediate threat was averted, and he told himself all would be well.

But Buddy was not well. He was beginning to come apart in ways he had hinted at earlier, when he spent days in the woods. Not long before Mom was due to come home—although I don't think he knew that—he came to the house in the middle of the night, unable to sleep, frantic with tension and restlessness. The temperature was fifteen below zero, although he wore neither hat nor gloves. He went into the garage and took the chain saw he had bought to practice cutting down trees. One of his many plans for himself was to go out West and become a logger. In a kind of trance of confusion, he decided to cut down a tree—that would be something new, he'd never logged at night. He entered the woods behind the house and tried to start up the chain saw, but it was out of fuel. So he returned to the garage and found the gas container. In the driveway he poured gas into the chain saw and spilled some on his hand. Back in the woods, he started up the saw and put it to a tree. He began to calm down as sawdust spewed out from the dark trunk, barely visible in the moonlight that threaded through bare branches. Strange, though, he heard a rattling and didn't know what it was. He stopped the saw and looked at his hands. Gasoline had covered his left little finger, and it was frozen solid. The rattling was his finger knocking against the saw.

A few days later Dad drove to Naugatuck to pick up Mom. They had a loving reunion and started on the trip home. As they were approaching Amherst, Dad said, "I've been afraid to tell you something. Buddy is having his finger amputated tomorrow."

"That can't be!" Mom gasped.

"I'm afraid it's true."

"What happened? I'm sure something can be done to save his finger. How did this happen?"

He told her everything, but she was not convinced. At home, Buddy was waiting to greet her. She asked him to remove the bandage so she could see for herself. When he pulled the gauze away from his hand, she saw that his finger was a deep, unforgiving black. She knew that the damage was beyond her powers. The helplessness she'd been fighting for three months once more engulfed her.

The next day at Cooley Dickinson (our home away from home) they removed his finger and part of the edge of his hand. It was done. Buddy was now visibly disfigured.

CHAPTER THIRTY-ONE

Dr. Virgil Brollier
Gould Farm
Monterey, Massachusetts

March 10, 1967

Dear Dr. Brollier:
    ... Mother and Father are now under the same roof in Amherst;
nothing explosive has happened yet (Daddy seems to be drawing from a
heretofore unknown well of sanity), but I'm afraid I expect the worst ...

Sincerely,
Leslie Ann Garis

After Buddy lost his finger, Mom and Dad were shaken, but they lived together in peace. Mom, still too sick to drive, spent her time moving slowly through the house, straightening, dusting, doing a little cooking. She was too dizzy to read for more than a few minutes at a time. Buddy, now nineteen, went back to live with the Williams family and continued school, doing such minimal work that he was barely passing. He took the loss of his finger in stride and in fact seemed calmer. The shock and violence of his accident had taken the edge off his agitation.

This was Brooks's time for going to New York and playing his guitar in coffeehouses in Greenwich Village. He was twenty-one and rarely in Amherst.

Money was the constant worry. Dad—at last!—sold his crazy Lincoln and bought a tiny Renault. That transaction reflected in Dad a move toward reality that was the effect of his stay at Gould Farm and his wife's pleas. Mary and Bud Hewlett came to see them, Mary often bringing dinner so Mom could rest. March in New England is a dreary, breath-holding time. Days are cold and often gray, but then the sun will come out and deliver a few hours of the sort of warming sunlight that lifts the spirit. This March, Dad and Mom watched each other warily in their lovely old house on January Hill. Dad went to his converted stable to write each day, and he did his best to stay on an even keel. Reverend Price wrote to him about collecting maple syrup at Gould Farm. "The sap came up one warm day, got scared and went back for five. Today it is warm enough to pry it up all over again."

Inevitably, however, Dad slowly reverted to higher doses of drugs, which led to more blackouts and ambulances.

I dread describing what happened next. My mother's ignorance of the nature of my father's illness, her desire to fix things simply, my father's egocentric inability to face his addiction, his desperation to ward off depression, and the unavailability of better psychiatric drugs in 1967 all came together one catastrophic afternoon.

It started in the morning. Mom took Dad's bottles of barbiturates from the medicine cabinet. At first she thought she would throw them out, but she hit on another plan that seemed less drastic. Upstairs, behind a bathtub pipe, there was a space in the wall with a crossbeam behind it, making a hidden shelf. There she put Dad's pills.

Downstairs, blood pounding in her temples, she waited. It happened around one o'clock.

She heard him coming, and she was afraid.

"Where did you put my pills?" he demanded furiously.

"I don't know what you're talking about."

"Where are they?"

"I don't know."

"I'm going to ask you one more time. Where are they?"

"I don't know, Roger."

He moved toward her threateningly, his hands outstretched as if he were going to strangle her.

"Where are they, Mabel?"

"I don't know."

She backed up as he continued to move toward her. When she was against the wall, he put his fingers around her neck and squeezed.

"Where are they?"

"I don't know! I don't know!"

Tears streamed down her face.

"Tell me!"

"I don't know."

Suddenly he let out a sob and dropped his hands. He moved away from her in horror at what he had almost done, knocked over a chair, and lurched out of the house. Hysterical, Mom called the Hewletts, who came immediately. Mary helped Mom pack her clothes, and they brought her to their home to stay.

A few hours later Buddy arrived at the house to pick something up. The front door was wide-open. One look at the overturned chair in the living room told him that something dreadful had happened. He thought there had been a robbery. When he reached Mom at the Hewletts', she tried to tell him what happened, but she couldn't stop crying. His understanding was that Dad threw a chair at Mom and tried to strangle her. This is the absolute end, he thought. I am no longer his son.

Buddy told Brooks. They were united in their condemnation: Mom must be protected, and Dad must be prevented from doing any more damage.

WHERE DID DAD GO when he left the house? My brothers believe he went to his workroom, as if to continue writing. He would have been shaking, possibly crying. He would also have called the Hewletts, but Mary wouldn't have let him talk to my mother. I don't know what else happened. I only know two facts: out of the rubble of his life he got an idea for a new novel, and he worked up a plan to go somewhere soothing.

CHAPTER THIRTY-TWO

One could, indeed, live in loneliness and live in strangeness, and in living there was victory.

—THE STEPPING STONE

I n recent years Dad had fled from home often to places other than hospitals. He went especially to a little inn in Wellfleet, and in fact, he had spent almost the entire summer of 1966 there alone in a room, so that by March of 1967, when he frightened Mom away with his strangling episode, he hadn't actually been with her very much for almost a year. That's why her homecoming from Naugatuck had been so important to him. With the improvement he made at Gould Farm in January and February, he had been hoping to resume the happy married life he remembered from long ago. He began to dwell on their first house. It was in Cheshire, Connecticut, near New Haven; he wondered if he would ever have anything resembling that happiness again.

Such happiness that neither could quite believe in it, and when they would awaken in the morning in the little house just outside New Haven, they would lie quietly, not speaking, savoring their delight.

—THE STEPPING STONE

He knew that his marriage was in serious jeopardy. Not a man to lose hope, however, he continued to try, through letters and phone calls, for a reconciliation. Meanwhile, he was desperate. True to his pattern, he went away, but this trip managed to enrage his wife and sons even more.

Dad picked up his American Express card and charged a round-trip plane flight and two weeks in a hotel on Montego Bay in Jamaica. He went on the April day when the prices dropped to off-season, but my mother at this point was living on the generosity of the Hewletts, with no money of her own. When she found out he was in Jamaica, she was stunned—as were my brothers. *How could he be so irresponsible? He's crazy!* (Well, yes.) *This is absolutely the last straw!*

For some reason—maybe the reason that has made me a writer—I was unable to blame my father. The entire situation was tragic, and we all had our roles to play. Mine was that of an observer from a fairly safe distance. I wasn't now dependent on family life the way the others were. I was on my own, horrifically disturbed by seeing those I loved so hurt, but not directly involved except for offering sympathy and kindness when I could. For $125 a month, which I could barely afford on my paltry salary, I had created a miniature home for myself in a one-room ground-floor apartment on West Seventy-fifth Street. I furnished it with an old bed and table from my parents, and I rented an upright piano. I switched from publicity to editorial (as an assistant) at Viking and brought work home almost every night, which filled my life well even though I had no love life. Literary readings at the Poetry

Center of the YM-YWHA on East Ninety-second Street con-
stituted a large chunk of my social world The rest was filled with
friends—mostly male, although none inspired romance in me—with
whom I went to plays and movies. I felt young and energetic, but I
also carried a deep, sad fatigue well below my daily operating surface.

Meanwhile, in Jamaica, Dad abandoned his novel *The Actress*,
which had now been turned down by McGraw-Hill and Crown,
and took up his new idea. It would be called *The Stepping Stone*, a
novel of academia, set in a town just like Amherst at a university
just like the University of Massachusetts, a land-grant agricultural
school expanded to encompass liberal arts and sciences. To this
backward university, with an overloaded, underpaid, discontented
faculty, comes Paul, a recent Yale Ph.D. whose wife's sudden death
has plunged him into unrelenting despair. A friend on the faculty
invites him to come in order to hibernate and heal. There is much
intrigue with the brash president, who wishes to create a vast library as a monument to himself but knows very little and cares less
about what's inside those books. Dad was able to use the knowledge he gained writing "aggie" pamphlets to advantage, with lots of
telling details, but the main connection he had with this book—
and I believe it was the deepest he ever made to one of his works—
was with Paul's despair at losing his wife and his loneliness at being
set adrift, living in a rented room.

From Jamaica he wrote to me asking if I could help him by
telling him what he could do to make Mom happy.

I know it was right for me to come down here, because I am
writing furiously and I think well—a new book. I could never
do this in the house alone . . . Mother and I would be fine if we
were left alone to work out our own problems. This is the sort of
thing which hits every marriage . . . Mother and I belong to-
gether. Any other conclusion would be disaster for us both.

He even had a plan for her to join him in Jamaica, although Mom was appalled by the notion. *What is he thinking? Has he at last no sense of reality at all?* His understanding of what was going on in the minds and hearts of those he loved was as opaque as it was self-protective. Without blinders, he couldn't put one foot in front of the other.

Meanwhile, in the bizarre way my family's narrative wove together present and past, reality and fiction, I had a momentous encounter in New York.

Although I was removed from my family's immediate company, I was haunted almost beyond bearing by my father's undoing, my mother's frantic despair, and my brothers' dysfunction. On the night I'm writing of, I spent several hours crying and writing a letter to Thayer Greene, who was now my therapist, having left the ministry, studied Jung in Zurich, and set up a practice in New York. (I know, I know . . . How does everything circle back like this?) I told him I was at a breaking point.

About 10:00 p.m. a friend phoned to invite me out for a drink. I told him I was in no shape for a date. Even though our relationship was platonic, I thought I would make lousy company. But he insisted, so I brought him to a new place I had recently discovered called Elaine's.

It was after eleven when we walked in. The place was packed, and there was the usual jolly din of silverware, conversation, and laughter. It was the sort of room you plunged into, rather like jumping into the ocean and holding your breath. There was at that time (as there still is) a large round table toward the front of the restaurant, known then as now as the Big Table. It was the table where Elaine—the quick-witted, tough, rotund, writer-loving owner—placed her current favorites. As I entered with my friend, I saw Frank Conroy at that table. Frank had just published his memoir *Stop Time* at Viking. His editor, Aaron Asher, was the man for whom I worked. Frank waved me over and asked me to join him at the table. He motioned to a chair next to a tall, swarthy man with broad shoulders. I noticed his finely tailored shirt, which defined the curves of his back, and as soon as I sat down, I took in his sculpted, sensual face. I felt an immediate, visceral, intense attraction. Frank introduced him as Arthur Kopit.

I looked at him in wonder. Arthur Kopit, the man who wrote the "mother play" that Dad sent me to when I was a college sophomore. My, he was handsome. Who would have thought the author of *Oh Dad, Poor Dad, Mamma's Hung You in the Closet and I'm Feelin' So Sad* would be handsome? The central character was a nerdy, introverted, stuttering, maturationally delayed young man. Was that young man inside this young man? So this is the playwright. Well, well, well . . . We talked. Our conversation was cryptic, humorous. I didn't tell him I knew his play, or that my father had asked me to see it, or that it was the only play he told me I had to see. We talked about his visit to Vassar my senior year when he was a guest speaker. I went away that weekend, so I missed his speech, but on Sunday night one of my friends said, "Guess what I did this weekend." When I rose to the bait, she said, "I went home with the guest lecturer." And she had, but then Nancy was the most brazen and sexually free of us all. So I opened my conversation with Arthur Kopit by saying that we had a friend in common, then named her. That got his attention. I felt reckless. After a while he asked, "Are you free Tuesday night?" My answer: "Not anymore."

Our first date was to the opening of Jules Feiffer's play *Little Murders*. I wore a daring dress. At the party, Arthur and I were so aware of each other that I perceived all else dimly. As the spring wore on, we fell in love. I felt as if I had tumbled into a land of safety and laughter. He was amazingly funny; I hadn't laughed so continuously ever in my life. His rhythms—urban, Jewish, theatrical—were new to me and kept catching me off guard. Layers of dread, sadness, and defensiveness dropped away. I was almost literally delirious with delight.

He wanted to introduce me to the most important people in his life: his mother and father; his best friends, Jack and Carol Gelber; his publisher, Arthur Wang; and his agent, who had signed him a few months after he graduated from Harvard. He was devoted to her. Her name was Audrey Wood. I told Arthur about Audrey's place in my life, and she was prepared for me when I walked into her office. Even so, it was as if in a dream that Audrey took my hand and said, "My dear, you have lived through a gothic story."

In that instant I felt myself being eleven years old, standing at her desk, fascinated by her box turtle sleeping in the miniature green rockery of its glass house, while I luxuriated in the warm bath of her words: *Your father has written a very good play. You should be proud of him.* I remembered dinners at The Dell when Mom told Dad he simply could not call his agent again that day and he certainly must not bother her at all hours. And the day he "fired" her. And here I was, years later, standing with her, in circumstances I never could have invented. "A gothic story." Her words shocked and comforted me. Audrey Wood, the diminutive powerhouse with a voice so soft you had to lean toward her to hear it, and her clients—Tennessee Williams, Carson McCullers, and, yes, William Inge—gladly bent their heads down to Audrey to hear words that would guide their volatile careers. This Audrey Wood stepped out of my past and reentered my life with words as important to me now as was her reassurance in my childhood— that reassurance having meant so much to me that it became a Technicolor memory. And her turtle, although perhaps not the same one, was still there in its aquarium, as if it had been waiting for me all these years.

CHAPTER THIRTY-THREE

Hope springs eternal in the human breast;
Man never Is, but always To be blest:
The soul, uneasy and confin'd from home,
Rests and expatiates in a life to come.

—*Alexander Pope,* An Essay on Man, *Epistle 1, 1733*

Today my mother doesn't remember much about that time. She stayed partly with the Hewletts and partly with her friends Nat and Bill Merrill. She had no money. She was still sick, still experiencing debilitating bouts of dizziness. In June, as soon as Buddy completed high school, he went west to try his luck as a logger. Brooks was around, with a job at a bookstore, but he was not often at the Leverett house. Dad was back at Gould Farm. My mother set her teeming mind to the task of saving herself. She had three ideas: a year's separation from Roger, resettlement to a new town free of bad memories, and selling the house to raise money to start again. At fifty, even with her illness, she looked ten years younger. My brothers and I thought she had a lot of life ahead of her.

But when she began to float the idea of selling the house, we were all alarmed. Or I should say my brothers and I were alarmed. Dad went into a tailspin.

July 31

Dearest Daddy,

Despite your fears, you will never have to live in a furnished room in a strange town . . . This business about Mother selling the house sounds very scary . . . But I think that if she does it (and it won't be for a long time if she does) it won't be nearly as frightening as it sounds . . . She'll find a place where we can all go . . . Mother's wanting to move is a very positive thing . . . Her search for a new town means that her attitude is positive . . . that she looks forward to a good future . . . You are not left out. She loves you still very much she has told me. Your letters touch and sadden her and she would like to help you . . . Wait until she is more confident and stops having nightmares . . . You must NEVER allow yourself to believe that you are being turned out into the cold . . . What you are going through now is NOT a conclusion. Not at all. You have a lot of time left and it is possible that you can live it happily.

Your letter made me cry. When you say "It made me wonder just what sort of a life that was, and whether I was there while it was being lived," I have no answer for you. Of course it WAS your illness . . . What I am trying to tell you is not to feel GUILTY the way you obviously do. You were sick. Very sick. And the fact that we suffered was not your fault—it was built into the situation . . .

. . . Please try to keep up your spirits. Don't drive yourself with dark thoughts . . .

All my love,
Leslie

My father's thoughts were indeed dark. At Gould Farm, alone in his room or walking across the fields, his imagination wandered through bleak scenarios and he understood that his illness was taking on new colors. His despair was now in sync, or so he thought, with the events of his real world. He couldn't sleep, and he barely ate.

He bit with deliberate savagery into the sandwich. Whether or not he was hungry was insignificant. He believed that he was not hungry, but he could not be certain. It had been some time since his body's welfare had been of interest to him.

—THE STEPPING STONE

On August 5 he wrote to Reverend Seth Newton, an Amherst minister who had preached at Gould Farm:

You may recall that during your most helpful visit to Gould Farm, I spoke with you after the service . . . I mentioned that I lived in Amherst, and that my wife and I were undergoing a domestic crisis. You said you would be very glad to talk with her.

Since then she has emphasized her opposition to talk with anyone, and I fear our marriage is at an end, but this is not certain, and since I love her very much I still hope, remembering the first line of "Hope springs eternal" etc., but not repeating the second line, which I think is the most bitter in all poetry.

Although I still am at Gould Farm, I am scheduled to leave tomorrow, Sunday . . . I would appreciate very much a chance to talk with you . . . I have been taking to myself as much of the realization of God that I can, helped immensely by Rev. M. Fraser here. I do not want to lose what I have gained—I'd like to increase it, if possible.

I'm sure you are aware of the desolation which haunts me at the thought of losing not only my wife, but two of our three children, who seem against me, and my home.

From Leverett on August 14 he sent a one-line letter.

Dear Mabs:
This is to ask you to come back home, where you will be wel-
comed with love and opened arms.

Knowing very well the punctuation rules for letters, he chose to use a formal colon instead of a comma after the opening. He must have been stiff with anger and resolve. You *will* come home. My strength of character will make you come home.

What he didn't know was that on that very day, Mom was in a lawyer's office filing papers to take a drastic step. He would learn of her extraordinary move eight days later.

CHAPTER THIRTY-FOUR

On August 18, I drove up to Amherst with Arthur to introduce him to my father. The speed with which my romance had progressed had an eerie sense of inevitability. Dreamily, I moved in with Arthur and left Viking during the summer in preparation for going to Europe with him in September. It was a precipitous leap to leave the safety of work and take a chance on the uncertainty of love. And with a playwright! Hadn't I said when I was an adolescent that I would never marry a playwright? And this particular playwright—the one who wrote the "mother play" that my father found so electrifying. What story was I part of? Was someone else writing my lines? Everyone who falls in love experiences an exhilarating loss of control, but in my case it made me dizzy with powerlessness. And yet I was, indeed, in love and happy.

Before we went to Europe, I wanted Dad to meet Arthur. Arthur had met Mom in July, when we went to Amherst while Dad was at Gould Farm. They took an instant liking to each other. But this paternal introduction had more gravity. Even though I would be gone only a few months, I wasn't sure I would ever see my father again.

I hadn't seen him for a long time. Earlier in the summer, when I wrote to say I wanted to visit him at Gould Farm, he answered,

I don't feel it is self-pity to say I had been alone, lost and had a sense of abandonment. Your letter brought me again into the family, made me realize that I was not alone. I suppose the feeling of family life is strong in me. It had been cut from me suddenly, and you restored it . . . As to coming to see me, darling, it's a long trip, and I'm not as you remember me. I've lost weight, and I suppose I look ill . . . That you want to see me is reward enough . . .

It was a still, humid August day. As we pulled into the Leverett driveway, I saw Dad and Brooks sitting on lawn chairs in front of the house, both affecting repose, both tan faces wearing a particular covered version of anxiety. I remember that the grass was a little long and lushly green, and when we walked toward them, it was spongy-soft underfoot.

Brooks jumped to his feet. Dad rose slowly. I hugged them both. It was shocking to put my arms around the collection of bones in soft clothes that was my father. I could feel his skeleton. Brooks, with a shy smile, offered to bring out lemonade and disappeared into the house.

"It's perhaps too hot out here," my father said. "Shall we sit inside?"

Arthur made the old living room with its low ceiling look too small. He was almost six feet four inches, and somehow, with his oversize feet on the weathered floorboards and his packed energy in the quiet of a New England room, our home looked like a fragile model instead of the solid house that had withstood a century and a half of storms. I could see that Arthur was charmed by everything around him, not least by the graceful man in his decades-old white shirt and tan slacks and his worn loafers that he wore with no socks. The room was full of books; the furniture was antique. The light was shadowy, the way it is at the end of summer, when tree branches, laden with the full growth of their leaves, bend to the windows. Dad put on a light tweed jacket; he had too little body weight not to be cold most of the time. When we sat down, Brooks brought the lemonade, then left us alone.

Dad sat far back in his chair. Arthur leaned forward. Dad told Arthur that *Oh Dad, Poor Dad . . .* was brilliant. And then, shaking his head in faint bafflement, he said, "I could never have written that play."

Arthur smiled and began to demur, but Dad repeated, "I could never have written that play."

As they spoke together, I watched the two most important men in my life: Arthur relaxed and confident, Dad quietly intense and uneasy; Arthur at the beginning of his life, Dad near the end of his; Arthur successful, Dad . . . the thought was too painful to finish. Dad's anxiety was belied by his smooth manners, but his hands were shaking. Perhaps the shaking was from the effects of cutting back his drugs enough to be in the right shape for the occasion. I could not imagine fully what form that effort had taken, or how difficult it was for him. And Brooks had come over, I now realized, to make sure Dad was on track.

Their words went by me in a haze. Arthur told Dad that his new play, called *Indians*, was being premiered in London by the Royal Shakespeare Company next spring. My father nodded in understanding, but in fact he was stunned by the achievement. Arthur was leaving in September—and I was going with him—to meet with Trevor Nunn about rewrites. He wanted to stay in Europe while he worked on the play. We had the idea that we would live in Mallorca during the winter. Dad remembered the time he spent in Mallorca at the Hotel Formentor. "We might go there," Arthur said. They talked about Ives's Fourth Symphony, which Dad knew. It was while listening to the symphony that Arthur had had the idea for *Indians*. Dad wanted to know more about *Oh Dad*. Arthur told him that he wrote it in the summer after college for a $250 prize. If he won the prize, he'd be a professional writer. Dad laughed softly at that.

I was uncomfortable that my living with Arthur before marriage was in the open. My father was very old-fashioned about such things. Modern life, in the form of this large, vigorous man his daughter had brought home, was overtaking him. But he already knew he was overtaken long before Arthur walked through his door.

"I could never have written that play," he said again, and it was years before I fastened on the obvious. It wasn't just that Dad had been trying to write "well-made" plays in an old-fashioned three-act structure, whereas *Oh Dad* was absurd, nonrealistic, broadly comic. What Arthur had done, and Dad could never do, was make fun of an annihilating mother. Dad's annihilation was too entrenched and had caused too much damage for him ever to be able to hold it up to ridicule. The man in his daughter's life had slain the beast.

I tried to pretend this day was momentous because I was honoring an age-old ritual by introducing the man I loved to my father. Yes, there was that. But there was another reason for the true searing momentousness of the day. I was leaving my father here, in his loneliness and incurable despair, while I was starting a new life with a man not of our tribe, a man whose strength was his ability to discard tradition and rewrite the rules, while my father was being pulled into oblivion by the undertow of his past. I listened to his voice, which was so devoid of strength as to be almost inaudible. I looked at his skeletal hand with its onyx ring (had I ever seen him without it?) resting on the knee of his crossed leg. Even with his hair gray now, you could tell, somehow, that he had been blond, like Brooks. His mustache was still a sandy color. I noticed everything in the room, the faint smell of bay rum aftershave on my father, the reading glasses in his shirt pocket, the darkening light as the day waned, the etchings of Dickens characters on the wall over the maple desk—a legacy of my grandfather's—the sound of birds outside. I noticed all this because I was trying to hold on to the short breath of a moment that would soon expire, and when it was past, I doubted I would see my father again.

We couldn't have stayed more than an hour. The strain on Dad was obvious, and we didn't want to tax him. He walked us to the car. At the last moment he gripped Arthur's hand, gave him a passionate, watery look, and told him he was "exceedingly happy" to meet him. He didn't say "take care of my daughter" or anything like that. Everything was in his look. He trusted Arthur.

As we pulled out of the driveway, I said bleakly, "I will never see him again."

Arthur disagreed. "He looks like a man who has lived through a bad bout, but he doesn't seem on his last legs. Believe me, Les, he has a lot of life left in him."

"You don't know," I said. "He's a shadow of himself. He's not going to make it."

"I think you're wrong."

After a while, after we pulled onto a main road, he said that when I left the room, he told Dad he loved me very much and would always protect me. My white knight had truly arrived, and yet all I could think about at that moment was how grateful I was he'd said that to my father, because I didn't want to add to his worries.

CHAPTER THIRTY-FIVE

Tuesday, August 22, 1967, began like other days for my father. He awoke with his usual headache. The only sounds came from convivial summer birds. Inside, all was stillness and absence. He wished he could hear the voices of his family, but he was alone. He made his way to the bathroom and took the first pill of the day. Without it he would, on top of the headache, begin to experience nausea, abdominal pain, sweats, shaking, spiraling anxiety, and perhaps even hallucinations. Those are the torments of a barbiturate addict without enough of the drug.

He ate his usual breakfast of canned apricots and an egg on toast. Not far from the table was the old collection of his parents' books, one of which was Lilian's *Barbara Hale: A Doctor's Daughter*, with a happy seashore scene on the cover. Dad had planned to be in Wellfleet this week, but he had been unable to arrange it. The last time he was there, he'd had a mild heart attack, tachycardia being another symptom of barbiturate addiction.

After breakfast he walked across the driveway to the patch of grass on which stood his studio. He took up where he left off the day before, reworking the scene in *The Stepping Stone* in which

he describes Paul's falling in love with his wife. Into Paul, griev-
ing for his newly dead wife, my father poured much of his current
feelings. He called the wife Ann, my middle name, although
she was an exact stand-in for Mabel. Lately he had been thinking
a lot about his marriage and his parents and how they all intertwined.

*What had he found with Ann? What want had been fulfilled—
what torment had been put to rest by her presence? The discom-
fiture, the loneliness of childhood. His mother would have helped,
but he had early sensed in her an uneasiness, a fear of life; the
fear increased so swiftly, turning into terror, it was like a train
roaring toward a destroyed bridge . . .*

*. . . His father had been, as long as he had remembered, a
stranger. He had not wanted to be a stranger and yet he was. He
had tried so hard not to be. But he could not understand his son's
young uncertainties, since he had few of his own. He was one
who adjusted, he was made for the world, and the world had
treated him well, as it always treats its kin. It gave him achievement and money and comfort.*

*. . . The arrival of Ann upon Paul's isolation had been almost
unnoticed, for she was not with him and then she was with him.
And it seemed that she was with him without interruption
thereafter until the severance . . . Both knew a completion . . . It
had been curious to experience with Ann a home-coming when
he could not remember ever having felt at home as a child; Ann
resurrected for him a happiness which he could not recall ever
having possessed. What she gave him must have been the recreation of a past that was not part of his natural life; how else
could the resumption be explained? . . . What had come to them
they accepted as children accept and they were blessed by it as
children are.*

He heard a car pull into the driveway. When he looked out his window, he saw a late-model Chevrolet, from which emerged a man in a suit who walked purposefully to the front door and rang the bell. It occurred to him that he could stay where he was and the man would go away. If he did that, though, he would worry about what the man wanted, so he decided to come out.

The man, named Stanley Cummings, turned to greet my father, smiled sheepishly, and held out a manila envelope for my father to take. The smile and the envelope were alarming. *What is this?* my father asked. Mr. Cummings answered that he was sorry to be the bearer of bad news, but perhaps it would all work out for the best.

Trembling, Dad opened the envelope and pulled out an official document, which, in his panic, he tried to read but didn't understand until he came to "mentally ill person."

"What the hell *is* this?" he howled to Mr. Cummings, using the nastiest tone he could, trying to frighten this predator enough to take away his noxious paper.

Mr. Cummings said that his client, Mabel Garis, believed that because of his mental illness, Mr. Garis was not competent to handle family funds. He explained that she was petitioning the court to become his legal guardian and be made custodian of the finances. My father told the man to get out and take his filthy paper with him, and Mr. Cummings obliged by agreeing to leave, but he said that regretfully he couldn't take away the paper. Mr. Garis had now been legally "served."

Dad took the document into the living room and collapsed on the couch, closing his eyes and moaning. Then he sat up and looked at the page again. Here is what he read:

COMMONWEALTH OF MASSACHUSETTS

FRANKLIN, SS.   *PROBATE COURT*

TO ROGER CARROLL GARIS of Leverett in the County of Franklin, and to his wife, Heirs apparent or presumptive and to the Massachusetts Department of Mental Health.

A Petition has been presented to said Court alleging that said ROGER CARROLL GARIS is a mentally ill person, and praying that MABEL R. GARIS of Leverett in the County of Franklin, or some other suitable person, be appointed his guardian.

If you desire to object thereto you or your attorney should file written appearance in said Court at Greenfield in said County, before ten o'clock in the forenoon of the fifth day of September 1967, the return day of this citation.

Witness, SANFORD KEEDY, Esquire, Judge of said Court, this fourteenth day of August 1967.

LAWRENCE A. COMINS, Register.

Stanley L. Cummings, attorney, presented this petition to Roger Garis at 11 a.m. Tuesday, August 22.

Since Dad had recently published a book and negotiated a new contract for the Uncle Wiggily Game and a deal for a television show with United Artists, and since he carried on a brisk business correspondence, he was flabbergasted and furious. Here in his hand was a paper saying that everything he had feared, everything his mother told him about himself, was true. He was a pathetic failure, unequipped to handle even basic financial affairs.

At some point during his hospitalizations he had given his wife power of attorney, but on August 7, two weeks before receiving this petition, he had revoked that right. He must have been afraid that she was planning to sell the house out from under him, so he'd made a preemptive move. But he never saw this coming.

What should he do? He decided his first move would be to hire his own lawyer and fight. To his mind, in those first moments of sickening awareness of what Mabel was trying to do, having her appointed his "guardian" was tantamount to losing his manhood. His rage swelled. He would not give up his place in the world. Nothing could persuade him to hand over the reins to his wife.

By early afternoon he had engaged a local lawyer, Paul Ford, and that evening, in black tumult, he made a list of people who would vouch for his sanity. It was a long list, reaching back into his early life, written in large, wavering letters. These people would tell the court that he was not "a mentally ill person," that he was as competent and normal as anyone. He would bring in heads of companies, agents, clergymen, psychiatrists, friends, who would all say he was an excellent man. He would gather big guns to slaughter her.

As the days wore on, he began to feel a new desolation. His wife was the woman who had always believed in him. She was his antidote to his mother's attempts to instill her own self-hatred in him. He would fight on, but his best warrior had joined the enemy.

CHAPTER THIRTY-SIX

The Hewlett household was the essence of taste, prosperity, and comfort. There was just enough disarray to suggest a busy family, and enough silver—place settings for fifty—to maintain elegance on a large scale when Bud's job as alumni director for Amherst College called for entertaining. Bud and Mary radiated an air of easy generosity, and they enfolded my mother into their lives, giving her a room in their home and unfailing love.

Still suffering from the tail end of labyrinthitis, Mom spent her time there devising a plan to remove her security, and that of her children, from the hands of an irresponsible, selfish, occasionally dangerous drug addict. Hadn't he tried to strangle her? Hadn't he vacationed in Jamaica when she and the boys had no money at all? Didn't he, right in front of her, arrange to get drugs the minute they arrived in New York for the *Today* show? Hadn't he—the list of transgressions whirred around in her mind like her spinning vision at the height of her illness. For years she had watched him alienate business contacts, including firing the esteemed Audrey Wood. When his career didn't go the way he thought it should, he would find someone to blame, send scathing letters, or make hysterical phone calls, and leave a trail of blood behind him. Before he made the deal with United Artists for the Uncle Wiggily television show, he fired Desilu Productions and yet another agent. He always found a way to justify lashing out, but it frightened his wife. Grampy, at the end of his life, had told my mother that he wanted her to manage Uncle Wiggily and write new stories, but in the will, everything was technically in Roger's name. Legally, she was totally dependent on her husband. If she could make the courts understand how unstable he was, she could take over their dwindling bank accounts and just possibly turn around the family fortunes.

Having a husband declared incompetent was nearly impossible, especially in Massachusetts, where the courts were still socially conservative. By the time she went to Stanley Cummings, she had gathered lists of his hospitalizations, pharmaceutical reports, testaments from doctors, ambulance summonses, statements from friends, as well as her own lengthy narrative of the history of their marriage. Stanley Cummings would not have been able to procure the petition without an enormous amount of evidence. It had taken Mom a long time to put it together, but still she hesitated. It was, finally, Dad's behavior over the last year that prompted her to go forward. The Hewletts' encouragement shored up her courage. She wasn't afraid of Roger now, and she wasn't concerned about the blow it would inflict. She was just going day by day, trying to improve her chances in life.

The rest of her plan was simpler: a year's separation from her husband, after which they would come together under her financial guidance. Selling the house would be necessary to support them both in separate dwellings during the coming months. She planned to go back to Washington, D.C., where I was born, a city in which she remembered being happy. Dad could find his own accommodations. After the year, they could buy a small house in a town less expensive than Amherst. She didn't want a divorce; her greatest goal was to keep the family intact, which she thought could be accomplished in the future of her dreams.

CHAPTER THIRTY-SEVEN

E arly in September, Crown turned down my father's unfinished novel *The Stepping Stone*, so the two books he'd been working on in the last two years, *The Actress* and *The Stepping Stone*, had both been rejected by the publishers Dad thought most likely to take them. With all his difficulties, he had always had good representation, people of judgment and taste who believed in him. To the eminent Carl Brandt, his agent, he wrote, "I know the two set-backs aren't fatal—how many books have gone on to success after many rejections? So let's keep going." My father was a fighter.

Of all the battles he was waging in those weeks, the one that preyed most on his mind was keeping his house. He wrote to his lawyer:

I am a writer, with 30 years of pretty fair success behind me . . . A writer must have a comparatively peaceful environment. It is true that some can write in a garret. I can not. I can write in my workroom here, which is a short distance from the house. You spoke of a few men moving my manuscripts, etc. I hope you will come to see the house, and my work room, and understand how impossible this would be—or at least, most difficult.

. . . my keeping this house is necessary to my livelihood. If I
had to move to another town, or an apartment in this town, it
would be a year before I could so adjust as to feel at home there,
and write successfully. In fact, it might kill the spirit which in-
spires writing.

He was not being disingenuous, even though in recent years he
had spent so much time not only at Gould Farm but in seaside
inns. In his lifelong struggle for success, he was always searching
for the magic room whose atmosphere would confer inspiration.
With his family scattered, his wife threatening his ability to write
checks and telling her friends she wished to move away from
Amherst, he felt besieged to his core, and he fastened on the one
tangible in his present circumstances: his home.

Feeling beleaguered made him wildly combative, and at the
time when he most needed support, he alienated every member of
his family—except me. The disparity between the way he treated
his daughter and how he treated his sons is part of the mystery of
his affection for me. On the most obvious level, he was proud of
me for making my way in the world, but he disparaged his sons'
less clear-cut progress. He belittled Buddy's job as a logger and
scathingly accused Brooks of being a coward for siding with his
mother, all of which prompted a full-scale break with his sons.
When they aired their grievances against him, he wrote them a letter full of self-pity, self-justification, and outright fantasy. And yet,
in his febrile state, he thought he was telling the truth.

September 13

Dear Buddy and Brooks:
  There is little chance, I feel, that you will believe anything in this
letter. But it is impossible for a man to allow his sons to go on believ-

ing things about him which are untrue without making an attempt at defense, even though he knows the defense will be useless.

These are some of the things you both accused me of, and which had not the slightest truth in them: that I tried to strangle mother. This is so fantastic as to make one ill from simply hearing it. I never in my life touched mother except in love.

That I took "the family's money" to buy the Lincoln. It was not the family's money, it was mine. I earned it the hard way.

That I did not earn my money myself, but that in some strange way it was my father's money, because some of it came from a game he invented. Don't you realize that when a man dies, his son or sons take over the business he started?

(Two paragraphs followed along those lines, describing the work he did to continue *Uncle Wiggily*.)

It is horrible for a man to have his sons hate him so, when he knows in his heart he has done nothing to deserve hatred. This is probably the last letter I'll ever write to you. Maybe one day you'll know the truth—but you may not. I only know that I have no guilt for anything I did, that I brought my children up as well as I knew how, that I did not deprive them of anything, that I sent them to schools as long as I could, that I did not take anything of them by going to Jamaica because I had that money for years back, and besides I worked in Jamaica on a book which will be published, some money of which you will get. I did not drink, not even smoke. I never "took pills" for fun. Those I took were ordered by doctors, mostly for XXXXXXX violent headaches. If I took too many once or twice, when I had an especially bad headache, does that make me a drug fiend?

. . . for a family to break up over such misunderstandings and lies is, I think, something that is evil.

Every day that September he worked on prevailing over the forces aligned against him. He found a lodger to move into the house and wrote to Mom about the sterling qualities of this man, thus demonstrating her folly in accusing him of irresponsibility. In the same letter he said sarcastically that he was sorry she was spending money on such a "useless project" as this petition, since she was sure to fail. He increased the pills, but stopped short of blotting out consciousness altogether.

Paul could feel the violence of his grief drain from him. As always it left him spent and weak. The weakness he did not mind. During its tenure he could not think actively.

—THE STEPPING STONE

The court date was set for the end of September, but he told his lawyer to try to get it postponed to sometime after October 3, when he expected a check from Parker Brothers. That way he could pay a portion of the lawyer's fee and settle other bills, so that when he appeared before the judge his accounts would be square. He continued to work on his list of character references, but I don't think he actually approached any of them, nor did the lawyer. The case was in suspension because Ford and Cummings were talking to each other, trying to work out a compromise. Counselor Ford was a much stronger opponent than Counselor Cummings, who was beginning to wonder what he'd gotten into.

Meanwhile, with no news coming his way, Dad paced the floor, fulminated to the air, his mood alternately angry, despairing, and hysterically restless. He phoned his wife, begging her to come back to him. He couldn't believe his marriage had come to this pass. In his book he wrote,

Christ, how could it have been over, how could it be ended? And yet it was ended . . . and there was now not only loneliness but a strange unfathomable sense of abandonment.

Yet Mabel, unlike his character Ann, was still alive and just across town. She said she only wanted a year apart. A year apart. He looked out on the blasted landscape of his life and couldn't see more than a few days ahead. She was either with him now or she was beyond his reach and would never come home. Toward evening, when he experienced the numb heaviness of a day's drug accumulation, he could believe that she would come back to him and their life would resume as before. When he considered what it was they would actually resume, he pictured their early marriage, the love they had, the young children who adored their parents, the nights when his family gathered around their new television set and watched his plays. The recent past floated further and further away from him. With drooping eyes he watched television, then stumbled to bed, where he endured another sleepless night, finally falling off before dawn, then waking to another day like the last.

What would he do if he lost everything? He decided to be proactive. He would need a place to live, so he should look for one.

On September 18 he wrote to a Mr. Chot Kemper at Pine Knoll Inn, Westport, Connecticut.

You may recall talking with me on the phone Sunday night about a bedroom and sitting room with some kitchen facilities which were available at Pine Knoll Inn. I'll be quite frank with you, and tell you my situation:

I am a somewhat well known writer, although not so famous as my father, Howard R. Garis, who wrote the Uncle Wiggily stories, and under pen names the Tom Swift series, Baseball Joe,

The Motor Boys, and some 700 books all told. My mother, Lilian Garis, wrote The Bobbsey Twins and some 300 other books.

Let me say here that those numbers are inflated. Even more disturbing than the needless hyperbole, though, is the pitiable fact that this late in his life he still depended on his parents' accomplishments for his own legitimacy. But to continue:

All this is told in my latest book, My Father Was Uncle Wiggily, available at all book-stores and libraries. Most of my work has been in the adult field—plays, novels, television, etc. All told, our family wrote over 1,000 books.

Now I find myself in a peculiar position. Married 25 years, with three lovely children, my wife has left me and is suing for money, although I am not sure how she intends to get it. She is a lovely person herself, and I think she is temporarily not mentally well, going through the change of life.

This, however, affects me greatly, because she is determined to sell our house in Amherst, a beautiful spot, but not one to live alone in. I am therefore looking for a place which I can call home, and in which I can go on with my writing. I am in the middle of a new novel.

From your description of the rooms available at Pine Knoll Inn, I thought this would do. But the $150 a month is a bit more than I can pay now, since with meals added this would amount to about $200 a month or more. It may be that when this business with my wife is settled, I will have this money. But I'm afraid to take a chance. Money will be available, as my agent, Carl Brandt of Brandt & Brandt, 101 Park Avenue, NYC, has a completed book of mine and is anxious to get the one I have started.

I wonder if the price could be a bit lower—say $140 a month? This would be temporary. When the money comes in, as it will, I will pay the $150.

I'd like to drive up Sunday to see the accommodations. I await your answer.

I wonder if he could possibly have believed that it was Mom who was the mentally ill person in the family. And I am continually amazed at the hope he expressed in his work. He moved in his own reality.

I don't know what answer Mr. Kemper gave to my father, but I imagine he wouldn't lower the price, probably finding my father's letter alarming. All I know is that Dad never stayed there. He was yet to find the right place for his escape.

CHAPTER THIRTY-EIGHT

A s the court date approached, Dad grew more and more frantic. The tone of his letters to his attorney, Paul Ford, alternated between aggressive ("We should move from a defensive
position to an offensive one") and delusional ("Due to Mabel's
moods and constant demands it was difficult for me to make a living writing"). He also fired the attorney in one letter, which the
canny lawyer chose to ignore, knowing the emotional volatility of
his client. In fact, Ford laid out Dad's case so effectively in conversation with Cummings that Mom's lawyer advised her to drop the
suit.

It was over. I don't know how Dad reacted to the news, but he
had to have been pleased. The danger was past: he would not
be dragged through the public ignominy of requiring a guardian,
and he was no longer at risk of losing his house, since it was in
both their names. In view of what happened over the next few
days, though, his spirits must have plummeted almost immediately.
He had his honor and his home, but he was alone, intolerably
alone.

*He felt then, unexpectedly, the sudden tidal wave of grief, the surge of
complete desolation.*

—THE STEPPING STONE

The next morning, he called the Hewletts. Mary answered and
said that Mom was out. Years later Mary told me about their
phone conversation, which went as follows:

"I have an important question to ask you, and it is imperative
that you tell me the truth. Is Mabel coming back to me?"

Mary answered gently, "No, Roger. She isn't coming back."

There was a silence on the phone. After a while Dad said,
"Then I have no choice."

Mary started to ask him what he meant, but he had hung
up.

I was surprised that Mary had said Mom wasn't coming back,
since she had always insisted she only wanted a year's separation.
But Mary may have realized that a year to my father was a lifetime,
and she probably thought it would be good for Roger to face the
fact that effectively he was on his own. That way he could begin
building a new life for himself. She couldn't have anticipated the
consequences of her words.

WITHIN DAYS—perhaps even hours—of talking to Mary, he decided to flee. His agitation must have been extreme.

He was used to packing. Into his open suitcase he would have
put the same necessities he'd had in Europe, in the Caribbean, at
the seashore in New Jersey and New England, in hospitals. I don't
know where he got the name of the guesthouse in Norwalk, Connecticut, but he made the required arrangements, put his leather
suitcase, portable typewriter, manuscript, typing paper, coat, and

fedora in the car, and started off. He always felt better when embarking on a trip.

It was late September, so Amherst students would have been playing Frisbee on the Common as he passed through town and headed south toward Northampton.

After a few false turns (he was always getting lost) he found the Norwalk street on which stood the Victorian house that had been described to him. The landlady later told my mother that she had a pleasant conversation with Dad, who showed her a picture of Brooks in his Tabor uniform at graduation. The woman led Dad to an upstairs front room with plenty of light.

> *In the room Paul stood motionless and was suddenly overwhelmed with memory. Their room, his and Ann's in the house near New Haven, the honeymoon house where impossible ecstasy came blindingly, where each sight and sound and touch emerged with new significance. A house like this house. A room like this room. It poured floodingly, bitterly, over him, the tide of recollection. But this room, far from his own and Ann's, was another room, another house, disparate. The bed there near the window, a strange bed. The paper on the wall, the rug on the floor, the bureau, the two chairs, the desk, all remote, all unrelated. He forced acceptance of this reality upon himself and he was again ready to contest.*
>
> *Deliberately, he placed his suitcase on a chair and opened it. Meticulously he unpacked the shirts, the socks, the handkerchiefs, the suits, stored them methodically and began his possession. Then when all was done he stood motionlessly, he let the relics of love fall from him, and he was a man alone in a rented room.*
>
> —THE STEPPING STONE

Although Dad wrote those words before checking into the Norwalk house, they perfectly anticipated what he must have felt that day in September when he entered yet another rented room. He had just turned sixty-six.

NO ONE KNEW that Dad had left Amherst. Brooks was living with a friend from Tabor in Greenwich, Connecticut, and was meeting expenses by painting houses. Buddy, who had left his logging job in Montana after his father's plea to come home and keep him company, was now staying with the Williams family and working in a box factory in Montague. The ferocious arguments between father and sons and the letter he had sent them kept both brothers away from the Leverett house.

Mary Hewlett had not told my mother the specifics of Dad's last phone call but had said merely that he had tried to reach her. Mom was shattered over the collapse of her suit. Not only was she back where she started, but she was sure Dad would now be so angry that he might refuse altogether to give her any money. She knew he would receive the Parker Brothers check on October 3. He'd have to pay his lawyer. Where would she get the money to pay *her* lawyer? He certainly wouldn't write a check for that. She also remembered that he'd mentioned going to the beach to work on his novel. Spending money to pay for a hotel and eat at restaurants would put her in more financial jeopardy. She was in despair.

I was in London with Arthur, and we were about to leave for Mallorca, where he planned to rewrite *Indians*. It was a tricky time for me, because after working for a career, my identity was suddenly that of the girl on the playwright's arm. My time alone with Arthur was exhilarating—we were still in the first throes of romantic love—but out in the world with him, I often felt untethered and adrift. And I couldn't stop thinking about my family. On September 29 I mailed this letter:

Dear Mother,

I'm so worried about you. PLEASE send me a line and tell me what's happening to you. If you don't have time to go into detail, just send me a little outline or something. AM GETTING DIVORCE. HEARING AVERTED. HOUSE STILL OFF THE MARKET. FATHER ILL. Something like that. Please. Send it to American Express, Palma de Mallorca, Spain, as we're leaving for that place tomorrow night. We will rent a villa when we arrive.

On that same day, Dad awoke in his room in Norwalk. Had he worked on his book the day before? Had he considered writing someone a letter and decided against it? By the morning, he must have thought that his words were all used up, that there would be no more.

It is easy to imagine what happened next. But I am sure of only two things: he swallowed the entire contents of a bottle of pills, and he said a prayer for forgiveness before he closed his eyes, waiting for release.

Around midday his landlady, downstairs at the time, heard a loud thump from the floor above. She later told my mother that it was an awful sound. After a few minutes she knocked on Dad's door but got no response. She knew he was in there; he hadn't been out since yesterday. She opened the door. The shades were drawn, the sheets were rumpled, but no one was in them; the room looked empty. She walked to the other side of the bed and saw him on the floor, lying on his side, his eyes closed, his breathing loud and labored. He must have had a convulsion that propelled him off the bed. She took in the empty pill bottle and realized that he had tried to commit suicide in her house. She was enraged. Cursing the fate that had brought this depraved man into her life, she called an ambulance.

The next evening, while Brooks and Mom collected Dad's things, the woman griped, "This is a respectable house! I'm a good Catholic. If I'd known he was that type, I'd have sent him away. He tricked me. He even showed me a picture of his son!"

Late in the day of Dad's hospitalization, someone from Norwalk Hospital had tracked down my mother. Roger Garis was in a coma. His condition was critical. He was stable for the moment, but they couldn't tell her whether he would pull through.

Mom hung up the phone. A weariness more deadening than anything she had ever felt overtook her. She couldn't go to him; she didn't have the strength. He'd landed comatose in hospitals many times. How was this different? He'd recover; he'd be discharged and go back to the drugs. It was all so hopeless. She had no more to give him. It was already getting dark, too late for a long drive.

Mary found her curled up on a sofa, crying. Bud Hewlett came home for dinner, and the three of them talked into the night. By the time my mother went to bed, she had decided to drive down the next day. Brooks was living not far from Norwalk and would meet her at the hospital. She wouldn't tell Buddy, because he seemed more unhappy and less stable than Brooks. Why add to his troubles? She and Brooks could handle it. Mary and Bud Hewlett both offered to drive down with her, but she said she'd be all right.

At one o'clock she and Brooks met in the hospital lobby. They were directed to the ICU and found Dad in a small room that was crowded with tubes and machines. He was gasping and shaking from muscle spasms. Each breath dragged and scraped from his depths.

The hospital scene has been described to me many times over the years by both Brooks and Mom. Surprisingly, the details have remained the same, and both tell nearly identical versions of the story.

They stood on either side of him and held his hands. Mom

said, "I'm here, Roger. I'm here." But there was no sign he heard her. Still, she repeated the words over and over, hoping her voice would comfort him. "I'm here, Roger. Brooks is here, too. We're here." She also said, "I love you."

After a while Mom and Brooks looked at each other across the bed in silent agreement to leave the room for a few minutes and collect themselves. But first she bent down and kissed his forehead. The second her lips touched his skin, he opened his eyes, and it seemed to Brooks that in that brief instant Dad had grasped everything. And then his eyes closed again, and Mom moved out of the room. Brooks wasn't sure she had seen what he had. Unwilling to leave his bedside yet, Brooks looked down at his father, who was much quieter now. Most certainly a change had occurred. Brooks walked into the hallway as if in a trance, trying to compose himself and find words for his mother, but at that moment the doctor came to them.

"You understand," he said as soothingly as he could. "When someone tries to take his life, we can't release him out into the world. He will have to be in a locked institution until the doctors agree he is no longer a danger to himself."

Mom clutched Brooks's arm.

Then, suddenly, medical staff began running down the hall toward them.

"Excuse me," the doctor said abruptly, and disappeared.

Mom and Brooks realized with horror that all the rushing people were disappearing into Dad's room.

After a few minutes the doctor returned.

"I'm sorry to tell you this, but your husband has passed away."

A wail broke from Mom that reverberated down the hall. Brooks put his arms around her. She sobbed for a long time, great heavings as loud as screams. After a while, when she was quieter,

Brooks found the words he'd searched for moments ago: "He waited for us." Mom raised her pounded, baffled face to him.

"You saw that, didn't you?" he asked.

"What do you mean?"

"He opened his eyes."

Mom stepped back in amazement. "Are you sure?"

"Positive."

"When?"

"When you kissed him."

They stood silently, taking that in.

Finally Brooks said, "He knew you were there. He was waiting. He didn't want to die alone. When you came to him, he let go."

EPILOGUE

We, the survivors, began the ordinary business of making lives for ourselves after Dad's death.

I think that of the three children, I had the easiest time in adulthood because I had the longest childhood with a relatively well father. Brooks had a few good years with Dad, but by the time Buddy was of an age to notice, his father was already sinking.

It took a long time for Buddy, who is now called Dalton, to find his way in the world. He tried manual labor, but his stint working for an electric company ended when he was repairing a high wire and fell forty-two feet, permanently injuring his back. He returned to school, first earning a master's degree in agricultural engineering, then a Ph.D. in economics. He is now living abroad, teaching at a university, having become an expert in oil markets. The BBC interviews him frequently on television for their business report.

Brooks tried a career in radio, but while he learned production and even hosted his own show on the Amherst NPR station, he eventually turned to the business of finance, and he works for a large investment firm. Brooks is less troubled than his brother by memories of his father. His anger and resentment haven't entirely faded, but he is relatively at ease with those emotions, tempered as they are by his underlying optimism and even-tempered nature. Dalton, a much more tormented person, still has searing nightmares and the kind of irrational guilt young children feel when they can't cure a sick parent. Memories cause him pain even now, and I don't think it is a coincidence that of all of us, he lives the farthest from Amherst.

Soon after the funeral, Mom left town, settling first in Washington, D.C., then in Lyme, Connecticut. But she missed her friends, so she moved back to Amherst, bought a small house, and lives there still. She had opportunities to marry again but chose to remain alone, saying to me many times that nothing could compare to the love she shared with Dad. But also I think she felt too bruised and weary to take care of another man, and her male friends were of a generation that demanded considerable attention. She would take care of herself from now on. That would be enough. As of this writing, she is ninety. Last week she painted the floor and walls of one of her rooms. If she'd wanted wallpaper, I'm sure she could have done that, too. In her sixties she wrote a long biography of Martha Root, a woman who traveled the globe for the Baha'i faith, a religion founded in nineteenth-century Persia. My mother became a Baha'i a few years into widowhood, and it has given her much solace.

Still, she is haunted by memories. "I was so naive!" she has declared many times, wishing she had understood Dad's illness and addiction better. "I had no experience of anything like that. I was a babe in the woods." She will be in the middle of an everyday conversation when suddenly a stray reference catches her off guard and her eyes fill with tears. At those times I have heard her murmur, sounding like a breathless child, "It's still so close. It's as if it happened yesterday."

I have had a long, bumpy, loving marriage and three children with my own beloved playwright. I cannot explain how it is I married into the very profession I vowed early on never to go near. Was I trying to give my father's story a happy twist? I was aware of no such idea when I fell in love. My husband has had a productive and distinguished career in the theater, yet he, too, like all our theater friends, has suffered bad reviews and canceled productions. Public scoldings are common and wounding, though rarely crippling. Now that I've spent more than thirty-five years inside the life my father so desperately wanted, I have come to believe that he couldn't have borne the day-to-day realities of a working playwright. You cannot survive without a healthy ego—something he conspicuously lacked.

MY CAREER STARTED in the dumbwaiter. All my professional life, especially as a profile writer, I have been exceedingly alert to the world around me, and I have tried not to judge. I am either blessed or cursed with a hyperactive mind that relentlessly processes so many impressions that it can be exhausting. Also, I have to add that I inherited major depression. My memory lapses in high school, the breakdown I had in college, the peculiar loss of consciousness in Paris, were all certainly precipitated by events in my life, but they were also symptoms of an underlying illness that plagued me in my twenties and thirties, and engulfed me in my forties. I was fortunate; today there is medicine that works.

I was also fortunate to find a career that I loved. In the 1970s I started writing book reviews for *Ms.* magazine and *The Washington Post*, then progressed to long profiles of literary figures for *The New York Times Magazine*—a profession to which I was particularly suited. I knew how to listen—how to draw out ideas and secret thoughts from artists with intricate internal lives—and I had a sympathy for them that I never tried to hide. I worked on a freelance basis, because my children and my depression often kept me home.

Unfortunately, the genes passed down to our children proved challenging. Alex has dyslexia, Ben has some dyslexia plus attention deficit hyperactivity disorder, and Kat, our youngest, inherited depression and anxiety. She spent the second half of sixth grade on the depression floor of Columbia Presbyterian Hospital. With Arthur's help, I devoted myself fiercely to their welfare, spending hours with them on their schoolwork and searching out whatever aid was available. I wasn't going to watch my own family succumb. Alex had years of tutoring and went to Dartmouth. Ben attended Eagle Hill, a school for learning disabled children, then went to Choate Rosemary Hall and Columbia University. Over the years, I have wondered how my brothers would have fared with the help available to my sons.

As for Kat, she had superb psychiatric care and psychopharmacology. By the time she started Wesleyan University she was stabilized, and as she has matured, her true personality, which is affectingly sunny, has bloomed.

I suppose it was preordained that they would be drawn to the arts. Alex is an editor of feature films; Ben, who writes and acts, is now working in media for the Metropolitan Opera; and Kat, like her mother at the same age, is an editorial assistant in book publishing. All three, in specific ways, turned their struggles into strengths.

Years ago, when we had only one child, I was still connected enough to my own childhood to be jolted by flashes from the past, which appeared as if from a parallel universe. Those juxtapositions once made me wild with grief, but something happened six years after Dad's death that had a surprisingly healing effect.

Arthur and I had been living in Vermont for five years and had a two-year-old son. We had tired of rural life and wanted to come back to New York, but it was financially beyond our reach.

Audrey Wood came to our rescue. When I told her our plight, she called an old friend, the Irish actress and New York resident Maureen O'Sullivan, the original Jane in *Tarzan*, who had just accepted a theater role in London. Audrey asked if she would like a responsible young couple to take care of her New York home for a nominal fee while she was gone. And thus, to our amazement, we landed in one of the most exquisite apartments in Manhattan: a high-ceilinged, light-drenched, mahogany-paneled urban mansion. It was the same apartment in which Woody Allen would film *Hannah and Her Sisters,* starring his then companion, Mia Farrow, Maureen O'Sullivan's daughter.

We had not been there long, but its magic had already seeped into us. The bones of its architecture reminded me of The Dell, and that association conferred on me the energy and hope of childhood.

My favorite space was the enormous pale bedroom. One morning at about 5:00 a.m. I pitched out of sleep and sat up straight in bed. I had no idea what awakened me. Light filtered dimly through the gauzy drapes, which, dropping to the floor like a theater curtain, covered a wall of windows. With a shudder I saw a man standing there. The backlight cast him in shadow. Before I had time to be afraid, I recognized him. He was my father. Was I dreaming? It didn't seem so. I felt entirely awake. I knew he couldn't be here, and yet he was. I sensed that there was an urgency to his appearance and that he had come to tell me something. I am not a particularly spiritual person. I don't even believe in God. But something beyond reason was happening, and I paid attention.

As he approached the foot of my bed, I was amazed at how well he looked, years younger than when I last saw him. His face was relaxed, his eyes clear, and he wore a calm smile. He let me know without speaking, but by a kind of thought transference, that I must never be unhappy about him again. He was blissfully at peace. Then he disappeared. I was still sitting up in bed, Arthur asleep beside me. The sun was rising behind the curtains, and I felt, for the first time in many years, completely serene.

Naturally that level of serenity didn't last, but a new and surprising tolerance for looking back began to grow inside me. Once I accepted the possibility that my father could have shed his misery and ceased to be in pain, I was able to think about him rationally and begin trying to understand. Whether his dawn visit was a dream or a vision, the narrative of my father's life—as I understood it—had taken a new turn.

ACKNOWLEDGMENTS

Along the way, many friends have helped me. I am grateful to John and Nina Darnton, Paul and Myrna Davis, Mary Peacock, Gayle Hunnicutt and Simon Jenkins, Rick Hawkins, Patricia Bosworth, Felicity Bryan, Tom and Kay Cottle, Walter Murch, Jake Slichter, and John Lahr.

The researchers of early American popular literature with whom I met were unfailingly willing to share their work with me. These include cellist and ghostwriter expert Geoffrey Lapin; Tom Swift specialist and series book collector Jack Dizer; J. Randolph Cox, editor of the magazine *Dime Novel Round-Up*; children's literature professor Deidre Johnson; American history scholar and Uncle Wiggily collector Joel Cadbury; and James Keeline, chronicler of the Stratemeyer Syndicate. Jim Towey provided the Tom Swift dust jacket photograph for the photo insert page of Garis books.

I have also received help from Fiona Russell at the Amherst History Museum; Peter Nelson and Marian Walker at Amherst College Library Archives and Special Collections; and the Syracuse University Library Special Collections Research Center, in particular Diane L. Cooter and Nicolette A. Schneider.

I would like to give particular thanks to Tevis Kimball, Curator of Special Collections at Jones Library. Kate Boyle and Kirsten Kay, aides to Ms. Kimball, were also enthusiastic and knowledgeable archivists who gave time to my project. The collection's meticulous historical record of Amherst life enriched my book with vital authentic detail.

Polly Longsworth, author of *Austin and Mabel: The Amherst Affair and Love Letters of Austin Dickinson and Mabel Loomis Todd*, provided crucial information about the Dickinson connection to The Dell, both privately and from her luminous book.

Friends from my childhood who were generous and candid with their memories include Jack Coughlin and Joan Hopkins, Thayer Greene, Betsy Hewlett, the late Mary and Horace (Bud) Hewlett, Bea Madeira Edmands, and Doris Abramson.

I am also indebted to two extraordinary organizations: The MacDowell Colony and The Writers Room.

My peerless editor, Jonathan Galassi, worked his elegant mastery on my manuscript, for which I will be forever grateful. And his assistants—Corinna Barsan at the beginning, and Jim Guida, who carried on—were both spectacularly helpful. Courtney Hodell's insightful advice helped me see the book through new eyes. Kathy Robbins, my agent, provided invaluable aid at every stage, as did her present and past assistants, Coralie Hunter and Kate Rizzo.

Most generous of all was my family, especially my mother, who, for my sake, courageously tapped her phenomenal recall to relive painful memories. Without her help I could not have written this book. I owe a huge debt to my two brothers, Brooks and Dalton, whose care and honesty in answering my relentless questions helped me beyond measure. My cousin Carroll (Mrs. Sheldon Brooks) added important insights from a family source not directly involved in these events.

Both my daughter, Kat, and my husband, Arthur, spent untold hours editing my manuscript, improving it enormously. Arthur has encouraged my writing from the beginning, and this book particularly. My gratitude to him is unending.